International Library of Psychology
Philosophy and Scientific Method

ARISTOTLE'S THEORY OF
CONTRARIETY

International Library of Psychology Philosophy and Scientific Method

GENERAL EDITOR—C. K. OGDEN, M.A. (*Magdalene College, Cambridge*)

PHILOSOPHICAL STUDIES	by G. E. MOORE
TRACTATUS LOGICO-PHILOSOPHICUS	by L. WITTGENSTEIN
PSYCHOLOGICAL TYPES*	by C. G. JUNG
SCIENTIFIC THOUGHT*	by C. D. BROAD
THE MEANING OF MEANING	by C. K. OGDEN and I. A. RICHARDS
INDIVIDUAL PSYCHOLOGY	by ALFRED ADLER
SPECULATIONS (*Preface by Jacob Epstein*)	by T. E. HULME
THE PHILOSOPHY OF 'AS IF'	by H. VAIHINGER
PSYCHE	by E. ROHDE
THE GROWTH OF THE MIND*	by K. KOFFKA
THE MENTALITY OF APES	by W. KÖHLER
THE PSYCHOLOGY OF A MUSICAL PRODIGY	by G. REVESZ
PRINCIPLES OF LITERARY CRITICISM*	by I. A. RICHARDS
METAPHYSICAL FOUNDATIONS OF SCIENCE	by E. A. BURTT
THOUGHT AND THE BRAIN*	by H. PIÉRON
PROBLEMS OF PERSONALITY	in honour of MORTON PRINCE
COLOUR BLINDNESS	by M. COLLINS
THE HISTORY OF MATERIALISM	by F. A. LANGE
PERSONALITY*	by R. G. GORDON
EDUCATIONAL PSYCHOLOGY*	by CHARLES FOX
LANGUAGE AND THOUGHT OF THE CHILD*	by J. PIAGET
SEX AND REPRESSION IN SAVAGE SOCIETY*	by B. MALINOWSKI
RELIGIOUS CONVERSION	by S. DE SANCTIS
THE SOCIAL INSECTS	by W. MORTON WHEELER
THEORETICAL BIOLOGY	by J. VON UEXKÜLL
POSSIBILITY*	by SCOTT BUCHANAN
THE SYMBOLIC PROCESS	by J. F. MARKEY
POLITICAL PLURALISM	by KUNG-CHUAN HSIAO
INTEGRATIVE PSYCHOLOGY*	by W. M. MARSTON
PLATO'S THEORY OF ETHICS*	by R. C. LODGE
HISTORICAL INTRODUCTION TO MODERN PSYCHOLOGY	by G. MURPHY
BIOLOGICAL PRINCIPLES	by J. H. WOODGER
THE TRAUMA OF BIRTH	by OTTO RANK
FOUNDATIONS OF GEOMETRY AND INDUCTION	by JEAN NICOD
THE LAWS OF FEELING	by F. PAULHAN
THE MENTAL DEVELOPMENT OF THE CHILD	by K. BÜHLER
EIDETIC IMAGERY	by E. R. JAENSCH
THE FOUNDATIONS OF MATHEMATICS	by F. P. RAMSEY
THE PHILOSOPHY OF THE UNCONSCIOUS	by E. VON HARTMANN
OUTLINES OF GREEK PHILOSOPHY	by E. ZELLER
THE PSYCHOLOGY OF CHILDREN'S DRAWINGS	by HELGA ENG
INVENTION AND THE UNCONSCIOUS	by J. M. MONTMASSON
THE THEORY OF LEGISLATION	by JEREMY BENTHAM
THE SOCIAL LIFE OF MONKEYS	by S. ZUCKERMAN
THE DEVELOPMENT OF THE SEXUAL IMPULSES	by R. E. MONEY KYRLE
CONSTITUTION TYPES IN DELINQUENCY	by W. A. WILLEMSE
THE PSYCHOLOGY OF ANIMALS	by F. ALVERDES
BENTHAM'S THEORY OF FICTIONS*	by C. K. OGDEN
THE NATURE OF LEARNING	by G. HUMPHREY
THE INDIVIDUAL AND THE COMMUNITY	by WEN KWEI LIAO
THE NATURE OF MATHEMATICS	by MAX BLACK
INFANT SPEECH	by M. M. LEWIS
IDEOLOGY AND UTOPIA	by K. MANNHEIM
AN EXAMINATION OF LOGICAL POSITIVISM	by J. WEINBERG
THE LOGICAL SYNTAX OF LANGUAGE	by R. CARNAP
PLATO'S COSMOLOGY*	by F. M. CORNFORD
CHARLES PEIRCE'S EMPIRICISM*	by J. BÜCHLER
THE LIMITS OF SCIENCE	by L. CHWISTEK
THE CONDITIONS OF KNOWING	by A. SINCLAIR
BERTRAND RUSSELL'S CONSTRUCTION OF THE EXTERNAL WORLD	by C. A. FRITZ
TREATISE ON INDUCTION AND PROBABILITY	by G. H. VON WRIGHT
WHAT IS VALUE	by E. W. HALL
PLATO'S PHAEDO	by R. S. BLUCK
ANALYSIS OF PERCEPTION	by J. R. SMYTHIES

* Asterisks denote that other books by the same author are included in this series. A complete list will be found at the end of the volume.

ARISTOTLE'S THEORY OF CONTRARIETY

by

JOHN PETER ANTON

Assistant Professor of Philosophy,
University of Nebraska

Routledge and Kegan Paul

LONDON

First published 1957
© *by Routledge & Kegan Paul Limited*
Broadway House, Carter Lane, E.C.4
Printed in Great Britain
by Butler & Tanner Limited
Frome and London

CONTENTS

	PAGE
PREFACE	vii
ACKNOWLEDGMENTS	ix

CHAPTER

I. APPROACHING ARISTOTLE

1. Aristotle in Perspective	1
2. The Setting of the Problem	5
3. Definitions of Terms	9
4. Difficulties in the Theory of Contraries	14

II. THE ONTOLOGICAL FOUNDATIONS OF CONTRARIETY AND ITS RELATION TO SUBSTANCE AS NATURE

1. The Field of Contrariety and the Speculative Sciences	19
2. The Nature of 'Nature' and the Four Levels of Distributive Being	22
3. Nature as the Locus and Principle of Processes	25
4. First Philosophy and the Study of Contrariety	28

III. FROM THE COSMOLOGICAL TO THE ONTOLOGICAL USE OF THE PRINCIPLE OF CONTRARIETY

1. The Basis of Aristotle's Reconsideration of the Principle of Contrariety	32
2. The Inadequacies of the Dialectical View of Contrariety	35
3. Cosmological Theory and Contrariety	37
4. Contrariety in the Pre-Aristotelian Stoichiologies and in Aristotle's Theory of Elements	42

IV. CONTRARIETY IN THE LOCUS OF PROCESS AND IN THE CATEGORIES

1. Basic Propositions in the Theory of Contraries	49
2. The Uses of Contraries	55
3. Contrariety as Related to Prior and Posterior	58
4. The Categories and Their Contrarieties	61

Contents

CHAPTER		PAGE
V.	THE PRIME CONTRARIETY AND THE ONTOLOGICAL ANALYSIS OF DETERMINATE OR LINEAR PROCESSES	
	1. Ontological Analysis and Contrariety	69
	2. The Principles for the Analysis of Process	72
	3. The Prime Contrariety as Actuality and Potentiality	77
	4. Privation and the Meaning of Matter	79
	5. Potentiality and the Types of Matter	81
VI.	CONTRARIETY IN THE THEORY OF OPPOSITION IN LANGUAGE AND AS THE FOUNDATION FOR THE LAW OF NON-CONTRADICTION	
	1. Contrariety and Difference	85
	2. Contradiction, Privation, and Contrariety—Their Differences and Relations	87
	3. The Four Types of Opposition	90
	4. Language and the Subject-in-Process	97
	5. Contrariety and the Law of Non-Contradiction	100
VII.	PROCESS AND THE PRINCIPLE OF SOUL	
	1. Scientific Foundations of Aristotle's Psychology	104
	2. Process and Organic Nature	111
	3. The Soul as the Principle of Organic Unity	114
	4. The Nutritive Soul and Contrariety	120
	5. On the Nature of Sensation	124
VIII.	BEING AND THE RANGE OF KNOWLEDGE	
	1. Common Features of the Particular Senses	136
	2. Contrariety and the Particular Senses	140
	3. The Faculty of Common Sense	150
	4. The 'Mesotis' of Common Sense and the Empirical Grounds of the Categories	156
	5. The Threshold of Intelligence	163
IX.	CONTRARIETY AND THE RANGE OF CONDUCT	
	1. Antecedents of the Aristotelian Theory of Ethics	171
	2. The Teleology of Conduct and the Appetitive Principle	177
	3. Contrariety and the Eventuation of Virtue	185
	4. Morality and Intelligibility	193
	EPILOGUE	200
	APPENDIX	203
	BIBLIOGRAPHY	242
	INDEX	247

PREFACE

THE present volume is the result of several years of research in ancient philosophy. It began with the main purpose of elucidating the theme of contrariety and the role it played in the Aristotelian treatises. But the many vexing problems which made their appearance as my inquiry progressed led me to extend my studies of this theme and look into its pre-Aristotelian history. A number of valuable ideas came to light as a result of the investigations into the concept of contrariety and its place in the various types of philosophical thinking from the early pre-Socratics down to Aristotle. This work in no wise claims to be an exhaustive study of contrariety in all ancient Greek thought, for a task of this kind would doubtlessly require the space of many volumes. The bulk of this work is centred around the philosophy of Aristotle with whom the principle of contrariety received, I believe, its most clear and classical formulation. The discussion on the pre-Aristotelian uses of this principle is so designed as to throw only what historical light was required for the full appreciation of the main theme. At the same time I have tried to avoid doing injustice to Aristotle's predecessors by paying as close attention as possible to their own original writings, fragmentary as they are.

ACKNOWLEDGMENTS

I WISH to express my gratitude to those teachers and friends without whose generosity of mind this work could not have been what it is. Professor John H. Randall, Junr., of Columbia University, whose intellectual compassion and profound knowledge of philosophy saved me from many an error, gave me the courage I needed to complete this philosophical undertaking.

For many valuable suggestions and sound criticisms I am indebted to Professor Paul O. Kristeller, to the late Irwin Edman, and to Professors James Gutmann, Herbert Schneider, and A. Hofstader, all of Columbia University. The German scholars Dr. K. von Fritz and Dr. E. Kapp brought to my attention a number of problems connected with the interpretation of the texts. Professor Werner Jaeger of Harvard University has helped me not only indirectly through his valuable contributions in recent Aristotelian scholarship, but also with sound personal advice during the initial stage of my research. I express my appreciation for the discussions on many crucial problems I had with Mr. A. Juffras and Mr. Emerson Buchanan, both of New York City. Miss Bessie Colocousis, formerly of Haverhill, Massachusetts, read the manuscript with admirable care.

This note of acknowledgments would not have been complete without mention of my gratefulness to Mrs. Helena H. Wurlitzer, founder of the Wurlitzer Foundation, and Dr. Henry Sauerwein, Junr., Director of the Wurlitzer Foundation, Taos, New Mexico, for granting me a Residence Fellowship at this Foundation during the last two summers for the purpose of bringing this work to its end. The last three chapters and the final revisions were written in Taos, New Mexico.

I should like to express my thanks to the publishers and authors

Acknowledgments

who have been kind enough to grant me permission to print quotations and translations, in which they hold the copyright:

Appleton-Century-Crofts, Inc., New York, from E. G. Boring's *A History of Experimental Psychology*, 2nd Edition, 1950.

Beacon Press, Inc., Boston, from J. Dewey's *Reconstruction in Philosophy*.

Cambridge University Press, New York (American Branch, manager Mr. F. Ronald Mansbridge), from R. D. Hicks's *Aristotle's De Anima*, Introduction, Text and Commentary, 1907; and G. R. T. Ross's *Aristotle, de Sensu et de Memoria*, 1906.

Dover Publications, Inc., New York, from Ernst Cassirer's *Substance and Function and Einstein's Theory of Relativity*, 1953 ($1.95).

Harvard University Press, Cambridge, Mass., from G. Sarton's *History of Science*, 1952. The Loeb Classical Library: *Aristotle, on the Soul, Parva Naturalia, on Breath*, tr. by W. S. Hett, *Aristotle, The Organon*, tr. by H. Tredennick, and *Aristotle, Physics*, tr. by P. Wickstead and F. M. Cornford.

The Johns Hopkins Press, Baltimore, Maryland, from H. Cherniss's *Aristotle's Criticism of Pre-Socratic Philosophy*, 1935.

The Library of Living Philosophers, editor Paul Arthur Schilpp, The Tudor Publishing Co., New York, from Professor John H. Randall's essay 'Dewey's Interpretation of the History of Philosophy' in *The Philosophy of John Dewey*, 1951.

Methuen & Co., Ltd., London, from W. D. Ross's *Aristotle*, 1949.

Oxford University Press, London, and New York, from *The Dialogues of Plato*, tr. by B. Jowett, 1937; W. Jaeger's *Aristotle*, 1948; J. I. Beare's *Greek Theories of Elementary Cognition*, 1906; *Aristotle's Metaphysics*, a revised text with introduction and commentary by W. R. Ross, 2 vols.; *The Works of Aristotle*, by W. D. Ross and J. A. Smith, editors, 11 volumes.

Presses Universitaires de France, Paris, from O. Hamelin's *Le Système d'Aristote*.

The University of Chicago Press, Chicago, from H. G. Apostle's *Aristotle's Philosophy of Mathematics*, copyright 1952 by the University of Chicago.

Acknowledgments

All translations, unless indicated as mine, are taken from the Oxford translation of *The Works of Aristotle*, except for the following: The quotations from the *De Anima* which appear in Chapters VII and VIII are from Hicks's *Aristotle's De Anima*, Cambridge University Press; the quotations from the *De Sensu* in the same chapters are from the Loeb Classical Library; other quotations from the Loeb translation are indicated in the footnotes.

The final preparation of the manuscript was made possible through a grant from the Research Council of the University of Nebraska. For this assistance I am deeply obliged to Dean H. Wise of the Graduate Faculty and to Professor Ch. H. Patterson, Chairman of the Department of Philosophy at the University of Nebraska.

Lincoln, Nebraska
November 7, 1956

JOHN P. ANTON

THE SEARCH FOR TRUTH IS IN ONE WAY HARD AND IN ANOTHER WAY EASY. FOR IT IS EVIDENT THAT NO ONE CAN MASTER IT FULLY NOR MISS IT WHOLLY. BUT EACH ADDS A LITTLE TO OUR KNOWLEDGE OF NATURE AND FROM ALL THE FACTS ASSEMBLED THERE ARISES A CERTAIN GRANDEUR!

Η ΠΕΡΙ ΤΗΣ ΑΛΗΘΕΙΑΣ ΘΕΩΡΙΑ ΤΗ ΜΕΝ ΧΑΛΕΠΗ ΤΗ ΔΕ ΡΑΔΙΑ. ΣΗΜΕΙΟΝ ΔΕ ΤΟ ΜΗΤΕ ΑΞΙΩΣ ΜΗΔΕΝΑ ΔΥΝΑΣΘΑΙ ΤΥΧΕΙΝ ΑΥΤΗΣ ΜΗΤΕ ΠΑΝΤΑΣ ΑΠΟΤΥΓΧΑΝΕΙΝ ΑΛΛΑ ΕΚΑΣΤΟΝ ΛΕΓΕΙΝ ΤΙ ΠΕΡΙ ΤΗΣ ΦΥΣΕΩΣ.... ΕΚ ΠΑΝΤΩΝ ΔΕ ΣΥΝΑΘΡΟΙΖΟΜΕΝΩΝ ΓΙΓΝΕΣΘΑΙ ΤΙ ΜΕΓΕΘΟΣ.
ΑΡΙΣΤΟΤΕΛΗΣ

Chapter One

APPROACHING ARISTOTLE

1. ARISTOTLE IN PERSPECTIVE

SCIENCE and philosophy in the mid-twentieth century have contributed in extraordinary measure to almost every field of human endeavour. Without doubt, we have made admirable progress in scientific matters and in philosophical inquiry, as well as in technological manipulation and purposive transformation of our natural and cultural environment. The second half of the nineteenth century and the early decades of the twentieth also had their successes, but they produced in various intellectual quarters a picture of man intoxicated with the accomplishments of the human mind, who, having taken quite seriously his faith in his triumphs, identified nature with progress. Our generation is still trying to overcome this error. However, the cultural advancements of our age—we tend to forget our social failures shortly after their occurrence—have supplied us with a sense of pride and have provided the pedestal from which the privileged contemporary may survey the past and draw favourable, if biased, comparisons which in turn he might use for premises from which to deduce his historical superiority.

The obvious danger in all this is the menace that our arrogant survey of our intellectual heritage may force us to become unjustly hypercritical and thus lose the desirable clarity of thinking with which alone we could assay our heritage and assign it its proper place in the living present. It is not difficult to find philosophers with a sceptical attitude toward the past, and

Approaching Aristotle

similarly one can find others who have become either enthusiastic or hypercritical of past achievements. The enthusiastic ones tend to exclaim with finality that all philosophy is but a series of footnotes on Plato or scholia on Aristotle. But again, there are the 'tough-minded' hypercritical philosophers who, in their emphatic concern with the present,[1] raise eagerly the axe of their vigorous and sweeping criticisms to cut off all the bonds which connect them with the major currents of the past. Were this attitude without consequence to the understanding of our own philosophical forces, it would remain significant only to the intellectual biographer. In passing judgment upon history, one need not become hypercritical by concentrating solely on its negative points and shortcomings. A more sober attitude is advocated and should prevail, for a critical evaluation of one's heritage has always proved a useful weapon in coping with present problems. That heritage should be regarded as material for reconstructive purposes.

The impact of Aristotle's thought on the intellectual history of mankind is uncontested. His name has been associated with the philosophical tenets of numerous schools and movements. He was the idol of the Middle Ages and the devil for modern tendencies which in many a case identified the road to emancipation and novelty with the rejection of his influence. Controversies and extreme positions have never been absent, thanks to the enthusiastic Aristotelians or the hypercritical anti-Aristotelians, or the unhappy misunderstandings of those who would reconcile the disputes. Numerous generations have misconstrued Aristotle, partly because of the inaccessibility of his works, partly because of the inability to evaluate and understand his real philosophical merits.

Historical circumstances did not permit the survival of all the writings his prolific genius produced. Again, the extant works which have come down to us demand the strenuous task of a life-long devotion by a promising mind in order to yield their secrets. Since we do not possess all his writings and since the systematization of the disputable points his teachings contain is still of interest—but the complete settling lies beyond anyone's reach—it seems that the task of coherent interpretation, in so far

---

[1] See Appendix: ch. 1, note 1.

Approaching Aristotle

as it is a challenge, appeals to all generations. Instead of saying that each generation discovers something new in Aristotle, it is much closer to the truth to say that each rather re-discovers Aristotle by finding in his teachings a great deal of what it is looking for. And consequently, when each generation reinterprets Aristotle, or attempts to settle the questions he did not face or simply did not answer, it does so by following the dictates of its own interests, predilections, and temperament, through a translation of his philosophical corpus into its own conceptual apparatus and linguistic idiom.

The problems about the Aristotelian corpus, whether philosophical or philological in character, have become the cherished study of many a scholar. Many valuable contributions have been made, especially in the last decades, toward a higher degree of satisfactory arrangement of the works of the Stagirite in terms of his intellectual development. A great deal also has been done in the direction of a critical edition of his writings. No doubt, much more will be done in the days to come. But what primarily interests the student of philosophy is the interpretive aspects of scholarship. The accumulation of new data, and the new emphasis they are likely to bring about, call for new interpretations, or re-interpretations. Needless to say, all interpretations are partial, biased, and selective.

This being the case, it is not altogether unwarranted to conjecture that the intellectual preferences, the philosophical and cultural climate which set the stage for interpretation are also largely responsible for determining the type of works that have come down to us. Apart from what was destroyed by historical accident, the past generations preserved what they thought to be of some significance to them.

Though only a fraction of the philosophical literature of antiquity has survived the vicissitudes of time, in the case of Aristotle's philosophical treatises we are in a rather felicitous situation. Moreover, the tradition of Aristotelian scholarship has been almost continuously kept alive up to the present. There have been shifts of emphasis on this or that aspect of his philosophy, but never did he disappear altogether from the scene of intellectual interest. He is still one of the most influential and effective teachers. His message and questions are still ringing in our ears, though the language in which he wrote is no longer

Approaching Aristotle

spoken. As an intellectual force in the formation of our philosophical heritage, he is too great to be ignored.

A good twenty-three centuries separate us from the days he taught and conducted his research at the Lyceum. The period of time that has elapsed is unimportant compared to the millennia of man's life on this planet. The cultural history of mankind has but a few thousand years of reflective life and detached scientific independence in its approach to nature and the products of human art. Meanwhile, in the last few thousand years, the basic structure of the human mind has changed but very little, if at all.

Throughout the period of reflective history, when radical changes have been wrought by the human hand in the structure of the environment, man has remained primarily a culture-building animal. At times he is engaged in ruthless destructive activity; at other times he is demolishing a static or obsolete portion of the past in order to reconstruct it; but in all cases he is expressing himself and is moving in a plurality of man-made universes. Coping constantly with co-operative and antagonistic forces of a complex environment, he is in the midst of a plurality of processes, the meaningful and intelligible articulation of which he has made one of his highest goals. And there are instances where either as an individual, as a group, or as a people in a given period, man holds firmly to the passionate belief that he is progressing or is ascending a ladder of Being and a scale of objectively existential value.

In this dramatic unfolding of mankind's effort to assert itself over a dynamic environment there appear, besides the co-operative contributions of social intelligence, certain personalities endowed with an extraordinarily acute sense of life and of unique intellectual powers who more than others become positively responsible for man's cultural development. They are the great thinkers who have devoted their lives to extending the comprehensive articulation of human culture within the framework of a conceptual language. Their ideal has been Intelligibility. Aristotle belongs to this category of unique and creative personalities.

His accomplishments, like all of their kind, share the quality of everlastingness and cultural immortality. They have, in this capacity, something of a didactic nature; they indicate the direction in which further progress may be found. They are reminders of the majestic compositions of the human mind and serve as invitations to similar tasks. But their richness of wisdom, their intimate message become evident only through a careful re-evaluation. When the approach is methodically detached and critically selective, it escapes the dangers of a destructive necrophilia to become real and constructive scholarship. As such, it becomes both appreciative and original.

2. THE SETTING OF THE PROBLEM

Socrates, in the opening scene of the *Phaedo*, in spite of his approaching execution and the sadness prevailing in the hearts of those who were present, maintained his philosophical calmness intact. His chains had just been removed, and this brought him relief. He sat upon the couch and, after the departure of his wife, continued his pursuits with unique detachment.

He was rubbing his leg.

Obviously he found delight in this little pleasure, for it became an occasion for reflection on the relation between pleasure and pain. He said:

'How singular is the thing called pleasure, and how curiously related to pain, which might be thought to be the opposite of it; for they are never present to a man at the same instant, and yet he who pursues either is generally compelled to take the other; their bodies are two, but they are joined by a single head. And I cannot help thinking that if Aesop had remembered them, he would have made a fable about God trying to reconcile their strife, and how, when he could not, he fastened their heads together; and this is the reason why when one comes the other follows: as I know by my own experience now, when after the pain in my leg which was caused by the chain pleasure appears to succeed.'[2]

Socrates raised a problem and offered a suggestion for its solution. The problem about the nature and the relation between opposites or contraries (ἐναντία) is one that invariably permeates the entire development of ancient Greek philosophy. This problem was not invented by Socrates. It is one whose philosophical antecedents can be traced easily in the early pre-Socratic writings. The relation between opposites as contrary feelings or

[2] *Phaedo* 60B, C.

Approaching Aristotle

contrary forces in nature has been treated by lyric and epic poets and is also found in the religious myths of the Orient.

The 'solution' Socrates is setting forth is attractive to the imagination, but far from explicit as to the actual way in which contraries behave, what their nature is, and why they manifest themselves in the way they do. Nor does he tell us here why it is that while the contraries exist independently they cannot co-exist simultaneously. However, this Platonic passage has at least two merits. First, by relegating the solution of the problem to God, Plato makes it a problem of utmost importance. From this, one might conjecture the following: if a human being should ever try to solve it, he must be one who is closest to God. In the Greek tradition, at least in Plato's eyes, the only such person is the philosopher.

The second point of interest is that Plato points out through Socrates' words the way in which the solution should be sought. Socrates' personal experience tells him that the two contraries, for example pleasure and pain, are distinct things which are joined 'by a single head'. Their bodies may be two, but their successive manifestation is contingent upon the presence of a third something which makes their occurrence possible. The Heraclitean notion of the unity of opposites reappears as a genuine as well as central problem to Plato who formulated it clearly. But it was Aristotle who first attempted a systematic analysis of the nature of the contraries as principles in process. He worked out what seems to this writer to be a carefully formulated theory of contrariety, which though never developed in a single treatise, is undeniably present in all his works and constitutes an integral part of his metaphysical thought.

The problem of the contraries is presented in the *Phaedo* in connection with Socrates' quest for grounds in support of immortality. In chapter 15, 70C, through chapter 16, 72A, Plato considers the question of whether the souls of men after death are or are not in the world below, and examines the whole question, not in relation to man alone, but in relation to animals generally, and to plants, and to everything of which there is generation.[3] And he advances his answer by resting the case on a theory of opposites.

[3] In phrasing this theory I have followed closely B. Jowett's translation, *The Dialogues of Plato*, New York, Random House, 1937, vol. I, pp. 453-6.

Approaching Aristotle

Here are the main points in the theory. All things which have opposites are generated out of opposites. Things like good and evil, just and unjust, and all the innumerable opposites are generated out of opposites. In all opposites there is a similar alternation. For example, anything which becomes greater must become greater after having been less, and conversely. Again, the weaker is generated from the stronger, and the swifter from the slower; the worse is from the better, and the more just is from the more unjust.

In this universal opposition of things, there are also two intermediate processes which are going on from one to the other opposite and back again; where there is a greater and a less, there is also an intermediate process of increase and diminution. There are many other processes, such as division and composition, cooling and heating, which equally involve a passage into and out of one another. And this necessarily holds for all opposites, even though not always expressed in words; they are generated out of one another, and there is a passing or process from one to the other.

Plato proceeds to build on this theory of opposites his view of the relation between life and death. Life is the opposite of death and the two are generated from one another, as waking is to sleeping, which in like manner are generated from one another. The conclusion is that the living come from the dead just as the dead come from the living. And this, if true, affords a most certain proof that the souls of the dead exist in some place out of which they come again.

What is of interest to our discussion is not a theory of opposites which provides the grounds for a proof of the immortality of the soul, but the way in which Plato conceived such theory.

Plato's influence on Aristotle is uncontested, especially with regard to the linking of process and generation to contraries. But Aristotle's view differs from Plato's in three main points:

1. Not all movements between contraries are reversible, for the bald man never does recover his hair, nor the blind his sight.

2. Not all pairs of contraries are essential to the analysis of beings in process. The essential opposites or contraries, for Aristotle, are only those which form the extremities of the prime contrariety Form-Privation, and in a wider sense, those

which form the *termini* of the metaphysical and categorical contrarieties.[4]

3. Aristotle, like all his predecessors, grants to the contraries the status of principles, but in his meaning of 'principle' it is impossible for one contrary to generate or cause another.

According to Aristotle, the contraries are principles in two senses.[5] First, they are physical points marking the extremities which delimit the entire life process of an individual substance and, therefore, they mark any given change present in a substance. Second, the contraries, as the *termini* of every change, can be generalized and stated in discourse and as such they are principles of understanding, generic concepts, employed in the analysis of any determinate process whatever. The contraries, being principles and generic concepts, cannot be generated, for then they would lose their status as principles.

It follows from this discussion that the two philosophers were using the term 'contraries' or 'opposites' in two different senses and in two different approaches to process. It is obvious, however, that both philosophers felt the need for a theory of contraries and both assigned it an important place in their own philosophies. But Aristotle, who followed Plato, in order to make use of contrariety as a useful instrument in the analysis of process, had to reconstruct it along lines necessitated by his own metaphysics and philosophy of nature. The principles of this reconstruction are discussed throughout this work. Thus, the main theme of this work is a detailed presentation of Aristotle's solution of the problem of contraries, which issue, in my opinion, received with Aristotle its classical solution in antiquity.

One would be justified in saying that there is in this essay an overemphasis on the concept of contrariety. If I were to write an exposition of Aristotle's entire philosophy, I would definitely refrain from making contrariety the 'key' to his analysis of process and would treat it as only one of the necessary conditions and factors required to render process fully intelligible. But by making contrariety central, I have been able to show how process can be examined from a variety of points of view and how all the Aristotelian 'distinctions' are relative to process itself, that is, the

---

[4] These terms are defined in ch. 1.   [5] See pages 12–14.

object of Aristotle's philosophy of nature to which the contrary principles refer and by virtue of which they exist.

The fundamental role of contrariety as the formal demand for determinateness and the grounds on the basis of which distinctions can be made for the cognizance of process have suggested the title of this book: *Aristotle's Theory of Contrariety*.

In this book, I shall try to demonstrate the validity of the position that contrariety, as the basis on which distinctions are made and as having a physical counterpart, provides a 'criterion' for the intelligibility of process. The term 'criterion', as used here, means distinguishing mark of process, the presence of which is a necessary condition for the full cognizance of process. The central place assigned to contrariety is obviously arbitrary. Its main virtue lies in the fact that by relating the fundamental metaphysical concepts in Aristotle's philosophy to the notion of contrariety, it is possible to state with new forcefulness and freshness the equal significance of all principles of knowledge as 'beginnings' of scientific inquiry and to treat satisfactorily this rather neglected principle.

Aristotle never wrote a complete and exhaustive essay on contrariety, although we are informed[6] that he composed one, probably of a limited scope. But so far as I know, this is the first time an attempt has been made to relate the various passages dealing with the contraries as principles and their significance and functions in Aristotle's philosophy. This limiting of the subject-matter has certain advantages as mentioned before, but it also engenders the presence of certain conclusions which perhaps will not convince every qualified reader. My predilections might have occasioned misinterpretations that I am not aware of, and for this reason I am ready to assume the responsibility for any discrepancy in the consistency of the argument.

3. DEFINITIONS OF TERMS

In the following paragraphs the definitions of some basic terms, important for the understanding of the argument of the thesis, are presented.

---

[6] *Diogenes Laertius* V, 21 (30); Hesychius, in onomatologos (ch. de Ar. libris, p. 49) s.v. (30) περὶ ἐναντίων ᾱ; *Simplicius*, in categ. f.t. 3a (p. 83 b7); chiefly see *Aristotelis Fragmenta*, collected by Valentinus Rose, Leipzig, 1886, pp. 109–14, 118–24.

Approaching Aristotle

(a) *The meaning of process.* The term 'process' is chosen as encompassing the meanings of the two Aristotelian terms 'movement' (κίνησις) and 'change' (μεταβολή).[7] Process is taken here in the sense in which it is *always* connected with individual substances that are subject to change.[8] Since we are concerned with sensible, individual existents on the sublunary level, we will not consider the cyclical or eternal movements of the heavenly bodies. The discussion is restricted only to the types of process present in substances which are subject to generation and destruction. Such beings are the four elements: the minerals, plants, animals, and human beings. There are four types of process or change in the sublunary level: in respect of substance, of quality, of quantity, and of place. Each type of process is marked by two contrary and delimiting extremities within whose boundaries it occurs.

(b) *The individual substance or the unit of distributive being.* The individual substance is at the centre of Aristotle's philosophy of process. This is the concrete individual which possesses a determinate principle of change or development inherent in it. This notion of 'being' must not be confused with those of other philosophies. Being or existence, in this sense of the Aristotelian term, is not to be used collectively as in the expressions 'being as a whole' or 'universe as a whole'. Being here is taken distributively,[9] meaning being of any kind, any subject-matter what-

---

[7] F. M. Cornford, recognizing the terminological difficulties, writes: 'There is no word in English that can be used consistently in its natural sense to represent this (i.e. in the wider sense) use of *kinesis*. "Motion" suggests to the English ear locomotion only.... "Movement" has been adopted as a conventional rendering; but as we do not speak of "movements" of quality or quantity, "change" has been frequently substituted where the chief distinction between "change" (metabolé) and "movement" (kinesis) is not important. Aristotle himself is not always careful to observe the distinction.' *Aristotle, Physics* (Loeb), vol. II, p. 3. W. D. Ross and P. Tannery also observed that there is a great deal of overlapping between the two terms 'movement' and 'change'. While P. Tannery takes the two terms as being equivalent, Ross is more convincing in his attempt to show that 'change' is a concept wider than 'movement'. Ross bases his view on passages which are found in the later works of Aristotle. See Appendix: ch. 1, note 2.

[8] *Met.* Λ, ch. 5, 1071a 2. The reference is to living things; also Z 1040b 5–10.

[9] The helpful and suggestive term 'distributive being' employed in this essay I have borrowed from Professor J. H. Randall's expression which appears in his article 'Metaphysics: Its Functions, Consequences, and Criterion', *The Journal of Philosophy*, vol. XLIII, No. 15, July 18, 1946.

ever, any substance which becomes the object of inquiry. The subject-matter of this essay is that which is in 'linear' movement. This is more clearly presented in Part 1 of Chapter Two, where the field of contrariety is discussed and contrasted with that of the other inquiries.

(c) *The subject-in-process.* All particular processes, changes, developments, fulfilments, or frustrations of potentialities are in all cases taking place by means of a subject (ὑποκείμενον). This is an affirmation which Aristotle states with sufficient clarity. The term 'subject' or 'hypokeimenon' has many meanings.[10] What is meant here by subject-in-process is not the grammatical subject of a statement but the individual substance, the unit of distributive being that is in process,[11] undergoes changes, develops, and actualizes its inherent 'end'. The individual substance by virtue of its being in process is subject to certain types of change. It has 'matter' or a substratum, which is the 'material' continually structured until the form is fully realized. This form is never generated as such. What is generated is a concrete individual whose form exists in the generating agent, and this form gives individuality to the substratum. Neither the form nor the substratum is created. What is generated is their unique union in each individual existent.[12] Each substance, as a subject-in-process, is connected with movement. 'It is necessary for all objects capable of any motion to exist (in the first place).'[13]

Subject-in-process is not identical with prime matter. The sense in which it is used stands for the sensible individual substance which is limited by its inherent formal determinations and whose boundaries are expressed in what Aristotle called 'prime contraries'. The subject-in-process and its prime contraries are

---

[10] *Met.* H, ch. 3, 8; also Θ, ch. 7. In one of its many meanings it is substance.
[11] *Met.* 1069b 3–9.
[12] 'Form' in a sense is the 'universal' as well as the 'essence', which is stated in the definition of a substance. What connects them is the meaning of τὸ τί ἦν εἶναι as 'first substance'; this combines both the universal element in the generation of the individual being. Thus, 'what-it-was-to-be' is the first substance, and hence it is only in this sense that a universal can be a first substance in the way in which first substance is defined in the *Categories* 2a 11–19, 2b 5–6. For 'τὸ τί ἦν εἶναι' see *Met.* 1028b 34; Z 4–6, 8; 1045b 3; 1074a 35. As οὐσία see 983a 27; 988a 34; 1031a 18; 1032b 2–14; 1035b 16; 1037a 23; 1038b 14; 1075a 2.
[13] *Phys.* 200b 33.

Approaching Aristotle

expressed in Aristotle's prepositional language through the terms 'by' (ὑπό), 'from' (ἐξ), 'to' (εἰς).[14]

(*d*) *Substance as the locus of process.* Each individual substance is also a locus of other processes. All developments and fulfilments of potentialities take place in this locus. The term 'locus of processes' (where each process within the locus is also bounded by contrary limits) was suggested by the Aristotelian expression δεκτικὴν τῶν ἐναντίων εἶναι.[15] Thus, all particular changes, qualitative, quantitative, and locomotive, occur by virtue of the substance as locus. While each of these changes is contained between two contraries, the fact remains that substance itself is encompassed between contrary determinations, namely those of generation and destruction, or coming-to-be and passing-away (γένεσις, φθορά) which delimit substantial change.[16]

(*e*) *The teleological character of process.* The unfolding of a process is a passage from one contrary *terminus* to an intermediate point or another contrary. This passage is witnessed in every fulfilment or realization of the potentialities and capacities inherent in a substance. Determinate developments or actualizations are conceived by Aristotle in teleological terms. 'Telos'[17] or 'end' is in Aristotle the point of culmination, the satisfactory fruition of a potentiality. The total actualization of a substance's *telos* is identical with its essence, its *eidos*. Complete fulfilment of an end or *telos* is possible only under certain favourable conditions precluding violent interference or interruptions.[18] Thus viewed, *telos* is the point of convergence of the fruitions of all delimited processes in an individual substance. Therefore, the understanding of process in either of its meanings, i.e. as subject-in-process and as locus of processes, involves the consideration of contrary determinations.

(*f*) *The concept of contrariety.* Contrariety as used here has three basic applications: (1) as a precondition of intelligibility, (2) as metaphysical contrarieties, and (3) as specific contraries. Only

---

[14] *Met.* Z, ch. 7, 1032a 14. *Phys.* 224b 8; 229a 25; 225a 1; 234b 11; 241a 27; 252b 10; 261a 33 ff.

[15] In *Cat.* 4a 2-4, Aristotle makes it very clear in the following statement: 'It is really peculiar to substance to admit of contrary qualities—to wit, by a change in itself' (Loeb translation). See also *Met.* 1018a 23, 29, 32; 1068b 25.

[16] *Phys.* 200b 33. μεταβάλλειν κατὰ τὴν οὐσίαν.

[17] *Gen. An.* 744b 16; *De Caelo* 291b 13; *Part. An.* 686a 22.

[18] *Phys.* 215a 1-6; 230a 29-31.

Approaching Aristotle

two of these are explicitly used by Aristotle. It is preferable for the sake of the argument to start with the first, implicit use, in order to render clear the comprehensive meaning of contrariety.

Contrariety as a precondition of intelligibility is a way of referring to, and describing in discourse, contrary *termini* of processes and contrary distinctions. Again, it is a way of relating concepts in order to delimit a subject-matter under consideration. Aristotle makes use of this most helpful application of contrariety but in no place does he state its foundations. Nor does he draw the connections between this use of contrariety and the presence of contraries as *termini* of substances-in-process.

As it will be pointed out in the chapters that follow, this meaning of contrariety is ontologically grounded and yields one of the preconditions of intelligibility. Theoretically viewed, contrariety constitutes a formal demand to be satisfied by all beings in process if their intelligible aspects are to be known. In chapter 6 of this book, contrariety, in the sense just discussed, is applied to language as part of the knowing process.

(g) *Metaphysical contrarieties*. These are general and inclusive contrarieties relative to substance or the generic trait made central for the purposes of analysis. The term 'metaphysical contrariety' covers a number of inclusive, most general pairs of contraries that delimit process in the sense of substantial change and its understanding. They display an utmost comprehensiveness and are the pairs of the most pervasive metaphysical distinctions in the analysis of process. From this point of view, contrariety is a first principle (ἀρχή) in the understanding of substance in so far as it is in process. Contrariety presupposes substance. Apart from this presupposition there can be no determinate context in terms of which contrariety as a distinctive characteristic, a criterion of process, can have any meaning. On the other hand, the full cognizance of substance as the locus of processes seems contingent upon this principle which states the *termini* of a movement or change.

The 'first' metaphysical contrariety, as Aristotle calls it, is that of 'form-privation'.[19] This pair of contraries is present in every individual substance throughout its career. The extremities of a

---

[19] Privation defined in *Met.* Θ, ch. 22, 1046a 32; also, as opposed to ἕξις and εἶδος, 1044b 33; 1055b 13; 1069b 34; 1070b 12. The study of the 'prime' or first contraries as principles belongs to philosophy. *Met.* K 1061a 19–1061b 17.

substance's career are indicated by the contrariety of generation-destruction. Another inclusive contrariety is potentiality-actuality (*Met.* Θ, ch. 3). Substance, finally, approached through the categories of quality, quantity, and place, discloses what is termed here the *categorical contrarieties*, which delimit particular processes in respect to quality, quantity, and place.

(*b*) *Specific contraries*. They are the contrary *termini* that delimit specific processes and functions in an individual substance. They are distinguishable within the area of qualitative, quantitative, and locomotive change and as such they are of incidental importance to the purposes of this essay. An example or two of the specific contraries will suffice. 'This particular part on the surface of this particular body displayed a change from white to black.' This specific process within the contraries of black and white does not affect the essential nature of the body in consideration and such contraries are negligible from a metaphysical point of view. The specific or particular contraries are of interest only for suggesting the metaphysical ones. Any failure to distinguish between the metaphysical use of contrariety and the specific contraries, which are the data to which the former refers and which it generalizes, leads to a fallacious analysis of this important Aristotelian concept.[20]

4. DIFFICULTIES IN THE THEORY OF CONTRARIES

One of the problems of philosophy to which Aristotle made a significant contribution, or at least rendered explicit, is the concept of ἀρχή. When compared to his predecessors, his use of the concept is strikingly original, for Aristotle's analysis is entirely consistent with his metaphysics of distributive being. In the same spirit he re-organized the principle of contrariety and made ample use of it for a critical reconstruction of his predecessor's views, as we shall see in chapter 3. In more precise terms, he shifted the philosophical employment of contrariety from the cosmological field to the ontological analysis of substance. However, as our inquiries will show, because of his limited views on chemistry and his crude empiricism in those matters, there is still a cosmological residue in his theory of elements. One must acknowledge that in spite of its artificial formulation it displays a high degree

[20] See Appendix: ch. 1, note 3.

Approaching Aristotle

of ingenuity, and in comparison with those of his precursors, his presentation of what one might call stoichiology,[21] or the study of elements,[22] is by far the most consistent and 'adequate' one.

But apparently, Aristotle was first to make a systematic study of the functions of 'elements' in the philosophical teachings of his predecessors. However, Aristotle, though he himself made use of elements (στοιχεῖα) in a somewhat similar fashion, was the first persistent critic of previous philosophers in the sense that he employed the concept as a tool for critical analysis of cosmologies, as well as for the construction of a theory of elements involved in the material cause. His scientific approach (through the prevailing 'chemical' views of his time) to the material cause gave to his theory the advantage of being the more accurate and less speculative one.

This success he owes to the attempt to present a 'stoichiology' by utilizing contrariety without deriving existence from, or reducing it to, its elements. This aspect of the Aristotelian application of distributive being has not been duly appreciated in this particular connection. Aristotle's Ionic predilections and his concern with *stoichiology*, in spite of the conscientious efforts to restrict the analysis within the limits of a theoretical and formal approach, lead him to the impasse of having two theories of contraries which are incompatible with each other.

The first is ontological; the second rests on the fiction of a theory of elements.[23] The former is sound and legitimate; the latter is artificial and fallacious. The ontological theory and application of contrariety is founded on the principle that contrariety

---

[21] στοιχειολογία, ὁ λόγος, ἐπιστήμη περὶ τὰ στοιχεῖα.

[22] Simplicius states that Eudemus, Aristotle's pupil and historian of geometry, noted that Plato was first to put into use the concept of stoicheion or element. See Simplicius, *Phys.* 7.13. See Plato's *Theaetetus* 201 E where 'stoichion' is metaphorically used for the elements of a complex whole. Empedocles used for elements the term ῥιζώματα. Diels, fr. 6. See also Hermann Diels, *Elementum*, eine vorarbeit zum griechischen und lateinischen thesaurus. Leipzig, 1889. Diels shows that the word is not found before 370 B.C. except in a tentatively metaphorical sense in Isocrates, Xenophon, and Plato (*Theaet., Soph., Tim.*).

[23] Aristotle did not emphasize the cosmological quests of philosophy in the way his predecessors did. This speculative aspect of philosophy became in Aristotle a theoretical analysis of elements. Of course, Aristotle did not separate these two aspects, the reason being perhaps that he was not aware of the problem.

is to be found in connection with a locus which is provided by the individual substance as a subject-in-process with a linear career marked by a beginning and an end. When contrariety is taken out of this, its only proper context, an insoluble difficulty becomes evident in the form of ungrounded speculation so abundantly present in most of the pre-Socratics.

The discrepancy lies in the application of the theory of contraries in the case of inter-elemental change, that is, how the four elements pass into one another. Actually, the notion of substantial change expressed through the contrariety of generation-destruction has two applications, one for the individual substances and one for the four elements. But it must be noted that the substances and the elements are in no case equivalent. Aristotle did not see that his theory of contraries needed modification in order to satisfy these two essentially different senses of the notion of generation-destruction. This problem is more fully treated in chapter 3.

There is another difficulty related to the application of the theory of contraries. It stems from the twofold conception of First Philosophy.[24] The conception, subject-matter, and extent of metaphysics are dealt with in books Γ and E (also K 7) of the *Metaphysics*.

In E 1 Aristotle explains what he means by a science of being *qua* being. He says that all sciences inquire into certain causes and principles of existents by marking off systematically a given portion of existence (ὄν τι) and a definite genus (γένος τι). None of them, however, discusses being in its own terms. This assignment is relegated to metaphysics which inquires into being *qua* being and the presuppositions of all particular sciences, which they themselves are in no position to investigate. This distinction between First Philosophy as universal science and the particular sciences is also brought out clearly in Book Γ (also in K 3), in which book he also includes in the object of metaphysics the inquiry into the ultimate principles of thought, the laws of non-contradiction and of excluded middle.

But this conception of metaphysics as the universal science in E 1 is followed by another one which states that the highest form of philosophy studies the highest type of being[25] which is both

[24] See Appendix: ch. 1, note 4.
[25] *Met.* E 1 1026a 19–32. There metaphysics is identified with theology. See ch. 2 of this essay.

independent and unmoved, and aims at knowledge of the highest type of being (περὶ τὸ τιμιώτατον γένος).

We are concerned here only with that portion of Aristotle's metaphysical theory that deals with the generic traits of being *qua* being, but not all being. Eternal being is excluded from this study for reasons that follow.

The question of the compatibility of the two functions of metaphysics[26] is beyond our present interests. In fact, our discussion does not depend on questions of the priority of either of them. The fact remains that both are present in Aristotle's works and both were treated extensively.

But with regard to contrariety, the theory of contraries applies only to that part of First Philosophy which concerns itself with individual substances in linear process. Contrariety applies neither to pure actuality and Nous nor to the heavenly bodies and their intelligences. By being eternal they are not subject to substantial change, nor are they developing any potentialities. This process resembles an eternal circular movement.

The difficulty is a serious one. However, the inapplicability of contrariety as a factor in the understanding of eternal motion does not prove conclusively that there is a contradiction in Aristotle's philosophy of motion. All it means is that there are linear processes as well as circular ones and that the two do not become known through completely identical means. Contrariety

[26] Werner Jaeger, *Aristotle*, Fundamentals of the History of his Development, trans. by R. Robinson, Second Edition, Oxford, 1948. Jaeger in this book talks about two levels distinguishable in the Aristotelian *Metaphysics*. In the first and older level we observe a type of metaphysics following the transcendentalism of the Platonists as a discipline concerning the supersensible and transcendental Substance. Here belong the books, A, a, B, Γ, E, K 1-8, Λ, M 9-10 and N. The second level and period is characterized by a definite tendency to institute an inquiry into the various meanings of existence; but now existence in the Platonic immaterial sense does not preoccupy his mind although it still appears to be the consummation of the realm of being. (See ch. 7, The Original Metaphysics, and ch. 9, The Growth of Metaphysics, pp. 167-227.) To this second level and period belong the following books: E 2-4, Z, H, Θ, I, and M. The connective link between these two periods is the inquiry about 'existence as existence'. In a previous book of his, Prof. Jaeger had already attempted to prove that there is no philological continuity in the *Metaphysics*, and, hence, it does not constitute a unity. (See his *Studien zur Entstehungsgeschichte der Metaphysik des Aristoteles*.)

Approaching Aristotle

is a precondition for the intelligibility of substantial change, but it is not so for the cognizance of the eternal movements of the heavenly bodies. The theory of contraries is not a necessary condition for the knowledge of eternal being. But this does not render the eternal processes any less real. Indeed, it seems to show the limitations of the principle of contrariety. Furthermore, we are reminded that the entire subject-matter of metaphysics, i.e. 'οὐσία', is wider than the distinctions found in it.

Chapter Two

THE ONTOLOGICAL FOUNDATIONS OF CONTRARIETY AND ITS RELATION TO SUBSTANCE AS NATURE

THE objectives of the present chapter are as follows: (1) To relate the subject-in-process as the ultimate unit of being to the subject-matter of the three speculative sciences, physics, mathematics, and theology, and to demonstrate the point that contrariety is relevant only to 'natures' which form the subject-matter of physics. (2) To determine through the various senses what the nature of 'nature' is and how Aristotle's meaning of 'synthesis' is related to the four levels of distributive being, and in continuation show that the increase of complexity from simple bodies to whole living organisms gives rise to additional contrarieties. (3) To study *ousia* in the sense of subject-in-process in its encompassing meaning as a locus and principle of teleological processes and then show how the four causes are meaningful principles of understanding only in reference to process. (4) To exhibit the necessity of the ontological priority of process distributively understood for any sound analysis of contrariety, which as a principle of understanding substance is the object of study of no other science than that of First Philosophy.

1. THE FIELD OF CONTRARIETY AND THE SPECULATIVE SCIENCES

Attention must be given to the conception of distributive being as applied to natural things. In the *Physics*, Book II, chapter 1,

The Ontological Foundations of Contrariety

Aristotle makes a distinction between things which exist by 'nature' and things which are the result of other causes, i.e. art (τέχνη), chance (τύχη), and choice (προαίρεσις). The kind of being which is ultimately identical with process and nature is that to which he refers in the *Metaphysics* as constituting the subject-matter of the science of physics. There he tells us that theoretical or speculative science is divided into three types of inquiry: physics, mathematics, and theology.[1]

Mathematics deals with a subject-matter where the unit of its speculation is of a kind of beings which are ἀκίνητα μὲν οὐ χωριστὰ δὲ ἴσως ἀλλ' ὡς ἐν ὕλῃ,[2] i.e. beings which are (*a*) not involved in any process nor themselves processes, (*b*) not separate, distinct, isolable existents, but which (*c*) possess being by virtue of being incorporated in matter, or rather, by being embodied in some kind of subject.[3] They exist through some containing locus.

Theology is concerned with a subject-matter which consists of beings that are χωριστὰ καὶ ἀκίνητα,[4] i.e. their fundamental characteristics are (*a*) that they have a separate, independent, individual existence, and (*b*) they are not involved in any kind of process or change as are other types of being, e.g. beings which are subject to the process of actualizing their potentialities. In order for independent and unchangeable beings to be altogether exempted from the process of actualization (such process necessarily involves the notion of 'matter') they must be pure forms. God and the pure intelligences that move the heavenly bodies are such pure forms. God is not involved in any change, because all changes *involve* contrariety, i.e. they conform to the demand that they must occur between two opposites[5] which are the polar extremities of a process of actualization. Therefore, God is not in change. God and the Intelligences are 'unmoved' on the basis of the inference drawn from Aristotle's position concerning the avoidance of infinite regress in respect to first causes. The eternal revolutions attributed to the heavenly bodies are causes of other

---

[1] *Met.* 1026a 18-19.

[2] *Met.* 1026a 15. *De An.* 431b 15; *Phys.* 193b 33.

[3] For the subject-matter of mathematics see *Met.* 1059b 16; 992b 1 ff. 'Intelligible. matter', i.e. of mathematics, is distinguished from 'sensible matter' in *Met.* 1036a 9. The problem is also discussed in *Met.* 1088b 14 ff. For further discussion on this topic see: Apostle, H. G., *Aristotle's Philosophy of Mathematics*, University of Chicago Press, 1952, pp. 41, 50-2, 106-7.

[4] *Met.* 1026a 16.   [5] *Phys.* 261a 31-261b 26; 264a 7-265a 12.

The Ontological Foundations of Contrariety

events, and in so far as they themselves have eternal causes, unmoved by other causes and not subject to change, these causes —the Intelligences—are unmoved and as such they constitute the subject-matter of theology.

The beings which comprise the subject-matter of physics are χωριστὰ ἀλλ'οὐκ ἀκίνητα,[6] i.e. they are (*a*) separate, concrete, individual, single subjects, and (*b*) their existence is such that it is not motionless, or to put it in positive terms, each subject in every instance of its career is bound up with motion, process, change, actualization and, therefore, it involves 'matter', or potential movement, and a form which is its 'end' and the source of movement. These two comprehensive features of physical entities set forth the concepts which physics as a theoretical science is concerned with: *change and process in the domain of distributive being*. This being the nature of the primary concepts of the subject-matter of *physics*, it is distinctly set off from that of both *theology*[7] and *mathematics*.

'For *physics* deals with things which exist separately but are not immovable, and some parts of mathematics deal with things which are immovable but presumably do not exist separately, but as embodied in matter; while the 'first' science deals with things which both exist separately and are immovable. Now all the causes must be eternal, but especially these; for they are the causes of as much of the divine as appears to us (i.e. movement of stars). There must, then, be three theoretical philosophies, mathematics, physics, and what we may call theology....'[8]

Since mathematics and theology deal with kinds of being which

---

[6] *Met.* 1026a 14. The manuscript reading ἀχώριστα has been defended by Bekker, Bonitz, and Schwegler, but the latter in his commentary changed the reading to the one adopted here. See Schwegler, *Metaph. Arist.* I, 130, and IV, 16. The emendation has been accepted by both Christ, *Studia in Arist. Lib. Metaph.*, pp. 40-1, and Ross, *Arist. Metaph.*, I, p. 355. This reading is accepted by W. Jaeger, *Aristotle*, p. 217. But ἀχώριστα is equally defensible, provided that it means 'inseparable from matter'. See Bonitz, *Index*, p. 131, where passages supporting the second reading are given. Compare τὰ πάθη τῆς ψυχῆς ἀχώριστα τῆς φυσικῆς ὕλης. *De An.* 403b 18.

[7] On 'theology' in Aristotle see A. Schwegler, *Metaph. Arist.*, III, 31-3; W. Jaeger, *The Theology of Early Greek Philosophers*, pp. 4-5; W. Jaeger, 'Proceedings of Xth International Congress of Philosophy', pp. 1069-71. 'Theology' for Plato means the true knowledge of God. *Rep.* 379 AC.

[8] *Met.* E, ch. 1, 1026a 13-19.

The Ontological Foundations of Contrariety

are unmoved, it follows that their consideration will not concern the present discussion. Evidently, and as further arguments will prove, the principle of contrariety is not applicable in their 'being', for their 'being' is not in process. Thus, physics is not concerned with 'matter' as such nor with 'form' as such. The account of form and matter as principles of process[9] is in its generality an object of metaphysical study,[10] since metaphysics is the science which inquires into the nature of *causes, principles*,[11] and the generic traits of being *qua* being. Metaphysics is First Philosophy, and only in a limited way is it theology.[12] The latter, by restricting itself to form *qua* form, is an abstraction from the analysis of form as *it is found* in the distributive sense of being of the *Physics* and the *Metaphysics*.

2. THE NATURE OF 'NATURE' AND THE FOUR LEVELS OF DISTRIBUTIVE BEING

The things that exist *by nature* are subjects-in-process which owe their capacity for development, their *movement and rest*, to an internal principle.[13] The entities that exist as a result of art, or of chance, or of choice, may possess movement and rest, but only as a consequence of a principle which is external to those entities.[14] Thus: 'nature is a source or cause of being moved and of being at rest in that to which it belongs primarily, in virtue of itself and not in virtue of a concomitant attribute.'[15]

The beings which exhibit such an internal principle are animals, plants, and their parts, and the four simple elements, air, earth, water, and fire. Entities which are the results of art, chance, or choice are things like clothes, beds, houses, but since they are composed of the four elements, they also share in the 'natural' movement of those elements.

Then, nature can be said to belong to four grades or levels of distributive being: (*a*) simple bodies; (*b*) inanimate compounds;

---

[9] *Met.* 986b 3; 1087a 30; 1061a 12; 1061b 5.
[10] The discussion of form and matter as related to contrariety is presented in ch. 5 of this essay.
[11] *Met.* Γ, ch. 1-3.
[12] *Met.* 1061b 5-25. For philosophy as equivalent to theology, see Appendix: ch. 2, note 1.
[13] *Phys.* 192b 13-14.   [14] *Phys.* 192b 16-19.   [15] *Phys.* 192b 21-3.

The Ontological Foundations of Contrariety

(*c*) parts of animals and of plants, i.e. tissues and organs (homogeneous parts); (*d*) whole organisms, i.e. plants and animals.[16]

Simple elements and the inanimate compounds which these elements generate through their simple mixture are natural objects in so far as their distinctive nature is a principle of movement, namely *up* and *down*. Plants and their parts, besides possessing the *up-and-down* movement of the simple bodies, also have an internal principle of their own which finds its formulation in the fundamental contrariety manifested by organic beings, that of *growth and decay*. On a higher level, animals possess an additional principle besides the above two. This new internal principle is the basis for a special kind of qualitative change, sensing, and for a special kind of locomotion peculiar to animals. Plants and animals have in common the principle of growth and decay, which is a principle of motion and is identical with the power of nutrition. But on a different level, animals have a distinctive principle which embraces operations and activities which include both those of elements and plants and those peculiar only to animals. This principle is the distinctive animal soul ($\psi v \chi \acute{\eta}$) that includes the nutritive, sensitive, and in man, the cognitive activities and functions.

There is a constant increase in the degree of complexity of operations and activities from the simple bodies to the higher organisms and finally up to man. It seems that the elements and their inherent principle of motion, which is expressed in the contrariety of *up and down*, prepare the foundations for a higher level of complexity. The principle of life displays new additional contrarieties. The whole organic level exhibits the principle of quantitative change expressed in the contrariety of *growth and decay*. The two previous contrarieties are presupposed by the type of life manifested on the animal and human level. Animal life has in addition to the previous principles, another of its own, reaching thus, through Man, the highest degree of complexity. The passage from one level of complexity to the other, i.e. from the elemental to the plant and the animal levels, is possible through three consecutive mixtures, compositions, or rather, *syntheses*.

'There are three degrees of synthesis; and of these the first in order, as all will allow, is synthesis out of what some call the

[16] *Phys.* 192b 9–11.

The Ontological Foundations of Contrariety

elements, such as earth, air, water, fire.[17] Perhaps, however, it would be more accurate to say synthesis out of the elementary forces; nor indeed out of all these, but out of a limited number of them, as defined in previous treatises. For fluid and solid, hot and cold, form the material of all composite bodies; and all other differences are secondary to these.... The second degree of synthesis is that by which the homogeneous parts of animals, such as bone, flesh, and the like, are constituted out of the primary substances. The third and last stage is the synthesis which forms the heterogeneous parts, such as face, hand, and the rest.

'Now the order of actual development and the order of logical existence are always the inverse of each other. For that which is posterior in the order of development is antecedent in the order of nature, and that is genetically last which in nature is first.'

Aristotle continues further along:

'In order of time, then, the material and the generative process must necessarily be anterior to the being that is generated; but in the logical order the definitive character and form of each being precedes the material.... So that it must necessarily be that the elementary material exists for the sake of the homogeneous parts, seeing that these are genetically posterior to it, just as the heterogeneous parts are posterior genetically to them. For these heterogeneous parts have reached the end and goal having the third degree of synthesis, in which degree generation or development often attains its final term.'[18]

Aristotle's conception of the process of development from lower to higher levels of complexity is intimately connected with his teleological structure of levels of being. He says:

'With organisms that possess life and also have sensation the structures (ἰδέα) are exceedingly intricate, and some organisms of this type have more intricate structures than others. The greatest complexity is characteristic of those organisms which are *not simply in possession of life*, but, in addition, their nature is such that they are capable of the *good life*; and such is mankind. Man alone of all the living beings known to us, partakes in the divine, or, even if others do too, he does so *par excellence*.'[19]

---

[17] The elemental synthesis is extensively presented in the treatise *De Gen. et Corr.*, Book I, ch. 6–10, and Book II, ch. 1–8.

[18] *Part. An.* II, 646a 12; 646b 10.

[19] *Gen. An.* II, 731b 24 ff. (translation mine).

The Ontological Foundations of Contrariety

In such a comparison, it is obvious that man, animals, plants, and elements form a succession of levels with a continually diminishing degree of complexity.[20]

3. NATURE AS THE LOCUS AND PRINCIPLE OF PROCESSES

The particular beings which have in themselves an internal principle of change are subjects-in-process and *their particular principle* exemplifies a contrariety. The three kinds of synthesis procure the conditions for higher levels of *organic* complexity and invoke the presence of new principles, but do not render contrariety inapplicable. Instead, its use increases significantly with each additional synthesis. Consequently, it is impossible to understand the operations and activities of natural processes without referring to elaborate explanations where the concept of contrariety plays a key role. In *Physics* I, chapter 6, Aristotle offers a rough analysis of his contention that *process as nature* is to be understood in terms of a subject involving a contrariety.

The subject-in-process plus the two extremities forming the poles of change are all the terms needed to define any particular process. If all natural results are fulfilments of determinable processes, then substance is the locus of teleological changes or movements between two contrary terms. Substance is process in which the intelligibility of all its actualizations and functions requires the principle of contrariety. While substance, as a subject-in-process, changes, the contrary terms which mark the *termini* of a change remain what they are, and are terms distinguishable in discourse. This analysis of nature and process is thus based on an ontology where being is distributively understood.

Such an approach to 'nature'[21] has provided the grounds for a new criticism of the various positions held by the pre-Socratics. This critical reconstruction which Aristotle offers in his various treatises could not take place unless a metaphysics of distributive being were presupposed. The need for a distinction between an ontological analysis of being and a cosmological account of its origin was clearly felt by Aristotle. The new orientation of metaphysical inquiry also made possible the reconstruction of the principle of contrariety itself.[22] It appears that the primary

[20] Compare *Hist. An.* I, 491a 19. [21] See Appendix: ch. 2, note 2.
[22] This is fully treated in ch. 3.

The Ontological Foundations of Contrariety

difficulty which led to the inconsistencies and other speculative embarrassment that Aristotle points out in the views of the early cosmologists, stems from a reductionistic insistency on their part.[23] Aristotle's 'nature' is the unity of form and matter which is disclosed in the individuality of the unit of *distributive being* with a complete career.

The shift towards, and the emphasis on, distributive being was a major and all-important advance in metaphysical thought. In *Metaphysics* A, chapter 3, where Aristotle sets forth the nature, the significance, and the objectives of First Philosophy, after he has stated the four causes, he embarks on a criticism of the entire philosophical tradition, viewing the contributions of the past on the basis of how his predecessors employed 'causes'.

There is no need here to recount his criticisms of the earlier philosophers. It is evident, though, that he makes ample use of the notion of 'nature' in the sense of distributive being. The criticism which starts from the notion of material cause is particularly emphatic in this respect. One could fortify the above statement by an analysis of the examples that Aristotle occasionally uses in illustrating his point.

Let us pause for a while to look into the issue more closely. There is a passage where he discusses what is the 'substance' of all things, i.e. what is that out of which everything comes into being and into which everything vanishes, while this *source-substance* suffers no changes of its original nature. What follows immediately is quite surprising. Instead of being explicit about the nature of the original cosmic substance, Aristotle refers to 'Socrates', i.e. a living organism and an individual substance. Socrates is a subject, and as such he remains an unbroken continuous unity throughout the course of his development, and is also the locus where all his particular qualitative changes take place. Socrates may become handsome or musical, but Socrates, the concrete individual, remains the locus of all his particular processes, becomings, developments, frustrations, and fulfilments. The only valuable conclusion one might draw through a serious consideration of the material cause is that it is *one* together with many other causes, and also that the existence of higher organisms depends on the organization of some kind of a more

---

[23] See Appendix: ch. 2, note 3.

The Ontological Foundations of Contrariety

general kind of 'matter' which is used in some special determinate way.[24] Therefore, a material cause apart from some locus, i.e. non-distributed, is an impossibility and a figment of the imagination. For if it is to be a cause and a principle it can only be so as a beginning in discourse, in which case temporal priority of the material cause becomes insignificant.

On the same grounds one may also note an argument which is advanced against Empedocles, who held the theory of the four material elements and the two efficient principles of 'love' and 'hatred'.[25] This position, according to Aristotle cannot in any way explain the phenomenon of change, simply because the elements are pure and unmixed from the very beginning. Aristotle then introduces subtly and cogently the solution of the embarrassment. What is particularly needed in Empedocles' position is a *nature*, a subject-in-process, a something that is capable of serving as the *missing* link between the elements. The individual nature which is *process* is capable of suffering the changes from one contrary to the other and can itself be contained between the boundaries formed by the two most general contraries. Only such a nature, whether *elemental* or *organic*, could undergo changes from *water* to *fire*, or from *earth* to *air*. But it is impossible for the elements, pure as they are, to become contrary to what they are.

'In general, change of quality is necessarily done away with by those who speak thus, for on their view cold will not come from hot nor hot from cold. For if it did there would be something that accepted the contraries themselves, and there would be some one entity that became fire and water, which Empedocles denies.'[26]

Empedocles begins his story with the assumed irreducibility of the first elements, which he also denies by using them as the stuff out of which the world was created. If Empedocles were a God and wanted to be consistent, according to Aristotle's criticism, he would never have made the world!

Similarly, Aristotle uses distributive being as his basic argument against the Platonic theory of forms and mathematics.[27] All his criticisms, those briefly discussed in the present connection as well as those that constitute a good portion of the next chapter, point to his fundamental view which makes central the notion of

---

[24] *Met.* A 983b 6–18.
[25] *Met.* A 1000a 24–1001a 2.
[26] *Met.* A 989a 27–30.
[27] *Met.* A 992a 24; 992b 18.

The Ontological Foundations of Contrariety

distributive being and forms the basis for a philosophy of process. In his consistent and systematic critique, Aristotle remains the first thinker who made explicit the philosophical consequences of the illegitimate assumptions employed by the early cosmologists in their philosophies of nature. Moreover, he stated with great clarity that a theory of process must rest its case on a view of nature which conceives of it in terms of a notion of being, where the individual natures are subjects-in-process always determinable by means of the principle of contrariety.

4. FIRST PHILOSOPHY AND THE STUDY OF CONTRARIETY

Where natural processes call for a metaphysical understanding and where process is always exemplified in a given locus,[28] there philosophical inquiry must pay due respect to the concepts of unity and oneness.[29]

Since contrariety is inseparable from the most inclusive and universal ways of talking about substance, the science of substance also inquires into contrariety.

'Now since it is the work of one science to investigate opposites, and plurality is opposed to unity—and it belongs to one science to investigate negation and privation because in both cases we are really investigating the one thing of which the negation or the privation is a negation or privation. . . . The contraries of the concepts we named above, the other and the dissimilar and the unequal, and everything else which is derived either from these or from plurality and unity, must fall within the province of the science above named. And contrariety is one of these concepts, for contrariety is a kind of difference and difference is a kind of otherness.[30]

The study of the particular contrarieties, as particular delineations of the determinate powers and functions of subjects-in-process, Aristotle relegates to the particular sciences, because it is the particular sciences that inquire into particular phenomena pertaining to specific contraries. The particular sciences concentrate on a given subject-matter, a given genus, and attempt to

---

[28] See Appendix: ch. 2, note 4.
[29] This theme is emphasized throughout this essay. See Appendix: ch. 2, note 5, and ch. 6, note 2.   [30] *Met.* 1004a 9-22.

The Ontological Foundations of Contrariety

deduce from the common undemonstrable axioms and assumptions the essential attributes of this subject-matter, and also to subsume all particularities under universal premises.[31] But the study of the metaphysical contrarieties and of the principle of contrariety falls outside the orbit of the particular sciences. If the generic traits of being are to be intelligible, they must satisfy the conditions under which intelligibility is achieved, and they must be capable of delineation after the pattern set by the principle of contrariety. It is not an accident that Aristotle called the contraries 'form-privation' the primary contrariety. This fundamental distinction, plus the necessary assumption of a subject-in-process as a locus, is all that metaphysical analysis requires to begin its analysis of being. This is affirmed in both the *Physics* and the *Metaphysics*.

Contrariety is both a generic trait and a principle of organization of the cognizable aspects of all functions and actualizations. It is a generic concept under which all cases of contraries are subsumed and also a distinctive mark necessary for the intelligibility of change and process altogether.[32] The distinctions which are applicable to the 'one', that is, the unbroken continuity and identity of the individual locus and subject-in-process, are also valid for the primary contraries. Whenever inquiry attempts to understand this oneness, it must also extend its interests to the 'other'. First Philosophy has as one of its functions to investigate whether one thing 'has one contrary, or what contrariety is, or how many meanings it has'.[33]

The study of contrariety belongs exclusively to metaphysics. Physics is necessarily interested in the concept of contrariety, and so is every branch of specific inquiry, since all of them assume it, because contrariety is indispensable for any explanatory generalization concerning the nature of process; but physics, strictly speaking, is not concerned with the investigation into the meaning of contrariety as such.

'Since the science of the philosopher treats of being *qua* being universally and not in respect of a part of it, . . . and since everything that is may be referred to something single and common,

---

[31] *Met.* 997a 20–5.
[32] A natural history of contrariety and its knowledge is suggested in *Met.* Θ, ch. 2, 1046b 1–29.
[33] *Met.* 1004b 3–4.

The Ontological Foundations of Contrariety

each of the contrarieties also may be referred to the first differences and contrarieties of being, whether the first differences of being are plurality and unity, or likeness and unlikeness, or some other differences; let these be taken as already discussed. It makes no difference whether that which is be referred to being or to unity. For even if they are not the same but different, at least they are convertible; for that which is one is also somehow being, and that which is being is one. . . .'

'. . . As the mathematician investigates abstractions . . . the same is true with regard to being. For the attributes of this in so far as it is being, and the contrarieties in it *qua* being, it is the business of no other science than philosophy to investigate; for to physics one would assign the study of things not "*qua*" being, but rather "*qua*" sharing in movement; while dialectic and sophistic deal with the attributes of things that are, but not of things *qua* being, and not with being itself in so far as it is being; therefore, it remains that it is the philosopher who studies the things we have named, in so far as they are being. Since all that is said to "be" in virtue of something single and common, though the term has many meanings, and contraries are in the same case (for they are referred to the first contrarieties and differences of being), and things of this sort can fall under one science, the difficulty we stated at the beginning (1059a 20–3) appears to be solved—I mean the question how there can be a single science of things which are many and different in genus.'[34]

[34] *Met.* K, ch. 3, 1060b 30–1061b 18.

Chapter Three

FROM THE COSMOLOGICAL TO THE ONTOLOGICAL USE OF THE PRINCIPLE OF CONTRARIETY

ARISTOTLE's position that contrariety is the object of metaphysical inquiry has been established on the basis that the proper understanding of contrariety as a principle presupposes being in the distributive sense. The purpose of this chapter is to carry this analysis further and show how Aristotle was able to arrive at his views through a criticism of his predecessors' erroneous use of contrariety. The topics that concern our discussion are as follows: (1) To state the conceptual apparatus which Aristotle used in his reconstruction of the principle of contrariety in terms of the historical antecedents of his ontological approach. (2) To draw the lines that distinguish Aristotle's analysis from Plato's dialectic treatment of contraries and to indicate wherein the fault of the latter lies. (3) To give an exposition of all the varieties and ramifications of the cosmological use of contrariety in the pre-Socratic philosophies, all of which had in one way or another hypostatized it and used it as a material cause. (4) To contrast, on the basis of a theory of contrary elements, Aristotle's stoichiology with the pre-Socratic ones, and to indicate in the light of contrariety the merits and shortcomings of his qualitative 'chemistry'.

The Use of the Principle of Contrariety

1. THE BASIS OF ARISTOTLE'S RECONSIDERATION OF THE PRINCIPLE OF CONTRARIETY

All the theoretical difficulties which Aristotle described in both the pre-Socratics and the Platonists must have had a definite effect on his formulation of his pluralistic and analytic metaphysics. His reconsideration and critical reconstruction of contrariety mark the transition and advance from cosmology to ontology. Most of the answers he gave to the problems he came across in the course of his reconstruction of the theoretical concepts requisite for such philosophical enterprise were implicitly and explicitly contained in his predecessors' views. However, surprisingly enough, none of them had the vision and the analytic power to find the healthy elements in each view and restate them in a new synthesis that could satisfy the demands of what was to become the soundest metaphysical position of antiquity. In his reconstructive synthesis, Aristotle worked with the rich suggestions of his predecessors' experiences, but he also added the findings and conclusions of his own research. He opened the way for the new solution first by extending the meaning of the concept 'principle',[1] and secondly by applying distributively the notion of 'nature', identifying nature with a pluralistic principle of change and process, so that its intelligibility forced the assumption of more than one principle and never an infinite number of them.

'What is common to all *archai* is that they are the beginnings and the first starts from which a thing either is, or constitutes a process, or is intelligible; but of these some are immanent in a thing and others are outside. Hence the nature of a thing, is a beginning, and so is the element of a thing, and thought and will, and essence, and the final cause—for the good and the beautiful are the beginnings both of the knowledge and of the movement of many things.'[2]

The conceptual apparatus which Aristotle employed for the reconstruction of the notion of contrariety involves, besides the above two general considerations, certain specifications concerning the meanings of contraries.

1. The contraries or any primary pair of extremities are raised

---

[1] *Met. Δ* 1012b 34; 1013a 23.
[2] *Met. Δ* 1013a 17–23. Also *Met.* K, ch. 1 (translation of lines 17–19 is mine).

to the status of principles, and as such, while they do not involve either each other or anything else in their composition, they are involved in the composition of everything else.[3]

2. A pair of contraries alone is not sufficient, although necessary (such as rarefaction and condensation, Love and Strife), for understanding any substance or process, because no given contrariety in itself can constitute a substance or a process. A contrariety always presupposes a substratum for its locus. Any thinker who has tried to assert the existence of contrary principles without stating what their locus is, is reducing the contraries to a material cause. Any philosophical theory which assumes that the contraries, or for that matter any other discursive distinction and abstraction, are prior to primary substance and locus, commits an irretrievable error which in turn becomes a source of all sorts of embarrassment. In Aristotle's view, all the pre-Socratics, including the Platonists, erred because they hypostatized certain attributes and aspects of being, however pervasive, before inquiring into what being is. They said more about being than their experience and point of view allowed for.[4]

3. The principles that are involved in a metaphysical analysis of any particular process are three, the subject-in-process and the two generic contraries that make the first contrariety.[5]

Before we begin an analysis of the basic ways in which the pre-Aristotelians used contrariety, reference must be made to the way in which the notion of *One* in its pre-Socratic cosmological connotation was related to the contraries. Aristotle states that it is possible in speculation to get through a successive reductive analysis, a set of ultimate contraries which can finally be arranged in two columns. At the top of them he places Being (contrary to) Non-being. The widest speculative contrariety of being in general is stated in terms of positive and negative contraries. However, this contrariety is not a contradiction, because the latter involves statements and not merely terms. Aristotle says in the opening chapters of *Metaphysics Δ* concerning this problem:

'Again in the list of contraries one of the two columns is privative, and all contraries are reducible to being and non-being, and to unity and plurality, as for instance rest belongs to unity and movement to plurality.'[6]

[3] *Phys.* 188a 28–30.
[4] *Met.* 1004b 7–10.
[5] This theme is treated in ch. 5.
[6] *Met.* 1004b 27–9.

The Use of the Principle of Contrariety

The contraries of the second column, i.e. non-being, plurality, and motion, would stand for *privation*. This seems to be the source of Aristotle's own use of *privation* as the contrary to *form* in a given substance; both of them, privation and form, gave him the model for the most inclusive contrariety, which is again connected with the first and basic category of *substance*. Non-being, plurality and motion, as typical of privation, are at the core of views like those held by the Eleatics, the Platonists, and the Pythagoreans. Aristotle's historical survey of the subject shows that all the pre-Aristotelians made use of contrariety. They assumed that all beings and all substance, the universe, are made up of contraries, and thus all of these thinkers directly or indirectly named the contraries as principles; the Pythagoreans in the form of *odd and even*, Parmenides (in his 'Way of Opinion') and Anaxagoras (as one of the contrarieties) in the form of *hot and cold*, the Platonists expressed them as *limit and limitless*, Empedocles as *Love and Strife*. The careful student of the pre-Aristotelian philosophical literature cannot but take note of the remarkable and pervasive use of the concept of contrariety in such a variety of ways that they present a very difficult problem of classification. Contrariety is used in connection with so many complex problems that even the most careful sorting out of its uses is not likely to do it complete justice. For the sake of clarity, in the development of our theme we shall present a set of distinctions which are closer to our recent terminological devices and somewhat different from those that Aristotle employs in his *Physics*, I, chapter 2.[7]

There are at least four inclusively wide applications of contrariety: (1) as a dialectical distinction where it has a logical aspect;[8] (2) as a principle of differentiation used invariably by the cosmologists in their various explanations of cosmic processes; (3) as a basic concept in the edification of the ancient theories of elements including the Aristotelian one; (4) as a fundamental assumption in the ontological analysis of being where it is taken

---

[7] *Phys.* 184a 15–22. For a valuable discussion on this topic see W. D. Ross, *Aristotle's Physics*, pp. 458–70.

[8] W. Jaeger states that: 'In Plato's school the method of referring (ἀναγωγή) all the affections (πάθη) of being to something simple and common (ἕν τι καὶ κοινόν) was division in the form of oppositions (ἐναντιώσεις) which were referred to certain most general or "first" distinctions in being.' *Aristotle*, p. 215.

The Use of the Principle of Contrariety

to be a distinctive mark of process serving as the criterion of intelligibility.

Only the first three applications are considered in the present chapter because of the immediate importance they have in understanding the transition from cosmology to ontology. It must be noted at this point that even Aristotle's theory of elements is in a sense the remainder of early cosmological thinking, and in spite of his earnest interest in a scientific treatment of the elements, his theory is not altogether innocent of dialectical and empirically unwarranted speculation. In view though of Aristotle's total attempt to achieve a thorough reconstruction of the notion of contrariety, his is a gigantic task with the best results finally attained in the originality that marks his ontological analysis of distributive being, a topic exclusively treated in chapter 5.

2. THE INADEQUACIES OF THE DIALECTICAL VIEW OF CONTRARIETY

Much of the criticism of his predecessors is carried through in the light of his reconstruction of contrariety. A great deal of our difficulty in understanding his criticisms is removed when they are seen as statements which are at once expositions and critical reconstructions. His interest in the ideas of his predecessors[9] is not that of a mere recording historian but the interest of a student who knows how and where to look for valuable suggestions. He constantly cautions the investigator to fix his eye on the locus, on the priority of the basic category of substance, and literally, on the first substances.[10] But his predecessors failed to meet this basic demand. Therefore, their philosophic visions can hardly fit into the scheme of a genuine metaphysics, though they contain valuable elements and suggestions. Similarly, but in a different sense, sophistry and dialectic are far from being metaphysics. Aristotle states that dialectic is merely critical where philosophy claims to know, and sophistic is what appears to be philosophy but is not.[11] We might compare this statement with Plato's remarks about the nature of dialectic: 'Dialectic is the truest of all sciences; its

---

[9] See Appendix: ch. 3, note 1.
[10] Compare *De Gen. et Corr.* II, ch. 1, 329a 1; 329b 6.
[11] *Met.* 1004b 25–7.

The Use of the Principle of Contrariety

knowledge has to do with being and reality and sameness and unchangeableness.'[12]

By definition, then, dialectic excludes contrariety from its realm of inquiry. Dialectic according to Plato is a noetic movement which distinguishes the 'being' from the 'non-being' of things by declaring what the things are and what they are not. This relation between being and not-being becomes evident in the *Sophist*. Aristotle knew well that at the core of the Platonic dialectic there was the incessant utilization of not-being and the constant questioning of the validity of every thesis; he knew it too well, since he referred to dialectic as 'being able to speculate about the contraries without knowledge of the essence of things';[13] i.e. dialectic is a kind of learning which works through 'apophora', denial, and removal.[14] However, this 'apophoric' trait forces dialectic to look into, and deal with, the realm of not-being and opinion. For as Aristotle says:

'In those types of predication where there is no contrariety inherent (e.g. relation), if nouns are replaced by definitions and the predicates are not accidental, belonging to the things in themselves, the individual may well be the subject also of the simple propositions. As, however, for that which is *not*, it is not true to say it *is* somewhat, because it is a matter of opinion. The opinion about it is not that it *is*; it is that it *is not*.'[15]

Aristotle had no objections to the logical use of the dialectical treatment of contraries. What he particularly regarded as fallacious was the fact that dialectic took contrariety out of context and deprived it of its necessary ontological foundations. If contrariety is a principle for understanding a given subject-matter, the subject of inquiry cannot be that of sameness and permanence and immobility. Change and process mean movement; and contrariety sets forth the extremities and limits within which any process whatsoever can be understood in any of its respects. Just as contrariety is inapplicable in the subject-matter of dialectic, since sameness excludes process, so is contrariety helpless in the search for the understanding of process and movement as a whole, i.e. on the cosmological level.

---

[12] *Philebus* 58 A. For the difference between logic and dialectic, see Appendix: ch. 3, note 2.   [13] *Met.* 1078b 25.

[14] *Met.* 1046b 14. For dialectic as a species of reasoning see Appendix: ch. 3, note 3.   [15] *De Int.*, ch. 11, 21a, 30–4 (Loeb translation).

The Use of the Principle of Contrariety

'Infinite' process, if one can imagine such a case at all, apart from individual entities, contradicts the notion of contrariety, since the infinite is indeterminate and escapes all consideration of limits and delineations. For this reason both 'sameness'[16] and 'infinite process' exclude the very conditions under which a criterion of intelligibility can be established. Sameness and infinite process may appeal to the imagination, they may serve as invitations to poetic visions and hence be valuable for their poetic suggestiveness, but so far as their value as tools for metaphysical analysis goes, they are, in Aristotle's view, inadequate, misleading, and enormously wrong, since they completely lack any determinate context to which they can apply and which in turn can sustain or support them.

3. COSMOLOGICAL THEORY AND CONTRARIETY

In cosmology, contrariety is an extremely complex notion which is present in all the cosmological positions formulated by the early thinkers.[17]

There are cases where contrariety is connected with the elements. Here it has either an *independent status* or *is the pattern of arrangement* of the elements. Thus, contrariety may be either an element itself or a principle of elemental organization. In the analysis that follows we will see how it is used in the various positions as to the elements, i.e. in monism, dualism, etc.

There are cosmologies where the status granted to contrariety is that of an *efficient cause*, as the principle of individuation causing the emergence of differences and giving rise to a plurality of substances and determinations. Contrariety as an efficient cause can be employed in two ways; either as *inherent* in the ultimate elements, or as having an *independent* absolute status of its own parallel to, and coexisting with, the elements.

There are cosmologies which employ contrariety either *monistically*, by making use of one and only one contrariety, or *pluralistically*, by employing many contrarieties, whether as material causes

---

[16] For the various meanings of 'sameness' see Appendix: ch. 3, note 4.
[17] The history of ancient Greek literature reveals that contrariety had its mythological antecedents, from which it was freed by the rationalization of the Milesian school. See F. M. Cornford, *Principium Sapientiae*, Cambridge University Press, 1952; especially ch. 11, 'Pattern of Ionian Cosmogony'.

or as efficient ones. There are only four possibilities of this case:

A (1) one element; one contrariety (Anaximenes)

(2) one element; many contrarieties (Anaximander)

B (1) many elements; one contrariety (Anaxagoras)

(2) many elements; many contrarieties (Empedocles).

Finally, contrariety, whether itself an element or an efficient cause, one or plural, presents again another important facet; namely, that whenever connected with process it exhibits three possible types.

1. As *rarefaction-condensation* (cosmological)—examples of this view are Anaximenes and Diogenes of Apollonia.

2. As *aggregation-segregation*, or mixture-unmixture (cosmological)—as in the views of Empedocles and Anaxagoras.

3. As *form-privation*, or (from other perspectives) as generation-destruction, as growth-decay, as motion-rest—as in the ontological analysis of Aristotle.

By definition then, no monistic view can employ contrariety as an independent principle, but rather as inherent in the nature of the substratum to give rise to a plurality of entities through an efficiency of the rarefaction-condensation type; such was the view of Anaximenes.[18] Nevertheless, a monistic cosmology could employ many contrarieties; for example, Anaximander's Boundless is the substratum in which two contrarieties inhere: a qualitative contrariety, like *hot-cold*, etc., and an efficient contrariety such as *rarefaction-condensation*.[19]

The main features of these two varieties of monism are (*a*) that the substratum they assume is something indefinite and undifferentiated in which all varieties of existents inhere potentially, and (*b*) all sensible things are derived by the efficiency of one or more contrarieties. But, in other positions, the employment of contrariety becomes a very complex notion, because it can be employed in different levels[20] and in both ways, i.e. independently and efficiently simultaneously; or as a principle of arrangement at two different cosmic levels. Cases of advanced and complex uses

---

[18] *Phys.* 187a 12 ff.

[19] Diels, *Die Frag. der Vors.* (Anaximandros), B 9, B 16.

[20] One level is the exposition of the nature of the elements, and another is the account of the cosmogonic process. This distinction is implicitly used by the early thinkers.

The Use of the Principle of Contrariety

of contrariety are the cosmologies of Empedocles and Anaxagoras. In Empedocles the principal elements are four and contrary to each other; there is also an independent and efficient pair of contraries, that of Love and Strife, which unite or mix and separate or unmix the opposite elements. But again, as Aristotle reports,[21] everything is in the cosmic *spheros* where the opposites are *united* by Love and *separated* by Strife.

In the Anaxagorean position we have an indefinite number of contrary qualities constituting the ultimate elements which are arranged in opposite pairs. But when movement is introduced and the universe is viewed as a *panthomou*[22] to be arranged by Nous, then, we find one pervasive contrariety, that of Air-Aether, which divides the infinite aggregates into two wholes, both of which are in turn infinite and equal. Therefore, whereas the elements present a plural contrariety, the aggregates show a single contrariety. It is known that Anaxagoras used Nous for the principle of efficiency, which is not involved in any contrariety at all. Hence, it is not surprising that Nous cognizes all, and in itself is pure and single!

Anaxagoras as well as Empedocles[23] could not use the rarefaction-condensation contrariety because they had assumed at the beginning distinct elemental and efficient principles. Anaxagoras explicitly refers to a contrariety involved in *becoming*, that of *generation-destruction*, as not used correctly by the Greeks, and he substitutes that of aggregation-segregation. In these two thinkers mixing is prior to unmixing and plurality is prior to unity. Obviously in their pluralism of elements they took substance out of its proper context; the same is true for their treatment of contrariety. Anaximenes and Anaximander were right in placing contrariety within the *one*, but this *one* again, on the level of cosmology, is used in a non-distributive sense of being.

Heraclitus is equally wrong in another way. His philosophy, being in a sense the counterpart of the Parmenidean position, amounts to a reduction of the pervasiveness of contrariety to the incessant nameless flux. Flux or change is made the ultimate

---

[21] *Phys.* I, ch. 4. Also Diels, *Die Frag. der Vors.* (Empedocles), A 28, 29, 32, 37; B 8, 17, 26, 27, 30, 35.

[22] *Ibid.* (Anaxagoras), B 1, 4, 6, 8, 12, 13, 17.

[23] Aristotle criticizes Empedocles for using the efficient contrariety of Love-Strife in an absolutistic way. *De Gen. et Corr.* 333b 22-6.

cosmological context within which all differentiations eventuate. Still, the opposites are ontologically real, but not as real as the flux, 'the hidden harmony'.[24] To the extent that he resolves all contrarieties in an inclusive, hypostatized, absolute Change, Heraclitus is not dissimilar from Parmenides,[25] who, in his dialectical efficiency, linked all differences to phenomena and opinion. Both Heraclitus and Parmenides had taken the One seriously; the former saw it dynamically, the latter statically, but both remained monists in their cosmologies. There appears on the surface a tendency to take substance seriously, but finally neither of them could say anything about it because both had reduced contrariety to the more ultimate notion of one substance.[26]

Anaximenes and Anaxagoras produced all discrete entities from a cosmic oneness through the implicit contrarieties which played the role of the principle of differentiation. Heraclitus and Parmenides, as a result of their negative critique of the Ionian thinkers, reduced all differences to the cosmic One. Heraclitus, being an Ionian, conceived the One physically; Parmenides, with a mathematical background, thought it logically; but both of them reserved contrariety for the world of plurality and individual changing things, and therefore, its cognitive significance, whatever its value, is reserved for the cosmos of change. Heraclitus, by making process absolute and ultimate, had attacked not only permanence as such, but along with it he rejected rationality and cognition and questioned the validity of the law of non-contradiction, for which he became the special target of Aristotle's criticisms.[27]

Parmenides, by reducing all reality to One,[28] made the laws of logic unnecessary, because the contemplation of the One required nothing but thinkability. The One yields no definition of itself in discourse, for it has no *differentia* to be stated in its essence or definition. The law of non-contradiction is valid only in so far as it helps discourse to arrive at the dialectic of the One; it is valuable only during the *process* of the argument. Once the result is established, nothing but pure vision of reality is valid—obviously,

---

[24] Diels, *Die Frag. der Vors.* (Herakleitos), A 1, 5, 16; B 1, 8, 10, 30, 50, 53, 67, 80, 91.
[25] *Ibid.* (Parmenides); Treatise of 'Physis' part one; B 7.
[26] See Appendix: ch. 3, note 5.   [27] *Met. Γ*, ch. 3; also K 1062a 32 ff.
[28] Diels, *Die Frag. der Vors.* (Parmenides), B 5, 6.

The Use of the Principle of Contrariety

because all differences and distinctions have been resolved and there is no change to understand.

The priority of the One is an essential character in the cosmologies of Anaximenes, Anaximander, Heraclitus, and Parmenides, but the role it plays in each of these cosmic stories is always non-distributive, inclusive, comprehensive, ultimate, absolute. These features of the One are altogether different from the *one* of the Aristotelian metaphysical unit of distributive being. However, their theories contain one healthy element with regard to contrariety: though contrariety is not thought of in terms of a distinctive trait that renders process cognizable, it is, nevertheless, conceived within the encompassing concept of One.

Later, in Aristotle's philosophy, the One became the locus, which, as a principle, sustains process, and is not to be confused with the other principles that are employed in the cognizing process. The cosmological monists did not conceive the advantages of a pluralism of principles. Empedocles, Anaxagoras, and the Atomists reacted against monism, but their efforts were restricted to the field of elemental speculation. They are pluralists regarding the material principle; in consequence, they continued to use contrariety as a *hypostasis*, whether they saw it as emerging from the One or as constituting the material principle itself. Contrariety was reintroduced by the pluralists, Empedocles, Anaxagoras, and other thinkers of that generation, because they not only took change seriously, like Heraclitus, but also took change as something to be explained and not to be reduced to some kind of an absolute.[29]

Whatever exists is never absolutely bare and without determinations. Even in the theory of elements, Aristotle states that there is no bare matter, but always determinate matter; therefore, when absolute matter is used as the first principle, there inevitably results a monistic reductionism, as in Anaximenes. The hypostatization of contrarieties (in which case they would have to be in process, like other substances) leads to a qualitative pluralism as in Anaxagoras, or to a non-causal material pluralism, as in Empedocles, who made contrarieties out of both the four elements and the efficient principles of Love and Strife.

The diverse and complicated treatment of contrariety in the

---

[29] Aristotle's criticisms of the monists from the point of view of contrariety are given in *De Gen. et Corr.* 329a 5–329b 2. See also *Phys.* I, ch. 6–9.

The Use of the Principle of Contrariety

early period of Greek philosophy was in need of systematic clarification and critical reconstruction. Aristotle was faced with this problem. He answered it through an analysis based on the solid grounds of his metaphysics of distributive being, which was in turn supported by the best available advance in scientific method. The Heraclitean One and the Parmenidean Whole were fused into one by Aristotle; the new combination became the first substance as the locus of process in his natural philosophy. Cosmology was replaced by ontological analysis. The basis on which the intelligibility of process could be re-established required an extension of the meaning of 'principle' to include in it the fundamental ways in which it could function as the starting-point of logos and meaningful discourse. The rudimentary Parmenidean logical suggestions and Plato's dialectical approach to 'difference' and contrariety could be turned into excellent instruments for understanding change; what was really required was a new approach to being. But before presenting the ontological reconstruction of contrariety, we must conclude our present theme with a comparative analysis of Aristotle's and his predecessors' stoichiologies.

4. CONTRARIETY IN THE PRE-ARISTOTELIAN STOICHIOLOGIES AND IN ARISTOTLE'S THEORY OF ELEMENTS

Aristotle's stoichiology has two main drives, the criticism of the older theories, and his actual reconstruction of the theory of elements.[30] It is essential to remember that the Aristotelian elements *are not prior* to the subject-in-process, but are only the final points of analysis of what seems to be involved in the material cause. They are what we might call chemical 'abstractions', existing only as constituents in given substances, as determinate powers within some kind of structure or formal organization. Aristotle's next point was to prove that the four elements change into each other, a point which Empedocles was not capable of demonstrating. In order to do so he proceeded to state what the contrarieties were, for in every change, in generation and destruction, there is a contrariety involved, with the reservation that contrarieties themselves do not suffer change.

[30] Aristotle (like Empedocles) recognized in the sublunary level only four elements: air, fire, water, earth.

The Use of the Principle of Contrariety

The contrarieties involved in elemental change are tangibly discoverable. They are the hot and the cold, the dry and the moist, the heavy and the light, the hard and the soft, the viscous and the brittle, the rough and the smooth, and the coarse and the fine.

After inquiring into their differences and relations, he shows that they can be reduced to the first two contrarieties, i.e. hot-cold and dry-moist.[31] The possible combinations of these four primary qualitative terms give six different couples, but only four are accepted, since those that are originally contrary, e.g. hot-cold and dry-moist, do not mix. Hence the pairs of the mixable four qualitative terms are (*a*) hot and dry, (*b*) moist and hot, (*c*) cold and dry, and (*d*) cold and moist.[32] Each of the four elements is characterized by one of these four possible pairs of combined qualities, which, it should be noted, are not themselves contrarieties. Fire is a combination of hot and dry; air, of hot and moist; water, of cold and moist; earth, of cold and dry. On the basis of these conclusions about the nature of the elements, Aristotle proceeds to criticize the early cosmologists in respect to the material cause. We have adopted here terminology which suggests the fundamental positions of these schools in terms of the number of elements used. They are as follows:

A. *Monistic Materialism or Elemental Monism.* Aristotle alludes to Anaximander.[33] In another connection,[34] he gives more extensive references to monism. In the *Physics*, he sees two types of monism: (1) where the 'one' is unchangeable (Parmenides and Melissus); and (2) where the 'one' is changeable (Thales and Hippo[35] called it water; Anaximenes and Diogenes of Apollonia,[36] air; Heraclitus,[37] fire). But to return to Anaximander, his Boundless generates the objects of nature through a fundamental contrariety, e.g. *dense-rare*. Therefore, Aristotle concludes, Anaximander is actually employing *two* principles; one is the *hyle*-substratum and the other is a pair of contraries, condensation-rarefaction, which in Aristotle's stoichiology is equivalent to hot-cold. The contraries are the 'formative forces'[38] while the One is the substratum. Consequently, this is a pseudo-monism.

---

[31] *De Gen. et Corr.* 329b 17 ff. [32] *Ibid.*, 330a 30–330b 1.
[33] *Ibid.*, 330b 7–8. [34] *Phys.* I, ch. 1, 2.
[35] Simplicius, *Phys.* 23, 22, 149 7; also *De Caelo* 615, 11.
[36] Diels, *Die Frag. der Vors.* (Diogenes of Apollonia), B 5.
[37] *Met.* A 984a 7. [38] *De Gen. et Corr.* 330b 12–13.

The Use of the Principle of Contrariety

B. *Dyadic Materialism or Elemental Dualism.* Parmenides, in his 'Way to Opinion',[39] offers two material elements, fire and earth, which are characterized by hot and cold; the intermediate elements, air and water, are mixtures of the first two. In the *Physics* Aristotle, through Parmenides, hints at the Pythagoreans as representatives of this type of stoichiology;[40] generation and destruction can be explained simply on the 'efficiency' ascribed to hot-cold, because there are no other determining factors that cause things to be.[41]

C. *Triadic Materialism.* The thinkers of this school are very similar to the dualists, since they regard two elements as the extremes, and a third intermediate one as a blend of the two. The only difference appears to be that the dualists split the intermediate element and relegate its divided portions to the contrary extremities, as in the case of air shared between fire and earth. Aristotle mentions Ion of Chios and Plato as maintaining this type of theory.[42]

D. *Tetradic Materialism.* The pre-eminent representative of this view is Empedocles. In a way, he also groups the four elements into two, i.e. air, earth, and water, together, as opposed to fire.[43] Aristotle objects to the Empedoclean tetradism: it is basically wrong in taking the elements to be pure and unmixed, and as such it makes change impossible.[44] In order to correct the shortcomings of this position he rearranges it in terms of the cosmic distribution and natural place of each of the elements;[45] thus, the extremities are occupied by fire and earth which are the least mixed ones. The intermediate regions are taken up by air and water. The elements now have become contrary to each other; fire is contrary to water, and earth to air.

E. *The Indefinite and Infinite types of Materialism.* Anaxagoras had employed, as we saw, an indefinite number of contrary qualities which comprise through their mixture the material substratum. The Atomists conceived of the elements in the form of infinite

[39] Diels, *Die Frag. der Vors.* (Parmenides), B 8, 53–9.
[40] See *Timaeus* 31 B; also Theophrastus, *Met.* 6b 25.
[41] *De Gen. et Corr.* 336a 1–12.
[42] See H. H. Joachim's *Aristotle's De Gen. et Corr.*, Oxford, 1922, pp. 214–17.
[43] *De Gen. et Corr.* 330b 19 ff; *Met.* 985a 31–985b 3.
[44] *De Gen. et Corr.* 315a 3–25.
[45] *De Caelo*, 268b 12–269a 9; 269b 20–9; 308a 14–33; 311a 15 ff.

The Use of the Principle of Contrariety

atoms. Aristotle believes that even the Atomists employed contrariety through making use of the *plenum and the void*.[46]

The pervasive cardinal error which Aristotle detected in all his predecessors' illegitimate use of contrariety in their speculative stoichiologies was due to the inability of these thinkers to inquire first into the concept of contrariety by way of a distinctive science. The ontological analysis of contrariety shows that it is not a material cause but a principle which has to do, not with the making, but with the understanding of process.

Let us now consider certain difficulties in Aristotle's reconstructed theory of elements. Besides the four elements (none of them infinite),[47] there is a fifth one, namely αἰνήρ, which has no contrary to it. Each of the four elements has a natural place and a motion which is linear, while *aither* is in perfect circular motion. These are again the four possible combinations of the contrary terms that determine the elements. This notion is based upon the assumption that these combinations are also the most elemental contraries perceivable in the material cause of the subjects-in-process, and that they form the material foundations for the derivability of all other contraries. The basic qualities of the elements, that is, hot, moist, dry, and cold, are consequently the ultimate characters.

At first sight, it seems that Aristotle is similarly reducing all beings to the formative character of the material cause. But however inadequate his stoichiology, this difficulty is resolved because he does not reduce to two contraries all the principles involved in the material cause of a subject-in-process. The four elements in their barest status as the mere potentiality of a substratum, are incapable of any actual change; *they are but the result of an analysis*, and abstractions do not change. Apart from being a potential substratum they are totally negative. As pure *termini* of a process of abstraction they are devoid of all determinations and are complete privation.

The second and genuine difficulty in Aristotle's stoichiology lies in his doctrine of elemental transformation, according to which the elements, though in principle mere privations, are curiously enough capable of changing into one another.[48] The elucidation of this confusion calls for an analysis of the role of

---

[46] *Phys.* 188a 19–27.   [47] *Phys.* 204b 35.
[48] *De Gen. et Corr.* II, ch. 4.

The Use of the Principle of Contrariety

contrariety in interelemental change, which must be clearly distinguished from any substantial process. Aristotle states:

'It is evident that all of them are by nature such as to change into one another: for coming-to-be is a change into contraries, and out of contraries, and the "elements" all involve a contrariety in their mutual relations because their distinctive qualities are contrary.'[49]

The transformation takes place through a substitution of one quality for another, provided that the new qualitative combination does not resolve into a qualitative contrariety. But the elements as such do not become, or, there is *genesis* but not *becoming*. The elements are in no process when isolated. Only 'natures', subjects-in-process become, in a sense that they actualize their potentialities, and by being *loci* of functions which are subsumed under the categorical contrarieties. The difference between an element and a subject-in-process amounts to this: an element contains no contrariety while the subject-in-process does. In point of fact, it is the presence of contrariety that testifies to process. It may be in theory that the elements change into each other, but this change is not of the type of process that experience discloses in the context of distributive being. This is a weak point in Aristotle.

Ultimately this is a result of an instance of *a priori* theorizing. Contrariety as a principle of understanding process is attributed only to 'natures'. A related consequence of this ontological approach to contrariety is that it enables him to avoid a progressivism in his theory of elements and of nature. Though 'nature strives for the better',[50] this natural impulse must be understood distributively. Aristotle did not attribute fulfilment to *nature as a whole*, because he made genesis an uninterrupted interelemental change and not the beginning of a total temporal evolution. Again, the conception of a stellar motion in a cyclical fashion prevented him from making generation rectilinear; the elemental transformation explains the reciprocity in up and down movement which keeps all things from being forced to land on the earth.

'That is why all the other things—the things, I mean which are reciprocally transformed in virtue of their "passions" and their

---

[49] *De Gen. et Corr.* 331a 14–16. [50] *Ibid.*, 336b 27–9.

The Use of the Principle of Contrariety

"powers of actions", e.g. the simple bodies—imitate circular motion. . . . It is by imitating circular motion that rectilinear motion too is continuous.'[51]

A major difference between his stoichiology and his ontology results from the way in which contrariety is used. In the stoichiology he assumes two primary contrarieties, while in the ontology he states one primary contrariety.

'Assuming, then, that the contrariety, in respect to which they are transformed, is *one*, the "elements" will inevitably be two:[52] for it is "matter" that is the "mean" between the two contraries, and matter is imperceptible and inseparable from them. Since, however, the "elements" are seemed to be more than two, the contrarieties must at the least be two. But the contrarieties being two, the "elements" must be four (as they evidently are) and cannot be three: for the "couplings" are four, since, though six are possible, the two in which the qualities are contrary to one another cannot occur. . . . Since the "elements" are transformed into one another, it is impossible for any one of them—whether it be at the end or in the middle—to be an "originative source" of the rest.'[53]

Though his avoidance of reducing the elements to an ultimate *one* is a sound pluralism, the assumptions of his stoichiology are of questionable validity. But, on the other hand, it was the best stoichiology of his time. The explicit and rational use of contrariety enabled him to refute the fallacies of his predecessors, but his crude empiricism in selecting the contrarieties on the basis of the senses (and especially touch), and in choosing the elements from the predominantly perceived types of matter (air, earth, etc.), made his stoichiology equally vulnerable. His success is to be found in his ingenious linking of contrariety to ontology where contrariety was introduced as a necessary condition for the intelligibility of process.

As to the problem of the transformation of the elements, he succeeded in offering the best solution by making use of the

---

[51] *De Gen. et Corr.* 337a 1–8.
[52] This is the opposite of what happens with subjects-in-process where the subject is one and the contrariety is one (with two extremities).
[53] *De Gen. et Corr.* 332a 34–332b 8.

The Use of the Principle of Contrariety

contrariety actuality-potentiality.[54] His main problem there was to demonstrate how, from the eternal transformation of the elements, one can derive the homogeneous organic substances, like bones and flesh. This task called for an elaborate theory of mixture.[55]

The Aristotelian stoichiology was discussed here because of its ample use of contrariety. By maintaining contrariety within every elemental mixture, Aristotle was basically demolishing the theories built on the primordial indeterminacy of the absolute elemental purity. Again, contrariety, as an indispensable factor in mixture, renders all cosmologies that appeal to pure elemental beginnings physically impossible.

The new usage of contrariety, in spite of the theoretical shortcomings of the entire stoichiology, marks a gain over his predecessors. There can be little doubt as to its significance for paving the road towards an ontological analysis of contrariety in a metaphysics of distributive being. Such was Aristotle's reconstruction of the cosmological and dialectical employment of contrariety for a more adequate theory of elements.

[54] *De Gen. et Corr.* II, ch. 1.   [55] See Appendix: ch. 3, note 6.

Chapter Four

CONTRARIETY IN THE LOCUS OF PROCESS AND IN THE CATEGORIES

THE purpose of the previous chapter was to clarify the grounds for Aristotle's reconstruction of the notion of contrariety. In this chapter the following themes are discussed: (1) To state and arrange those general statements in the theory of contraries that constitute a set of rules relating contrariety to the locus of process. (2) To make an exhaustive analysis of the uses of contraries as presented in the relevant Aristotelian passages and demonstrate the meaning of contrariety as a formal demand. (3) To relate the distinction of prior-posterior, as it fulfils the formal demand of contrariety, to change and development. (4) To show that the Aristotelian categories display fundamental and pervasive contrarieties, termed 'categorical', and are ultimate distinctions rendering substance intelligible.

1. BASIC PROPOSITIONS IN THE THEORY OF CONTRARIES

There are certain basic propositions or admissions which lay the foundation for a metaphysical analysis of the meaning of contrariety and its relation to process.

1. *The kinds of process are equal to the types of change related to the four categories: substance, quality, quantity, and place.*

'Since every change is *from* something *to* something—as the word itself *metabole* indicates, implying something "after" (meta)

Contrariety in the Locus of Process

something else, that is to say something earlier and something later—that which changes must change in one of four ways: from subject to subject, from subject to non-subject, from non-subject to subject, or from non-subject to non-subject, where by "subject" I mean what is affirmatively expressed. So it follows necessarily from what has been said above that there are only three kinds of change, that from subject to subject, that from subject to non-subject, and that from non-subject to subject: for the fourth conceivable kind, that from non-subject to non-subject, is not a change, as in that case there is no opposition either of contraries or of contradictories.'[1]

According to this passage, change may occur in four ways:
1. From a positive A to a positive term B.
2. From a positive A to its contradictory not-A.
3. From a negative not-A to its contradictory A.
4. From a negative not-A to a negative not-B.

Upon inspection, case 4 is ruled out since there is no opposition between two negative terms. There remain the other three cases.

Case 1. Only this case is process. Here change from A to B is possible in two ways: either A and B are contraries, in which case both are positive terms, or A is a contrary and the other is an intermediate point, positive again, between A and B.

Case 2. Change from A to not-A becomes equivalent to destruction or passing away, which in turn is of two kinds: (*a*) passing-away absolutely (φθορὰ ἁπλῶς) meaning destruction of a substance, and (*b*) passing-away in a given respect (φθορά τις) meaning that a substance comes to lose a certain quality, changes its size or location.

Case 3. Change from not-A to A is the opposite of case 2 and is equivalent to generation or coming-to-be, which is similarly of two kinds: (*a*) coming-to-be absolutely (γένεσις ἁπλῶς), meaning the generation of a substance, and (*b*) the coming-to-be of the things a substance comes to possess (γένεσίς τις), such as a given quality, an increase in size, or a change in its location. The movement from not-A to A, in the absolute sense, is not called *kinesis* but *metabole*, because that which is not-A was not a substance in the way in which an existing individual substance is. The distinctions between absolute and relative generation and that of absolute and relative destruction allow Aristotle to bring the notions of

[1] *Phys.* 224b 35–225a 12.

Contrariety in the Locus of Process

relative generation and relative destruction under that of process between contraries. In this way 'metabole' acquires an encompassing meaning and refers to two types of process: (*a*) process between contraries, and (*b*) process between contradictories, which is delimited by generation and destruction in the absolute sense. Relative generation and destruction, though formally expressed as movement between contradictories, is the same as process between contraries, that is, case 1.

In the light of the categories mentioned in *Physics* 225b 5–9, the kinds of *kinesis* are indeed three, but if we are to include in this list the 'metabole' of generation and destruction, then the types of process are four.

1. In respect of *substance*, which is not kinesis but metabole, because substance has no contrary to it.[2]
2. In respect of *quality*, which admits of contrariety; this change is called alteration.
3. In respect of *quantity*, which also admits of contrariety and is encompassed between growth and diminution.
4. In respect of *place*, which is called locomotion.

There is no movement in respect of *relation*, except in an accidental sense.[3]

The context in which all possible changes take place is provided, according to the passage quoted, through the existence of a *hypokeimenon*, a subject-in-process, which is a substantial entity and is the locus of quality, quantity, and place. This substance is presupposed in all change.

2. *Process apart from a given subject is a mere impossibility.*

'There is no such thing as motion *over and above* the things. It is always with respect to substance or to quantity or to quality or to place that what changes changes. But it is impossible, as we assert, to find anything *common* to these which is neither "this" nor *quantum* nor *quale* nor any of the other predicates. Hence neither will motion and change have reference to something over and above them.'[4]

W. D. Ross interprets this passage as meaning 'not the things that change but the various respects in which things may change'.[5]

---

[2] *Phys.* 225b 10–11; also *Cat.* 3b 24–7.
[3] *Phys.* 225b 11–13. [4] *Phys.* 200b 32–201a 3.
[5] W. D. Ross, *Aristotle's Physics*, p. 536.

Contrariety in the Locus of Process

This interpretation seems correct since Aristotle uses the expression τὰ ἐν οἷς ἡ κίνησις. It has been mentioned before that *kinesis* refers to substance as the locus of changes. Since process presupposes substance, it follows that there cannot be process in the abstract.

3. *There is no process of process.*[6]

'There can never be, process of process, or generation of generation, or in general, change of change. . . . If there is to be change of change and becoming of becoming, we shall have an infinite regress. . . . Since in an infinite series there is no first term, here there will be no first stage and therefore no following stage either. . . . On this hypothesis, then, nothing can become or be moved or change. Moreover, if a thing is capable of any particular motion, it is also capable of the corresponding contrary motion or the corresponding coming to rest, and a thing that is capable of becoming is also capable of perishing: consequently if there be becoming of becoming, that which is in process of becoming is in process of perishing at the very moment it has reached the stage of becoming: since it cannot be in process of perishing when it is just beginning to become or after it has ceased to become: for that which is in process of perishing must be in existence.'[7]

Generation and process as such do not exist. Aristotle correctly points out that to turn process in the abstract into a substance leads to infinite regress. Inevitably, an infinite series follows in which there is no first term, and thus movement and change become impossible. The upshot is that movement itself cannot be moved.[8] If it were, it would have to be one of the three mentioned kinds, in which case it ceases being 'in itself'. The absurdity is obvious.

4. *None of the primary types of change is either absolute or infinite.*

'It is evident, then, that a process of change cannot be infinite in the sense that it is not defined by limits. But it remains to be considered whether it is possible in the sense that one and the same process of change may be infinite in respect of the time which it occupies. If it is not one process, it would seem that there is nothing to prevent its being infinite in this sense; e.g. if a process of locomotion be succeeded by a process of alteration and

---

[6] See Appendix: ch. 4, note 1.   [7] *Phys.* 225b 15–226a 12.
[8] See also in *Aristotle, Physics* (Loeb), vol. II, p. 22, F. M. Cornford's comment (note b).

Contrariety in the Locus of Process

that by a process of increase and that again by a process of coming to be: in this way there may be motion for ever so far as the time is concerned but it will be not one motion, because all these motions do not compose one. If it is to be one process, no motion can be infinite in respect of the time that it occupies, with the single exception of rotary locomotion.'[9]

And elsewhere:

'... no process of change is infinite: for every change, whether between contradictories or between contraries, is a change from something to something. Thus in contradictory changes the positive or the negative, as the case may be, is the limit, e.g. being is the limit of coming to be and not-being is the limit of ceasing to be: and in contrary changes the particular contraries are the limits, since these are the extreme points of any such process of change...'[10]

There is *metabole* in a substance as a whole, while *kinesis* is in its parts. But in both cases process cannot be infinite, for all change is from something to something. The substantial change is between contradictories (not-A and A) while qualitative, quantitative, and locomotive changes occur between contraries, and therefore, both are determinate. The only movement not enclosed between boundaries is rotation, which alone is eternal and infinite.[11]

5. *Process does not have a contrary to it, i.e. process itself does not constitute a term of any contrariety.* 'Non-process' (ἀμεταβλησία) is not a term contrary to process (μεταβολή).

'Of all things that have no contraries there are opposite *changes* (viz. change from the thing and change to the thing, e.g. change from being, and change to being), but no *motion*. So, too, of such things there is no remaining though there is absence of change. Should there be a particular subject, absence of change in its being will be contrary to absence in its not-being. And here a difficulty may be raised: if not-being is not a particular something, what is it, it may be asked, that is contrary to absence of change in a thing's being? And is this absence of change a state of rest? If it is, then, either it is not true that every state of rest

---

[9] *Phys.* 241b 11–20.   [10] *Phys.* 241a 26–31; also see 265a 11 ff.
[11] This question is answered at length in *Physics* 261a 27–265a 12. The impossibility of infinite motion along an infinite straight line is stated in *Phys.* 265a 17–20.

Contrariety in the Locus of Process

is contrary to a motion or else coming to be and ceasing to be are motion. It is clear then that, since we exclude these from among motions, we must not say that this absence is a state of rest: we must say that it is similar to a state of rest and call it absence of change. And it will have for its contrary either nothing or absence of change in the thing's not-being, or the ceasing to be of the thing: for ceasing to be is change *from it* and the thing's coming to be is change *to it*.'[12]

The only contrary to process (in the sense of *metabole*) could be a 'non-process' (ἀμεταβλησία). We must now consider the possible ways in which non-process is contrasted to the extremities of *metabole*, i.e. generation and destruction. Let us take the case of a subject passing from a state of not-being to being, or not-A to A and *vice versa*. When the subject is in the state not-A, the non-process could only be contrary to the subject's non-process in the state of A, just as generation is contrary to destruction. However, since not-A as such does not have any existence at all, the alternative is to see what non-process is or could mean when the subject is in A, i.e. in being, and whether this non-process could be identified with *rest*. But non-process cannot be rest, for (*a*) the only contrary to rest is movement, and (*b*) it is not the case that non-process could be rest and have as its contrary the notion of absolute generation and destruction since the latter is not movement (*kinesis*) but *metabole*. Hence, non-process or absence of change, or non-*metabole* is not the same with rest, but only similar to a state of rest. If it is contrary to something, then either (*a*) it is nothing at all, or (*b*) it is contrary to non-process in the state of not-A, which again is impossible, or (*c*) at best, it is contrary to destruction, for only destruction is moving away from non-process, whereby non-process now means the permanence or unchangeableness of the essence of a substance throughout its career.

The conclusion seems to be that the only way in which non-process could have any meaning at all, if we are right in our interpretation, is to refer to it as absence of (substantial) change in the essential character and unity of an individual substance after its generation and prior to its destruction, in which case non-process could be contrary only to the latter, i.e. destruction. It follows

[12] *Phys.* 230a 7–18.

Contrariety in the Locus of Process

then, that in the final analysis, (*a*) process has no contrary to it, (*b*) both process and non-process are not substances, and (*c*) the meanings of these terms are relative to individual substances.

2. THE USES OF CONTRARIES

Although Aristotle devoted ample space in the *Categories* to discussing the various functions and applications of the term 'contraries', we still have to go to the *Metaphysics* to find a concise exposition of the plurality of meanings that the term 'contraries' implies. Chapter 2 of the *Categories* contains a brief but inadequate statement. For this reason it will be necessary to supplement it with the careful enumeration of the uses of 'contraries' given in *Metaphysics* Δ,[13] which may be grouped under two headings: primary and derivative.

A. *Primary contraries*. In this sense, the term 'contrary' is applied:
1. To those attributes differing in genus which cannot belong at the same time to the same subject. (Note that here Aristotle refers to the elemental substratum.)
2. To the most different of the things in the same genus.
3. To the most different of the attributes in the same recipient subject.
4. To the most different of the things that fall under the same faculty.

The first two meanings are also given in the *Categories*.[14] The apparent inconsistency between these first two meanings disappears if we bear in mind that a genus may be a species of a higher and more inclusive genus, in which case the contraries differing in genus are species of a higher one, and thus belong to the same genus again; and thus case 1 is reduced to case 2.[15]

---

[13] *Met.* Δ, ch. 10, 1018a 25–37.

[14] *Cat.* 14a 19–20; also *Top.* 153a 36. However, in *De Gen. et Corr.* 324a 2, a rule is stated that all contraries must necessarily be in the same genus. Also, *Cat.* 6a 17; *Met.* Iota, ch. 4.

[15] *Cat.* 14a 20–5. The reference is to justice and injustice as coming under the contrary genera of virtue and vice. This notion must be pushed farther in connection with *possession*, and this again with that of *hypokeimenon* or subject-in-process capable of possessing such contrary genera. Vice and virtue are genera of a moral type and are contained in the categorical genus of relation.

Contrariety in the Locus of Process

In the *Metaphysics*[16] we see that the contrary genera do not appear in the list of contraries. The reason, according to W. D. Ross, is that the genus is here conceived as a *summum genus*.[17] Since nothing can pass from one genus to another,[18] it follows that there cannot be contrary genera or contraries in different genera, especially in process. It seems that in Book Δ, 'genus' is treated rather loosely in order to include in it contrary genera like justice and injustice and vice and virtue.[19]

'All things which are generated from their contraries involve an underlying subject; a subject, then, must be present in the case of contraries, if anywhere. All contraries, then, are predicable of a subject, and none can exist apart, but just as appearances suggest that there is nothing contrary to substance, argument confirms this.'[20]

The question here is what underlies the contrary genera of virtue and vice. In the *Categories*[21] we are told that virtue and vice are contraries as *relatives*. Admitting that there is no change in relatives,[22] it is plausible to say that the term 'contraries' and 'genus' are here used in a particularly non-technical sense.

In another connection, Aristotle states explicitly that contraries necessarily belong to the same genus, and in fact, through a common subject-matter.

'So far then as concerns the sphere of connexions scientifically known in the unqualified sense of that term, all attributes which (within that sphere) are essential either in the sense that their subjects are contained in them, or in the sense that they are contained in their subjects, are necessary as well as consequently connected with their subjects. For it is impossible for them not to inhere in their subjects—either simply or in the qualified sense that one or the other of a pair of opposites must inhere in the subject.'[23]

The fundamental importance of the locus provided by the subject-matter lies in the fact that apart from it change from one contrary to the other becomes impossible.[24]

[16] 1055a 23-33.
[17] Compare *Met.* 1054b 29.
[18] *Met.* 1054b 29, 1057a 26.
[19] Also *Top.* 123b 14-16.
[20] *Met.* 1087a 35-1087b 3. The place of contrariety in ethics is treated in ch. 9.
[21] 6b 15-20.
[22] *Met.* 1088a 27-35.
[23] *An. Post.*, Book I, ch. 4, 73b 16-21.
[24] *Met.* 1055b 12-17; 1055a 30-31.

Contrariety in the Locus of Process

B. *Derivative contraries.*
1. They possess one of the types of primary contraries.
2. They are receptive of such primary contraries.
3. They are productive or susceptible to primary contraries.
4. They are producing or suffering primary contraries.
5. They are acquisitions or losses of primary or other contraries.
6. They are possessions or privations of primary contraries.

Contrariety, again, can be considered as the source of 'otherness' (not difference). Aristotle states this notion in an interesting passage which is worth quoting for the bearing it has on the present discussion.

'The term "other in species" is applied to things which being of the same genus are not subordinate the one to the other, or which being in the same genus have a difference, or which have a contrariety in their substance; and contraries are other than one another in species (either all contraries or those which are called in the primary sense), and so are those things whose definitions differ in the *infima species* of the genus (e.g. man and horse are indivisible in genus but their definitions are different), and those which being in the same substance have a difference.'[25]

So far we have encountered all the possible meanings of the term 'contrary'. It is only in one of the above meanings that we can use it intelligently. Whenever this locus is absent it must be sought and clearly stated through a series of reasonings which would connect the contraries as terms of a given contrariety and show that they belong to such a subject.[26] This locus may be explicitly stated at the beginning or tacitly assumed, but in all cases it must be accessible to the inquiring mind or the questioning interlocutor. The contraries, although they may be the object of a formal analysis, also state the pattern and the limits of all changes that the subject-in-process displays. It is not the contrary terms taken in abstraction, but the activities, operations, and functions of the subject-in-process that display *limits and extremities*.

There are certain formal conditions which, though implied by

---

[25] *Met.* 1018a 39–1018b 6. A brief and useful summary of the meanings of contraries in the light of 'difference' is given in *Met.* Iota, ch. 4, 1055a 16–33.
[26] *Cat.* 14a 6–19; also *Met.* 1055a 29.

Contrariety in the Locus of Process

the aforesaid meanings of 'contrary', must be stated with great care. It is necessary, if the contraries are to constitute extremities of an identifiable and continuous actualization of an activity, that they must conform to the following: *they must in every case constitute the extremities of a single kind or genus, for otherwise it is impossible to understand the change that a given activity undergoes in the process of its unfolding.*

3. CONTRARIETY AS RELATED TO PRIOR AND POSTERIOR

Since activities and functions are actualizations of some kind, the process which they display is a development from a given extremity to another extremity (or an intermediate). Change is a movement from a something to a something, and as such it involves the notion of prior and posterior. Whatever the sense of the term 'priority' may be, it must always be applied to actualizations of particular activities and operations of certain functions of a subject-in-process. The concepts *prior* and *posterior* form a distinction that again is patterned according to the formal demands of the principle of contrariety. They constitute a notion useful for the understanding of the linear character of various developments and actions, whether taken against the background of the locus provided by the subject-in-process, or taken separately in a comparison between distinct events.[27]

The uses of the distinction *prior-posterior* are given in this passage:

'... Other things (4) [are called prior and posterior] in respect of nature and substance, i.e. those which can be without other things, while the others cannot be without them—a distinction which Plato[28] used. (If we consider the various senses of 'being', first the subject is prior, so that substance is prior; secondly, according as potentiality or complete reality is taken into account, different things are prior, for some things are prior in respect of potentiality, others in respect of complete reality, e.g. in potentiality the half line is prior to the whole line, and the part to the whole, and the matter to the concrete substance, *but in complete reality these are posterior; for it is only when the whole has been dissolved that they will exist in complete reality.*) In a sense, therefore, all things

[27] *Met.* 1018b 7–1019a 14.
[28] See Ross, *Aristotle's Metaphysics*, vol. I, commentary 1019a 4, p. 317.

that are called prior and posterior are so called with reference to this *fourth* sense; for some things can exist without others in respect of generation, e.g. the whole, without the parts, and others in respect of dissolution, e.g. the part without the whole.'[29]

There are two particular meanings of priority that are fundamentally connected with the analysis of contrariety and process. First, as has already been stated, the contrariety of possession-privation necessarily entails the *priority* of possession. The assumed 'possession' of certain powers of a subject-in-process to act in certain determinate ways must be prior to the total development and fulfilment of these activities. Therefore, there are two priorities involved in process, (1) the priority of the locus within which the activities can be understood as particular processes, and (2) the priority of the possession of certain powers which under favourable conditions become actualities, i.e. the priority of form as *telos*. The particular functions of a subject-in-process are potentiality 'possessed' by virtue of the subject's essence or formal structure. This structure is logically prior in the sense that it is in terms of this structural determinateness that the subject is intelligible.[30]

Since the subject-in-process already possesses its determinations in their potential states, the developments of the latter can be fulfilled by proceeding from the prior potential to the posterior actual. The structural interdependence of the functions of a subject is prior to the developments of that subject's particular functional activities. All movement is essentially connected with the completion or career of the structural interdependence of all the functions present in a locus for the fulfilment of the subject's nature or *eidos* or *end*.[31]

The second meaning of priority has to do with the relation between contrariety and truth. This case is another application of the priority of substance. According to Aristotle, truth and falsity are meaningful only in so far as they belong exclusively to propositions, affirmative or negative. Whether a statement is true or false must be decided on the grounds of some empirical verification of what the statement states as its factual content. The statement 'a man exists' is either true or false. To be true, it is necessary to establish the fact of the existence of a man. In this

[29] *Met.* 1019a 1-14. [30] *Met.* Θ, ch. 8. [31] *Met.* 1050a 4 ff.

Contrariety in the Locus of Process

sense, the cause or grounds of the truth of the statement is the existence of the fact; in another sense, the cause is the establishing of the locus in terms of which the statement can be said to be true. This priority of the locus is the *cause* of the truth of the statement.

'The fact of the being of a man carries with it the truth of the proposition that he is, and the implication is reciprocal: for if a man is, the proposition wherein we allege that he is true, and conversely, if the proposition wherein we allege that he is is true, then he is. The true proposition, however, is in no way the cause of the being of the man, but the fact of the man's being does seem somehow to be the cause of the truth of the proposition, for the truth or falsity of the proposition depends on the fact of the man's being or not being.'[32]

The above discussion might suggest why Aristotle makes first substances prior to secondary ones; again in the category of relation he states that the *sensible* and the *knowable* are prior to knowledge and sensation. In general, if we observe the order in which the categories appear, the category of substance precedes all the others. But the passage just quoted is important in connection with certain deeper consequences.

This quotation presupposes the distinction between the *grammatical* (logical) and the *ontological* subject, i.e. the distinction between the subject of a statement and the subject-in-process. Only the latter is real or first substance. Aristotle has tried in the *Categories*, chapter 2, to give a detailed analysis of the various meanings of the term *subject*. The word *hypokeimenon* stands for two things: (*a*) a grammatical subject which has a place in a sentence, and (*b*) subject as a first substance, which is the ontological ultimate, the locus of processes; the second type of subject is said to be 'neither present in another subject nor predicable of another subject'.[33] If the ontological ultimate could be predicated of another subject-in-process or be present in it, then there could be process of process. This would contradict the foundations of his entire philosophy of nature.[34] For the same reason, the subject-in-process as a locus does not constitute the contrary term of any higher and more inclusive contrariety in a larger locus. If it did, then Aristotle would involve himself in an infinite regress of the 'third man' type. Instead, substance as the subject-in-process

[32] *Cat.* 14b 14–22.   [33] *Cat.* 1b 3–4.   [34] *Phys.* 225b 33–226a 12.

Contrariety in the Locus of Process

can always become a grammatical subject in a given statement, but grammatical subjects should not be uncritically taken as first substances. Attempts at the hypostatization and substantialization of all grammatical subjects do not merely result in philosophical calamities, but, in connection with *priority*, such attempts efface the conditions under which ultimate priority should be given to the substantial subject. Therefore, if the truth of a given statement is ascertainable, it is so by virtue of the substantial subject. The ontological priority of fact is a necessary condition for the truth and falsity of statements.

4. THE CATEGORIES AND THEIR CONTRARIETIES

The very fact that contrariety is necessarily joined with process, change, and development imposes the demand that it cannot occur in all the categories. Thus, contrariety is present only in those genera of categoriae which imply *change*:[35] *substance, quantity, quality*, and *place*. Within each of these four categories, there are two distinguishable *termini* which form the extremities of a distinct and inclusive categorical contrariety:[36] (1) in substance it is form-privation; (2) in quantity it is completeness-incompleteness; (3) in place it is up-down; and (4) in quality it presents no exhaustive general extremities; instead it yields a variety of contrarieties, such as white-black, hot-cold,[37] etc.

Each categorical contrariety when developmentally conceived stands for two directions or types of change characteristic of each category, as subsequent analysis will show.

A. *Substance*

In the *Categories*[38] substance in its primary and first sense is said to be that which (*a*) is not predicated of anything else, (*b*) nor can it be present in another subject. Then, it is always plural and individual. Each substance is integral and concrete; when developmentally conceived it is in process, possessing a plurality of functions through the co-operation of which it fulfils the potential

---

[35] See Appendix: ch. 4, note 2.
[36] *Phys.* 201a 3–9; *Phys.* I, ch. 6, 189a 13. μία τε ἐναντίωσις ἐν παντὶ γένει ἑνί,, ἡ δὲ οὐσία ἕν τι γένος.
[37] The qualitative pairs of contraries were hypostatized by Anaxagoras, who made them the ultimate constituents of the universe. See Diels, *Die Frag. der Vors.* (Anaxagoras), B 6; B 12.   [38] *Cat.* 2a 10–15.

Contrariety in the Locus of Process

ends imbedded in its structure. In the *Categories* Aristotle says: 'If it were not for the first substances it would be impossible for anything else to be.'[39] Also in the *Metaphysics*: 'Being is nothing apart from substance or quality or quantity ... to be one is to be a particular thing.'[40] All substances or subjects-in-process are equally 'substantial', and the notion of existence, strictly speaking, belongs exclusively to the beings signified by the category of substance, because: 'None of the categories other than substance can exist apart.'[41]

This central and supreme character of the category of substance will justify the supreme role which is assigned to its fundamental contrariety, i.e. *form-privation*. (In the *Metaphysics* Aristotle calls it the *primary contrariety*.) When substance is seen *in the light of movement*, it is the subject-in-process and it involves process from something to something. Therefore, once process is made the indispensable feature of substance, the principle of contrariety is automatically introduced as a necessary condition for the intelligibility of process, for apart from these limits process is wholly unintelligible and will remain unknown like Anaximander's original 'Boundless'. A given primary substance, or a subject-in-process, as taken by itself, *has no contrary to it*, but while it remains numerically one and the same it is capable of being the locus of contraries.

'Substances never have contraries, for how could something be contrary to them, e.g. to a given man or a given animal? Nothing is contrary to them. But this trait ... also belongs to species and genera and others such as quantity.'[42]

There is in the *Physics*, the following statement, among others, about contraries in relation to the substance that supports them:

'We do not find that the contraries constitute the *substance* of anything. But what is a first principle ought not to be the *predicate* of any subject. If it were, there would be a principle of the supposed principle: for the subject is a principle, and prior presumably to what is predicated of it. Again, we hold that a substance is not contrary to another substance.'[43]

[39] *Cat.* 2b 5–6. (By anything else he means, genera, species, categories.)
[40] *Met.* 1054a 18–20; *Cat.*, ch. 5.   [41] *Met.* 1069a 25.
[42] *Cat.* 3b 25–30 (translation mine).
[43] *Phys.* 189a 29–33. The contraries are principles not as constituents of substance, but of the intelligibility of substances.

Contrariety in the Locus of Process

Contrariety as the criterion of substance is stated in the following passage:

> 'But what appears to be *the most distinctive mark of substance* is that although it remains numerically one and the same it is capable of admitting contrary determinations. *From among things other than substance one could not possibly adduce an entity possessing that characteristic.* . . . It is by themselves being in process that substances admit of such contrary determinations. . . .
>
> 'Therefore, the most characteristic trait of substance is that it preserves its identity throughout, it remains numerically one during the course of its self-caused change and it is capable of admitting contrary determinations.'[44]

Now we may summarize the following important conclusions about contraries and their relations to substance and to statements about substances:

1. The contraries are not substances, but are *in* substances.
2. Substances are not contraries, nor are they reducible to contraries.
3. Substances are in process by virtue of a principle of their own; therefore, the contraries cannot be efficient causes.
4. Contraries are polar determinations which presuppose a subject-in-process; thus, they are *among* the principles.
5. Defined essences and opinions concerning substances remain unaltered, for they are not substances; they change only by virtue of the substance *being* in process. The truth or falsity of a statement depends on the given determinations, and not on any power of the statement itself of admitting contraries.

The fundamental contrariety in substance, *form-privation*, yields two types of change: (*a*) acquisition of form, coming-to-be, genesis; (*b*) loss of form, passing away, destruction.[45]

The ultimate presuppositions for the *generation* of any subject-in-process are two: (*a*) prime matter as the first substratum to each 'nature',[46] and (*b*) form (which will lead to the distinction of contraries). A third presupposition is admissible, i.e. the four elements.[47] However, the former two presuppositions are in no

---

[44] *Cat.* 4a 10–4b 19 (translation mine).   [45] *Phys.* 225a 33–4.
[46] *Phys.* 192a 25–32.   [47] *De Gen. et Corr.* 329a 32–5.

Contrariety in the Locus of Process

way concrete individual subjects-in-process, nor are they rudimentary stages of a cosmic development which precede the emergence of 'natures'. Rather, they are metaphysical in the sense that they are principles of understanding, pervasive traits of being. They are *archai* reached through analysis and must be presupposed as principles for a metaphysical approach to 'genesis'. The exclusive use of either one of the two presuppositions *at the expense of the other* leads to two kinds of reductionism in cosmological theory.[48]

In the sequel we shall deal briefly with the other three categorical contrarieties. They consider the subject-in-process not as *the total locus, but as a locus of processes*. They apply to discrete processes distinguishable within a given substance.

B. *Quantity*

The distinctive contrariety here is *completeness-incompleteness*. If quantity is considered apart from the notion of substance, an absurdity is inevitable.[49] If there are difficulties involved in the analysis of the contrariety in the category of quantity, they are the result of the fact that there are also mathematical 'existents' which are quantitative terms. However, quantities as such are not subjects-in-process. The notions of great and small appear to form a contrariety, but in the final analysis they do not, for when great and small are taken absolutely they are not quantities in any real sense except in a comparison and in reference to *homogeneous* quantities. Quantities were contraries, then:

'... it will come about that the same subject can admit contrary quantities at the same time and possess simultaneously both terms of a contrariety, which is absurd, for such a case would make a subject contrary to itself.'[50]

---

[48] The two kinds of reductionism are: (*a*) *Monistic reductionism* makes the matter or the substratum totally independent of the contraries; it renders contrariety subordinate, and makes matter indeterminate and temporally prior. The embarrassment is superficially avoided through a cosmic myth or story, as in Anaximander. (*b*) *Pluralistic reductionism* reduces the substratum to ultimate qualitative contraries. It allows for a variety of positions depending upon the number of contrarieties assumed, e.g. one, two, etc. The classic theory of this type is the Anaxagorean one, 'Panthomou', which hypostatized an indefinite number of qualitative contrarieties *prior* to any substratum.

[49] *Phys.* 185a 23.

[50] *Cat.* 5b 33–6; the entire ch. 6 deals with quantity (translation mine).

Contrariety in the Locus of Process

A subject may admit the quantitative terms of great and small at the same time only in an accidental sense; namely, in reference to two external objects. Substance *qua* process admits contraries only successively, and this involves an elaborate analysis of contrariety in terms of *actuality-potentiality*. But finally, *neither is 'great' contrary to 'small' nor 'much' contrary to 'little'*. In order to establish the categorical contrariety of quantity, it is necessary to take the subject-in-process as an *organic quantity* that is subject to growth and diminution by virtue of its internal principle of motion.

'Motion in respect of quantity has no name that includes both contraries, but it is called increase or decrease according as one or the other is designated: that is to say, motion in the direction of complete magnitude is increase, motion in the contrary direction is decrease.'[51]

Thus, to conclude, completeness is the direction toward growth and tends to coincide with the attainment of form, while incompleteness indicates lack of growth and privation.

C. *Place*

Its categorical contrariety is up-down. It gives rise to two kinds of natural locomotion: (*a*) *movement up*, and (*b*) *movement down*.

'Motion in respect of place has no name either general or particular: but we may designate it by the general name of locomotion, though strictly the term "locomotion" is applicable to things that change their place only when they have not the power to come to a stand, and to things that do not move themselves locally.'[52]

In another passage[53] Aristotle traces the natural movements of up-down to the inherent directional properties of the elements. Since every 'nature' has an elemental substratum, it follows that the natural contrariety of up-down is present in each subject-in-process according to the subject's 'chemical' composition. Rotation as locomotion is not considered here, because Aristotle reserves this type of movement for the heavens.

Rotation is not bounded by contrary *termini*, for if it were,

---

[51] *Phys.* 226a 29–32; *Met.* 1010a 23; 1069b 10; also for 'growth', see *De Gen. et Corr.*, Book I, ch. 5.
[52] *Phys.* 226a 32–5; also 229b 7–9.   [53] *Ibid.*, 230b 10 ff.

then it could not constitute a single continuous change.[54] There appears to be an Anaxagorean[55] influence on Aristotle in that he connects rotation with the prime movers.

D. *Quality*

This category lends itself to a series of qualitative categorical contrarieties which come under the heading of qualitative change. A variety of pairs of opposites marks the beginning and the end of certain distinctly qualitative changes always observable in a given locus of processes. Qualities abide necessarily in a subject as possessions, habits, qualified powers, and capacities,[56] and whenever a change occurs in them, it invariably takes the form of a motion between two contraries.[57]

Every change must take place between contrary poles that belong to a given *informed* matter.[58] If an aspect A changes into B, then A and B must be determinations of a single substantial substratum; again, if A and B are determinations of a single substratum then change of A into B is alteration or qualitative change.[59]

Once a given locus is identified and certain powers are in operation, there occur in the subject-in-process determinate changes which dynamically stated mark the *actualization of a potentiality*. The process of change takes place only while the given actualization is present and up to the point where completion—or frustration—is reached. Change is actualization only in so far as the development is yet *incomplete*. As Aristotle states: 'Motion is thought to be a sort of *actuality*, but incomplete, the reason for this view being that the potential whose actuality it is is incomplete.'[60]

---

[54] *Phys.*, Book VIII, ch. 8.

[55] According to Anaxagoras, 'Nous' is the only principle of motion, it displays no contrariety—it is aloof—and it begins the process of the cosmic formation through rotation alone, which once started, continues eternally. Diels, *Die Frag. der Vors.* (Anaxagoras), B. 12.

[56] *Cat.* 8b 25.

[57] *Cat.* 10b 11; *Phys.* 226b 1–10.

[58] *De Gen. et Corr.* 319b 6; 320a 7. For the relation between qualitative change and the elemental substratum in its oneness see: *De Gen. et Corr.* 314b 26; 315a 3.

[59] *De Gen. et Corr.*, Book III, ch. 4. Alteration as qualitative change is essentially distinct from generation-destruction, which is substantial change. Also, *Phys.* 224b 28–35.   [60] *Phys.* 201b 31–2.

Contrariety in the Locus of Process

The very instant that the actualizing process in a given substance reaches a given term of a pair of contraries, at that same instant this process is completed and that term becomes an actuality, a fulfilment. However, if the change is within the categorical contrariety of substance and *complete* privation is reached, then the subject-in-process ceases to be. Its negation negates all its particular processes, functions, and contrary determinations.

Chapter Five

THE PRIME CONTRARIETY AND THE ONTOLOGICAL ANALYSIS OF DETERMINATE OR LINEAR PROCESSES

THE theoretical background on the basis of which Aristotle was able to perform the reconstruction of the views of his predecessors has been amply presented in chapters 3 and 4. It was observed there that the pervasive use of the notion of contrariety in all types and branches of pre-Aristotelian thinking had led to a great variety of uses, and that all cosmologies as well as theories of elements including Aristotle's were not free from error. The general argument in this chapter is that the ontological reconstruction of contrariety in Aristotle's philosophy was a decisive advantage over all previous thinkers. By establishing a new science of First Principles, he was in a position to inquire into the nature of contrariety, detect its misapplications, and work with those uses which best contributed toward the understanding of being in the distributive sense.

The topics requiring elaboration here are the following: (1) To bring contrariety within the exclusive focus of ontological analysis in order to fix the conditions of its validity and meaningfulness. (2) To determine with precision the minimum number of principles needed for metaphysical analysis and inquire into their ontological status. (3) To consider the prime contrariety in its dynamic equivalent as expressed in the opposition of actuality-potentiality. (4) To clarify the applications of privation, as one of

The Prime Contrariety

the terms of the prime contrariety, to the related meanings of matter. (5) To discuss potentiality as a generic concept standing for various types of matter in the process of actualization of their relative forms.

1. ONTOLOGICAL ANALYSIS AND CONTRARIETY

First Philosophy is concerned with contrariety because the latter has the status of a principle and a generic trait of being. Form and privation are the contrary extremities of this first metaphysical contrariety, and together with the subject-in-process, as its locus, they constitute the minimum number of principles the most general analysis of process must employ in its course. The nature of the principle of contrariety is such that, negatively, it is not a factor involved in the bringing about of process, but positively, it is a factor in the understanding of process. This distinction needs to be emphasized, especially since it is a cardinal point of contrast, between Aristotle and his predecessors.

In *Metaphysics Λ*, ch. 10, Aristotle departs from a discussion of certain metaphysical aspects of the notion of the Good in order to advance a sweeping argument against all those theories of his predecessors that used the contraries as cosmological principles. He stated in the *Physics*[1] that all previous thinkers have made the contraries principles. Even for those who have explained the existence of all things by means of contraries like 'being' and 'not-being', the not-being does not really mean nothingness, and hence are really employing a definite contrariety.[2] It is true that the pre-Aristotelian thinkers talked about contrariety. However, Aristotle characterized their thought in this area as inconsistent, and in the light of his analytic metaphysics, inadequate.[3] Summarizing his main objections to his predecessors, Aristotle exposed at the same time their main fallacies:

'All make things out of contraries. But neither (*a*) "all things", nor (*b*) "out of contraries" is right; (*c*) nor do these thinkers tell us how all things in which the contraries are present can be made out of the contraries; for contraries are not affected by one

---

[1] *Phys.* 188a 19. [2] See Appendix: ch. 5, note 1.
[3] There are numerous passages in *Metaphysics* where Aristotle criticizes his predecessors primarily for the status they give to contraries as first principles, especially *Met.* N, ch. 1.

The Prime Contrariety

another. Now for us this difficulty is solved naturally by the fact that there is a third element.... These thinkers, however, make one of the two contraries matter; this is done for instance by those who make the unequal matter for the equal;[4] or the many matter for the one.[5] But this is also refuted in the same way; for the one matter which underlies any pair of contraries is contrary to nothing.'[6]

From this and the discussion of the previous chapters two notions stand out: first, the locus is not a contrary term in any contrariety whatsoever, or to state the notion differently, contrariety is not material-substantial in character, for substances do not have contraries. Secondly, if the contraries are to be accepted as *archai*, they must first of all be rid of all material connections, i.e. as such they are neither material nor efficient causes; neither cosmological principles nor elemental constituents. The contraries in their barest meaning are ultimate principles that constitute the foundations for the intelligibility of process. It is in this capacity that they are used by *logos* as 'beginnings' for the understanding of 'natures' and their actualizations. The main drive of the Aristotelian criticisms as they appear in the *Metaphysics* is to preserve the contraries as principles, and at the same time deprive them of the cosmological connotations they had had in pre-Aristotelian thought. The Aristotelian analysis is a valid and successful attempt to demonstrate the fact that contraries are principles and their presence in a substance is unmistakable evidence for a process in its actualization, but they are not identical with that process.

The pre-Socratics and the Platonists were right in making the contraries principles, because the contraries satisfy a basic demand which must be met by any system of axioms or ultimate presuppositions, i.e. *the demand for irreducibility*.[7] No principles or set of axioms can be deducible from other principles in the same set of axioms, for if they were deducible, they could not be principles. The contraries, Aristotle says, satisfy the canon of irreducibility of axioms.

'For first principles must not be derived from one another nor from anything else, while everything has to be derived from them.

---

[4] The Pythagoreans.   [5] The Platonists.   [6] *Met.* 1075a 27–34.
[7] This is what in modern logic is called the independence of axioms and concepts.

The Prime Contrariety

But these conditions are fulfilled by the primary contraries, which are not derived from anything else because they are primary, nor from each other because they are contraries.'[8]

But it is not sufficient to agree with the earlier philosophers that the contraries are principles. The analysis must be pushed in the direction of a metaphysical consideration of the requirements the contraries have to satisfy in order to acquire validity and accuracy.

Now if the contraries are principles, then monism leads to an obvious absurdity. Hence, a plurality of principles is necessary to begin with, and in the most austere economy of principles, the principles must be at least two.

The contraries, on the other hand, cannot be infinite in number, because no set of principles can assume an infinite number of determining factors in any cognizing situation, for then knowledge would be impossible. The possibility of an infinite number of principles must, therefore, be rejected.

A being, or a subject-in-process, would become unknowable, and consequently utterly indeterminate; or, as it were, it could not be a given being. A being with no determinations is not a being in the sense of a concrete individual instance of distributive being. Indeterminacy is avoided because discourse can refer to *ousia* not as a species of something else, but in such a sense that its oneness in genus is preserved and the demand for a plurality of principles is satisfied. Consistent meaningful relations between substantial oneness and plurality of contrary principles cannot be maintained by positions which advocate an infinite number of principles, because such positions automatically negate the grounds for substance, either by making substance indeterminate, or by making it merely one of the infinite species of principles. But in each of the categorical genera there is but one fundamental contrariety involved, and hence the number of categorical contrarieties is not infinite but finite because the genera of predication are not infinite either.[9]

Regardless of the number of possible contraries there must always be primary ones. This characteristic of 'primacy' does not necessarily mean reducibility in the Parmenidean sense or in the way of the Anaximandrean relapse of processes into the original

---

[8] *Phys.* 188a 28–30.   [9] *Phys.* 189a 13–14.

The Prime Contrariety

Boundless. Aristotle means here that it is possible to have a plurality of contrary pairs, where from the point of view of *particular processes*, each one of them is irreducible to another; but in so far as contraries are present in the genera of predication and since contrariety is a generic trait of being, all contraries can, by means of analysis, be referred to a primary pair of contraries. A similar situation prevails in the case of the categories, where there are many genera, but existentially speaking, they all refer to the primary genus of substance.

'That which primarily "is" is the substantial being, the "this one here", that which indicates the substance of the thing. . . . Then it is by virtue of this category that each of the others also *is*.'[10]

2. THE PRINCIPLES FOR THE ANALYSIS OF PROCESS

The principal character of the categorical contrarieties is compatible with the metaphysical need for a primary, generic, and fundamental pair of contraries, where the priority attributed to it is *logically* prior.[11] The inclusive type of contrariety of any substance contains[12] the following principles or extremities: form-privation.[13]

The essential point of Aristotle's argument is to demonstrate that any discussion about the axiomatic character of contraries is meaningful only when contrariety is connected with the intelligible aspects of process as substance. Substance is the ontological principle and contrariety is a necessary principle for its intelligibility, and in this respect, the latter is ontologically grounded in the essence of the former and only logically prior to it. Thus, the principles involved in any process are in one sense two, and in another sense, three.

Before further explanation is given of these two senses of the number of principles involved in process and its intelligibility, it is necessary to introduce two other distinctions that will facilitate the understanding of the relation between substance and contrariety. They are the differences between (*a*) having the power of

---

[10] *Met.* Z 1028a 13 (translation mine), 1028b 2; also *Met. Δ*, ch. 7; *Cat.* 14b 5; *Phys.* 261a 14, 265a 22; *Met.* 1050a 4, 1077a 19; *Part. An.* 646a 26. See also pp. 24–5 of this essay.   [11] *Phys.* 189a 11–20.
[12] *Cat.*, ch. 10, 12a 26–9.   [13] *Met.* 1022b 27; also Book Iota, ch. 4.

The Prime Contrariety

'being the subject of process' (ὑποκεῖσθαι) and having the power of 'coming-to-be' or the power of becoming (γίγνεσθαι); and (b) subject-in-process (ὑποκείμενον)[14] and opposite (ἀντικείμενον).

'But there are different senses of "coming to be". In some cases we do not use the expression "come to be", but "come to be so-and-so". Only substances are said to "come to be" in the unqualified sense.

'Now in all cases other than substance it is plain that there must be some subject, namely that which becomes. For we know that when a thing comes to be of such a quantity or quality or in such relation, time, or place, a subject is always presupposed, since substance alone is not predicated of another subject, but everything else of substance.'[15]

This quotation yields three important conclusions:

(1) 'Coming to be' is used in two general senses which should never be confused. The first sense with reference to *ousia* is an absolute one, where Aristotle means that a definite being, a whole subject or concrete unit of distributive being is generated, and a new substance has begun its career.

(2) The second use of the term interests us particularly, for it means having the power of 'coming-to-be' where this power belongs to a substance which comes-to-be in a determinate way in regard to a given capacity. It means the power of a substance to be the locus of determinate processes which are pertinent to its nature. This meaning is dependent upon and presupposes the first sense. The primacy of substance in Aristotle's philosophy of process is identical with the primacy of substance in the list of the *Categories*.

(3) Any particular being which undergoes determinate processes has the power of 'coming-to-be' (in the second meaning) and is a being in that it continues to exist through the entire course of its development and while it is process; it remains a *one*.[16]

'It is plain that contrary attributes must needs be present in subjects which belong to the same species of genus. Disease and

---

[14] The notion of the 'subject' as a principle occurs in the opening chapters of the *Metaphysics* A where Aristotle discusses the nature, significance, and objective of First Philosophy.
[15] *Phys.* 190a 31–190b 1.   [16] *Met.* 998b 22; 1045b 6.

The Prime Contrariety

health require as their subject the body of an animal; white and black require a body without further qualification; justice and injustice require as their subject the human soul.'[17]

Since no power of coming-to-be occurs apart from a subject-in-process that is capable of actualizing its inherent potentialities, and since all substances are subject to 'coming-to-be' in the absolute sense, then 'coming-to-be' is intelligible only in so far as it exemplifies determinate processes which in turn can be cognized only with reference to the genera of categories.

Now let us consider the implications of having the power 'to be the subject of process' in terms of the relation subject-opposite.[18] Two important notions are connected with this theme:

1. Apart from the subject-in-process[19] as the locus of its actualizations and fulfilments,[20] no meaningful discourse about, and no serious inquiry into, process is possible. All change occurs in a subject and involves an opposite. The factors that change requires for its understanding are three: (*a*) the subject, (*b*) the opposite or privation, and (*c*) the form or essence. All three together make a concrete instance of distributive being. Opposite is opposed to subject in the sense that the former might be regarded as the contradictory to the latter provided that 'opposite' is given the meaning of complete privation of a determinate aspect of the subject. But if opposite is taken in the sense of actual and absolute privation, then its assertion, if it is a true statement about a subject, implies the total negation of the subject or its destruction.

2. Any natural process is always something composite and complex having antecedents, and following a course of development the determinateness of which is pertinent to the nature of the subject-in-process.[21] This latter aspect has two sides to it: first, the entire unfolding of a given function can be identical with the subject-in-process provided that this function coincides with the essence of the subject; and second, a function can be identified with an outstanding aspect, e.g. a qualitative one which is not yet completed but is indicative of certain fundamental contrasts, like that of growth and the objectives of a 'nature', or that between

[17] *Cat.*, ch. 11, 14a 15–18.
[19] *Phys.* 190b 9–10.
[21] *Met.* 1011b 34; 1012b 26.

[18] See Appendix: ch. 5, note 2.
[20] *Phys.* 190b 3–4.

The Prime Contrariety

the substance as a whole and the gradual unfolding of its plural capacities.[22]

The subject-in-process is a composite nature possessing a plurality of irreducible functions which are capable of developing to a point of consummation. The processes of these functions are analysable in terms of an 'opposite' which indicates a determinate oppositional situation, the absence of which reveals essential aspects of a subject's irreducible functions. The opposite, however, has no existential import[23] because a substance actualizes itself by denying the privation and by becoming what it is not in actuality; hence privation stands for 'opposition'.

Metaphysical analysis finds in every process first principles and causes. If 'firstness' and 'principle-ness' are taken seriously, then terms like 'accidental' or 'incidental' must not be attributed to them. Regarding the logical and ontological constituents of natural occurrences, Aristotle feels that analysis can find no fewer principles than those of a subject-in-process and a structural configuration (form). Numerically expressed, the subject is one, but since the subject is intelligible by virtue of its structural configuration, the principles are thus two. The subject as the unity of matter-form is existentially indivisible, and only conceptually analysable. The form of a subject is really one, because it is a structural oneness that causes individuation. Concerning the place which the contraries occupy in this schematic analysis, it is clear that they are not participant causes in the efficient or material manner, but post-categorical inclusive distinctions. They presuppose the category of substance. This is the reason that Aristotle calls both privation and contrariety accidents to the individuated form in a given subject-matter.[24]

Every subject involves a structural configuration. The understanding of its fulfilment is what calls the contraries into the picture. The contraries suggest the necessity for employing principal points of departure in every act of cognition, and thus provide the framework by which processes can be grasped and limitations can become meaningful.

A perplexity arises when Aristotle tells us that the principles involved in the 'processes' as natural beings are in one sense two and in another sense three. By two, he means matter and form;

[22] *Phys.* 190b 11–24.   [23] *Phys.* 189b 13–21.
[24] *Phys.* 190b 27; *Met.* 1055b 3; 1004a 10–1005a 18.

by three, he understands the subject-in-process plus the two polar extremities of the metaphysical contrariety. Since the contraries are principles of analysis, they are in no relation of reciprocal affection.[25]

The contraries, being conceptual distinctions, are subject to analysis and subsequent classification. But from a given set of contraries it is impossible to produce another new set. For if such a distinction were possible, they could be turned into principles of generation, and also of destruction. Stating the matter positively, contrariety is (as was observed in a previous connection) a generic concept in ontological analysis. This fact throws further light on Aristotle's doctrine of contrariety, and it explains in addition how contrariety is conceptually inherent in the genera of predication. Its presence in each of the categories features fundamental distinctions which are limitations within which the cognizance of any course of action and development is possible.

When the contrariety form-privation is considered in terms of potentiality-actuality, the question as to the number of principles involved in process receives its final answer. The contraries, form-privation, are essentially different and conceptually distinct extremities of the metaphysical contrariety, in which case the principles are two. Another sense in which they are two is that the subject-in-process is never in absolute want of form; i.e. no subject exists in absolute privation, and privation *qua* privation is a meaningless term. Thus:

(*a*) From the point of view of the completion of structural configuration, there is always a substance which can be said to be in a stage of *relative privation* in every instance of its development and in every cross-section of the complex co-operation of its functions; hence the principles are two.

(*b*) From the point of view of the complete absence of the subject's total actuality, the subject is always in possession of configuration, for if it did not have form at all the subject could not be a natural being in process. And here again the principles are two: subject and relative form.

To conclude, from the point of view of process, privation and form are relative terms. It is only by virtue of the subject-in-

[25] *Phys.* 190b 33.

The Prime Contrariety

process that thes terms come to have meaning, for without their locus they could possess neither significance nor applicability.

Finally, it is important to see that *contrariety, as a principle, and the subject-in-process* when taken together, do not in any way form any other kind, or a new type, as it were, of contrariety. If they could make a new contrariety, then the result would automatically be an *infinite regress*. But such an absurdity is avoided because substance is an ontological principle, and contrariety a principle of understanding process. Therefore, since these two types of principle are generically different, they do not enter contrary relations, for there can be no *locus* for them, nor does the original Aristotelian assumption of pluralism of principles allow such confusion. In point of fact, he says that:

'This difficulty is solved by the fact that the subject-in-process is something else different from the contraries, for it itself is not a term of a contrariety. Therefore, neither can the principles, in a sense, be more than the contraries (i.e. two) nor again exclusively two, because there is a fundamental difference in regard to their nature[26] but there may be three principles.'[27]

3. THE PRIME CONTRARIETY AS ACTUALITY AND POTENTIALITY

The metaphysical contrariety, developmentally viewed, takes the form of *potentiality-actuality*. Process cannot be explained by potentiality alone, nor can analysis do without it.[28] Potentiality is the source of change in the sense that it expresses the 'from-ness'.[29] Nor is knowledge about the nature of existence possible apart from the movement exhibited by the subjects-in-process in the accomplishment of their ends.

Actuality is the principle that originates this movement and is identical with the complete structural configuration of substances. The final cause must be carefully distinguished from the efficient causes, because the point of formal consummation is an end and serves as the guiding aim, rather than as the efficient forcefulness of the interaction of certain determinate powers and functions of the living organism.

---

[26] He means the difference between the nature of a subject-in-process and the logical character of the contraries.
[27] *Phys.* 190b 33–191a 1 (translation mine).
[28] *Met.* Θ, ch. 3.   [29] *Met.* 1069b 15.

The Prime Contrariety

Structural configurations as outcomes are 'desired' ends which are not efficiently present in a given instant of process; they are accomplishments. As such ends, they possess the status of 'beginnings' of understanding, for it is in the light of configurations and final achievements that inquiry, discourse in general, states the essences of beings.

Actuality is a functional concept in the sense that it stands for the completeness and the formal integration of a subject-in-process. The existent does not exist for the sake of sheer process.

'The fittest mode, then, of treatment is to say, a man has such and such parts, because the conception of a man includes their presence, and because they are necessary conditions of his existence, or, if we cannot quite say this, which would be best of all, then the next thing to it, namely, that it is either quite impossible for him to exist without them, or, at any rate, that it is better for him that they should be there; and their existence involves the existence of other antecedents. This we should say, because man is an animal with such and such characters, therefore is the process of his development necessarily such as it is; and therefore it is accomplished in such and such an order, this part being formed first, that next, and so on in succession; and after a like fashion should we explain the evolution of all other works of nature.'[30]

Potentiality and actuality are always connected with particular beings. Consequently, outcomes and eventuations are distinct occurrences within structural configurations present within substance. The plurality of outcomes and purposes in connection with whole substances eliminates the possibility of a purpose to nature collectively. All that can be said is that *ends* are natural and particular; and hence that while there is no 'nature' that has no *telos*, there is no uniform *telos* for all beings. Since there is no particular form which is inclusively valid, and comprehends all other forms, actuality is not prescriptive but descriptive, in that it states the necessity of some configuration for every subject-in-process. Actuality and potentiality constitute a contrariety generic in character and universal in its validity.

The totality of natures does not afford significant content for potentiality-actuality, simply because there is no locus of loci nor is there a process of processes as such. This is probably the reason

---

[30] *Part. An.* 640a 33–640b 5.

The Prime Contrariety

that Aristotle speaks of pure actuality *alone*, but does not accept the case of any pure actuality in complete unity with pure potentiality. Such a commitment would inevitably entail both the hypostatization of contrariety and the denial of the plurality of individual substances. Furthermore, it is impossible to establish on empirical grounds an all-inclusive locus in the sense of a concrete individual wherein pure actuality and pure potentiality could be shown to constitute the most universal and necessary contrariety.

4. PRIVATION AND THE MEANING OF MATTER

Aristotle states that matter is other than privation.[31] This distinction calls for clarification. Matter can be identified with 'not-being' only accidentally. If absolutely taken, i.e. apart from determinations and as completely formless—which is an impossibility, according to Aristotle—it is unintelligible as such.[32] But apart from this negative view, he states positively that matter is potential being,[33] while privation is, indeed, in the absolute sense not-being. For Aristotle, all determinate processes are matter in relation to some type of form. In this respect, matter becomes a relative concept which acquires significance on the basis of its connection with a given structural configuration.[34] 'First matter' as such, does not exist in Aristotle. Whenever he uses the notion of first matter, the term is never altogether stripped of every formal relation, for the removal of all definitional grounds would render anything incomprehensible. Even in the theory of elements matter still remains an identifiable entity such as fire, air, water, or earth.[35] However, first matter is used by Aristotle as a first principle of understanding process.

Privation, as a principle in ontological analysis, acquires significant content in connection with a given locus in two possible ways: (*a*) it means relative absence of a determinate capacity in respect to degree of fulfilment, and (*b*) it indicates the complete absence of an aspect, or stands for a certain determinate incapability and loss.[36] On the other hand, matter in its most

---

[31] *Phys.* 192a 3.
[32] *Met.* 1036a 8.
[33] *Met.* 1050a 15.
[34] *Phys.* 194b 9.
[35] *Met.* 1015a 7; 1017a 5; 1023a 27; 1044a 18; and 1049a 25.
[36] See 'The Four Types of Opposition', ch. 6, section 3.

The Prime Contrariety

comprehensive and elaborate meaning is substance in that it is a necessary condition for the individuational efficacy of form, and in so far as matter is always given as determinate and intelligible, it is substance-in-process.[37] But privation as such viewed ontologically is a mere nothing.

'We distinguish matter and privation, and hold that one of these, namely the matter, is not-being *only* in virtue of an attribute which it has, while the privation in its own nature is *not-being*; and that matter in a sense *is* substance, while the privation in no sense is.'[38]

In the end of *Physics*, I, Aristotle states:

'The matter comes to be and ceases to be in one sense, while in another it does not. As that which contains the privation, it ceases to be in its own nature, for what ceases to be—the privation—is contained within it. But as potentiality it does not cease to be in its own nature, but is necessarily outside the sphere of becoming and ceasing to be. For if it came to be, something must have existed as a primary substratum from which it should come and which should persist in it; but this is its own special nature, so that it will be before coming to be. (For my definition of matter is just this—the primary substratum of each thing, from which it comes to be without qualification, and which *persists in the result*.) And if it ceases to be it will pass into that at the last, so it will have ceased to be before ceasing to be.'[39]

The contrary extremities are in a state of mutual exclusion such that, to use a metaphor, they desire the destruction of each other. To posit the one is to deny the other. This relation of mutual exclusiveness, when logically formulated and generalized, constitutes the law of non-contradiction. The completion of form or structural configuration is achieved through the co-operative process of a subject's functions in such a way that each instance of actualization *negates* the relative absence of form, and in that respect, it is *energeia* which diminishes privation. One contrary pole excludes the other in any given moment of functional development, because, of necessity, one of the terms of the contrariety that delimits theoretically a given process comes under the name of privation. These observations are in line with what

[37] *Met.* 1042a 25–1042b 7; also *Phys.* 225a 12–20; *De Gen. et Corr.* 317a 17–31.   [38] *Phys.* 192a 3–6.   [39] *Phys.* 192a 25–33.

The Prime Contrariety

was previously said about the non-efficient and inactive character of the polar extremities *qua* terms.[40] They also support two basic considerations concerning the relation between contrariety and the developmental character of substance.

1. The contraries are fixed points. A process is observable and renders itself a subject-matter for scientific inquiry if, and only if, it displays a passage from one contrary to another, i.e. from privation to the completion of its pertinent structural configuration.

2. The contraries do not possess the properties of causal agents; in themselves they have no significance aside from a mere verbal meaning. They are crucial conceptual instruments used by *logos* in inquiry to determine and render cognizable what has been already experienced and felt as potentially intelligible in a 'nature' and in all 'natures' in complex interaction. The highly complex and pluralistic 'nature' is revealed in discourse because it possesses determinate powers and operations and has in every instant of its career achieved a certain degree of integration which is termed a structural configuration. *Logos* uses the fixed extremities as conceptual terms which comprehend processes. In the light of the relations of contraries, science articulates the ways in which subjects-in-process can be said to be what they are.

5. POTENTIALITY AND THE TYPES OF MATTER

Matter as potentiality is understood only as relative to particular subjects-in-process. If matter can be said to have 'being', its being is a distributive term manifested in all functions of subjects-in-process;[41] its intelligibility is realized through its function as a contrary in the metaphysical contrariety of form-privation. In that respect, matter is equivalent to the relative configuration of given capacities in development.

Matter extends its range of application to psychic processes and includes within it non-sensible objects. Aristotle distinguishes many kinds of matter which he divides into two main types: sensible and intelligible. Sensible matter is divided into (*a*) movable matter, (*b*) changeable matter, and (*c*) matter involved in generation and destruction.[42] These distinctions follow the ones

---

[40] *Met.* 1075a 30. [41] *Phys.* 217a 20–26. [42] *Met.* 1042a 34.

The Prime Contrariety

he gives of the basic types of process. All natural occurrences necessarily involve matter in this sense.[43]

Again, there are the intelligible processes which also require a certain kind of 'substratum' as their matter. This intelligible matter exists in what may be termed non-sensible beings.[44] Aristotle states: 'In a formula there is always an element of matter as well as one of actuality.'[45] This type of intelligible matter is identical with that universal element which inheres in those conceptual entities that are called definitions or essences. In short, all the higher genera become potentially the matter for the essential definitions of the species.

Elsewhere Aristotle compares the genus to matter.[46] The genera are not material entities to be utilized or consumed by the species, nor are they a *material* substratum which partakes of the individual's composition. He means the unique capacities that are dormant, but inherent in the species, which comprise, in a way, what could be said to be the genus. In the final analysis it is in virtue of these capabilities that, in the case of man for example, render him able to achieve knowledge; and man's most distinct trait is that 'by nature he desires to know'. There is nothing strange about the fact that knowledge in Aristotle is connected with matter, and whereas matter is potentiality, knowledge is a matter of actualization and growth. We are told that the last stage of matter is identical with structural configuration.[47]

Mathematics also involves intelligible matter.

'And some matter is perceptible and some intelligible ... and intelligible matter is that which is present in perceptible things not *qua* perceptible, i.e. the objects of mathematics.'[48]

In the same sense he uses elsewhere the expression 'the matter of mathematics'.[49]

This new and generalized way of speaking about matter raises genuine questions, because only in the case where matter means potentiality have we seen the connection of matter with contrariety. Now the acceptance of the existence of intelligible matter demands an answer as to the way in which contrariety is applicable to it.

---

[43] *Met.* 1032a 2; 1042b 6; 1044b 7.   [44] *Met.* 1036b 35.
[45] *Met.* 1046b 35.   [46] *De An.* 417a 27, and also *Met.* 1022b 25.
[47] *Met.* 1045b 18.   [48] *Met.* 1036a 9–12.   [49] *Met.* 1059b 15.

The Prime Contrariety

Aristotle speaks the language of the trained scientist who trusts the plural manifestations of his subject-matters. Potentiality is a generic concept and matter is plural. The *locus* is what makes matter significant, and as such, it is an *arche*, an irreducible assumption and an undemonstrable beginning. So far Aristotle has told us what conditions have to be satisfied in order to have process in sensible substances. In *Metaphysics Λ*, chs. 6-10, in M, chs. 1-9, and in N he refutes the substantiality of mathematical objects and of ideas, but also establishes the existence of non-sensible objects, i.e. God and the pure Intelligences. Then, the problem as to the applicability of contrariety to non-sensible objects is a question which can be answered only in terms of the substantiality of non-sensible objects. As to God and the pure Intelligences, the answer is simple. Since their 'substantiality' is a kind that is divorced from all change and linear developments, their conditions are not identical with that of process; their nature is actuality, not actualization.

With mathematical objects the case is different. The useful distinction between sensible matter and conceptual matter can be pushed further. The *De Anima* contains the doctrine of the 'inception of forms' where the perceptive material is matter for further elaboration and is a potentiality for further cognitive industry. Then, the conceptual matter yields a contrariety within the dynamic cognitive process of potentiality-actuality. But since the mathematical forms are *achieved outcomes* of the cognitive situation, they are not in process, and hence they are in no need of a principle of intelligibility because they are already *known*. Being conceptual actualities, they are not in process except in an accidental sense, i.e. as being the objects in *mathesis* for learning individuals.

Chapter Six

CONTRARIETY IN THE THEORY OF OPPOSITION IN LANGUAGE AND AS THE FOUNDATION FOR THE LAW OF NON-CONTRADICTION

WITH the uses of contraries and the categorical contrarieties made clear, our inquiry is now focused upon the theoretical grounds that sustain the principle of contrariety as a formal demand which renders process intelligible. It is an analysis of how contrariety connects Aristotle's logic to his metaphysics and how the entire theory of opposition rests upon the principle of contrariety.

The chapter develops five central topics: (1) To draw the contrast between the concept of difference, in all its variety of meanings, and the cognitive primacy of contrariety. (2) To make explicit the basis for a clear distinction among the meanings of the key terms, contradiction, privation, and contrariety. (3) To give an exposition of the four types of opposition, relate opposition to the direct contraries and contraries with intermediates, and establish the rules concerning the logical relations of contrary statements. (4) To discuss what seems to be Aristotle's philosophy of language and its relation to process. (5) To establish contrariety as the grounds for the formulation of the law of non-contradiction and relate it to the understanding of being as process.

Contrariety in the Theory of Opposition in Language

1. CONTRARIETY AND DIFFERENCE

A number of problems have remained obscure owing to the condensed language Aristotle uses in *Metaphysics*, Iota, chapter 4. In chapter 3 of the same Book, the meanings of terms like unity, plurality, identity, likeness, otherness, and difference are presented. First Aristotle discusses the *meaning of difference*, and then proceeds to consider contrariety, privation, and contradiction in the light of 'difference'.

If anything whatever is to be considered 'different' from something else, it must be so only in some particular respect. Again, two things, *any* two things, when they differ, that in which they differ must be the same sort of thing, i.e. the same genus or species.[1] The conditions for difference in genus are satisfied only in those cases where the two differing entities (*a*) have no common matter, and (*b*) when all possibilities of generative transition from the one to the other are excluded, i.e. when the two entities are not capable of constituting terms of a common operation where passage from one to the other would have been possible; such would be the entities that come under different categories. *Specific difference* is attributed to those entities that belong to the same genus, where by genus is meant[2] that which is invariably predicated of both terms of a difference.[3]

Difference is given with different individual substances which are loci of different functions, operations, developments, interactions, and fulfilments. Difference can be best understood when scientifically treated, by pairing difference with similarity as constituting the grounds upon which scientific generalization may rest. There are different phenomena which exhibit structural similarities, and the latter form the basis for universals and for comprehensive classificatory concepts. The nature of language is such that the subject of a sentence can be either a substantial subject or an abstracted subject; hence it makes possible science and the rise of higher and more inclusive classificatory and explanatory generalizations and principles. Particularity and universality are thus linked immediately with ontological difference and similarity. The universe of discourse is selected from a highly complex and differentiated variety of subjects-in-process which

---

[1] See Appendix: ch. 6, note 1.　　[2] *Met.* 1054b 25–31.
[3] See Appendix: ch. 6, note 2.

exhibit structural similarities, where difference is displayed everywhere and is encountered along with every locus of processes. Change generates and implies difference. If change is to be rendered intelligible, then it must submit all the *differences* to which it gives rise to the principle of contrariety, which in turn becomes the pivot-point for relating, organizing, and systematizing differences.

In the opening of chapter 4 of Book Iota, Aristotle says:

'Since things which differ may differ from one another more or less, there is also a greatest difference, and this, I call contrariety. That contrariety is the greatest difference is made clear by induction. For the things which differ in *genus* have no way to one another, but are too far distant and are not comparable; and for things that differ in species the extremes from which generation takes place are the contraries, and the distance between extremes —and therefore that between the contraries—is the greatest.'[4]

From this and the foregoing discussion, certain fundamental notions follow that need careful restatement.

1. *Contrariety* is the greatest difference. And contrariety as a principle should not be confused with a particular contrariety, i.e. a given opposition of terms which states a given greatest difference.

2. A *difference* unless it possesses terms which can be arranged within the limits of *specific* difference, cannot be accounted for, because its differing terms remain unrelated to the same genus or species and do not form a given contrariety.

3. *Generic difference* is a necessary distinction because it enables Aristotle to establish the irreducibility of the *genera of categoriae*. The categories as ultimate types of predication are not subject to contrary arrangements. No two categories, taken separately, e.g. quantity and quality, can form, or need form, a contrariety. Being genera, they cannot be the species of another genus. This seems to be one of the main reasons that Aristotle maintained vigorously

---

[4] *Met.* Iota, ch. 4, 1055a 4–10. It is true that the term 'genus' is an ambiguous one. W. D. Ross writes: 'Aristotle doubtless calls many classes which are not categories genera, but in the strict sense the categories are the only genera, since they are the only classes that are not species.' *Aristotle's Metaphysics*, vol. 2, p. 289. The attempt to link contrariety to difference within the same genus suggests strongly the view that by genus Aristotle means here the genera of predication.

the distinction between generic and specific difference. The fact that the subject-in-process is also a locus of processes is the reason for insisting upon the ultimate types of predication.

It is not sufficient to say that contrariety is the greatest difference within a genus, nor is it enough to distinguish between generic and specific difference. The issue becomes more complicated when we come to state how contrariety differs from negation and privation; and again in what respect privation differs from negation so that their difference still differs from contrariety. Chapter 4 of Book Iota aims at such clarity. It states:

'That which is greatest in each genus is complete. For that is greatest which cannot be exceeded, and that is complete beyond which nothing can be found. For the complete difference marks the end of a series (just as the other things which are called complete are so called because they have attained an end), and beyond the end there is nothing; for in everything it is the *extreme* and includes all else, and therefore there is nothing beyond the end, and the complete needs nothing further. From this, then, it is clear that contrariety is *complete difference*; and as contraries are so called in several senses,[5] their modes of completeness will answer to the various modes of contrariety which attach to the contraries.'[6]

This being the case, Aristotle argues, it is impossible for a given term to have more than one term contrary to it, because there is nothing that is more extreme to an extremity nor can there be more than two extremes encompassing a given process; and this is what is meant by *complete difference*.

2. CONTRADICTION, PRIVATION, AND CONTRARIETY—THEIR DIFFERENCES AND RELATIONS

The first or fundamental contrariety is that whose contrary or polar terms are a positive state and a privation.[7] Privation in this

---

[5] See *Met.* 1018a 25–35.   [6] *Met.* 1055a 10–19 (italics mine).

[7] Chapter 4 has been misunderstood by both Ross and Zeller, because they missed the more basic meaning of contrariety. See Ross's *Aristotle's Metaphysics* (Text, Introduction, Commentary), vol. II, pp. 291–2, note on lines 26–7. He says: 'Thus, contradiction includes privation as a particular case, and privation includes contrariety as a particular case.' But this is absurd. For, (*a*) privation in all its functional aspects is but *one* term, while

Contrariety in the Theory of Opposition in Language

connection must be taken as complete. Thus, we are provided with an absolute measure by which all other particular pairs of contraries may be judged. Positive state and complete privation give a general formula to measure contraries, or rather given functions in action. The crucial difficulty is introduced at this point. It calls for distinguishing between (*a*) antiphasis (or contradiction) and contraries, (*b*) privation and antiphasis and (*c*) privation and contrariety.

1. *Antiphasis*.[8] Aristotle gives two characteristics: (*a*) it has no intermediate, i.e. it is either affirmation or negation, and consequently, (*b*) antiphasis cannot be the same as contraries, since the latter have intermediates. For example:

Antiphasis: 'x' has colour (aff.); 'x' has no colour (neg.).
Contraries of the affirmative: '*x*' *has colour.*
'x' has white colour (pole, extremity).
'x' has intermediate colours *a*, *b*, *c* (intermediate pole).
'x' has black colour (pole, extremity).

2. *Privation*. It is a kind of contradiction.[9] Indeed, if privation is taken absolutely, then its meaning is equivalent to the complete negation of a predicate. But, from the assumption that possession *always* precedes privation, it follows that a complete privation as a result of complete deprivation of a former possession amounts to a kind of antiphasis, for it yields definite instances of affirmation-negation. However, the fact is that privation is a generic term and it has other possible forms besides the antiphatical one, i.e. (*a*) it can mean a definite incapacity, like the house that can never become a plant; and (*b*) privation in a given situation in a given locus can mean deprivation of a previously possessed state, like the man who became bald or lost his teeth. Therefore, whereas there is *no third kind of statement* serving as an intermediate between affirmation and negation, the concept of privation can be stated in *three* ways: (*a*) absolutely, (*b*) as a determinate incapacity, and (*c*)

---

contrariety has two definite terms, and (*b*) Ross did not see that privation is *also* a generic concept. Zeller, again, is wrong in saying that privation is reducible either to contradiction or to contrariety. He simply did not see the contextual aspect of privation which along with possession forms a dynamic contrariety which is a generic one (the primary contrariety, 1055a 33). *Ibid.*, vol. II, p. 291.   [8] *Met.* 1055b 1–3; Book Γ, ch. 7; 1063b 19; 1069a 3.
[9] *Met.* 1055b 3–11.

as a given deprivation of a possession within a given locus. The analysis has shown that privation-possession as a form of opposition conforms to the principle of contrariety, and more specifically it is the *primary contrariety*. Privation when taken separately as *one* of the terms of this contrariety is shown to differ from contradiction in that privation is not altogether negation except in the sense of complete or absolute privation, and since it has other meanings, it has 'intermediates' in that sense.

3. *Privation and Contrariety*. There are two preliminary notions that form the background for the understanding of the difference between privation and contrariety. First, in the generation of processes that occur in a subject-matter, it is always the case that these processes fall within the delimitations of a certain contrariety. Second, the processes proceed either from the nature of a structure and the possession of such a form, or from relative privation of a certain structure and configuration. Every contrariety contains two extremities, but *only one* is possessed by the subject-in-process at a given time, whereas the other term is in the state of privation. It follows that every contrariety implies complete privation of the other term[10] but not every privation taken in itself can comprise a complete contrariety. Complete privation is not the efficient cause of any process. Since privation may be taken to stand for a complete lack, i.e. non-possession, it follows that in this sense privation alone is not sufficient to yield a whole contrariety. This is more evident in the case of movement and change, because here, there must be continuous development, uninterrupted unfolding, of certain powers in operation *between two extremities* which constitute the contraries within a genus.

Any *complete contrariety*, in order to be contrariety at all, must imply the privation of one of its terms at a given moment. This is a general rule for all the contraries within a genus. If the case of contrary genera be admitted for once, then the rule is not applicable to the contrary genera, like *equality and inequality, vice and virtue*. But we know already that this type of contrary is an admissible case of contraries only under certain conditions, i.e. that the contrary genera be the species of a higher genus.[11] *Complete or first contrariety* employs privation to characterize one

[10] *Met.* 1055b 13–19.
[11] Or if it be admitted that 'genus' is used in a sense different from its meaning as highest type of predication.

of its terms where privation is now used only in the sense of *determinate incapacity*.[12] However, when we take the other case where privation implies the loss of a previous possession (and therefore yields a given contrariety), then this specific reference to privation is applicable to one of the contrary terms with the provision that certain specifications are possible in respect to time, or to a certain function in operation, or to the entire career of the subject-in-process.

'This is the reason why in certain cases there are intermediates (for there are men who are neither good nor bad) and in others there are no intermediates (as a number must be either odd or even). Further, in some cases the subject to which the contraries refer is definitely stated, in other cases it is not. Therefore, it is evident that one of the contraries is always related to privation.'[13]

Once the theoretical difficulties involved in the concepts of difference, contrariety, antiphasis, and privation are removed, the understanding of the categorical contrarieties presents no major problems. From the assumptions that contraries are different and that contrariety is a kind of difference, Aristotle concludes chapter 3 of Book Iota with the following statement which is important for the reference he makes to the categories.

'The above is correct on the basis of induction. But the contraries are not merely "other"; there are cases of contraries which are "other" because they come under *another* genus, but "other" pairs of contraries could be found in the same line of predication[14] (i.e. in the same genus of categories). Thus, contraries are other in the same genus and the same in genus.'[15]

The above solidifies the argument that contraries must belong to the same type of predication.

3. THE FOUR TYPES OF OPPOSITION

We can now proceed to inquire into Aristotle's general conception of a theory of opposition and contrariety. The passages

---

[12] *Met.* 1055b 21.   [13] *Met.* 1055b 23–29 (translation mine).
[14] *Met.* A 986a 23. For the identification of genus with category see 1016b 33 and 1024b 12. Categories are the genera that are not species. This is a feasible interpretation, but one must not forget that 'genus' is an ambiguous term. See footnote, p. 86.   [15] *Met.* 1054b 31–1055a 2.

Contrariety in the Theory of Opposition in Language

where he most fully discusses opposition (ἀντικεῖσθαι) are the following: *Categories*, chapters 10, 11, and *Metaphysics*, Iota, chapter 4. We are informed that there are four kinds of opposition, (*a*) of relatives (ὡς τὰ πρός τι), (*b*) of contraries (ὡς τὰ ἐναντία), (*c*) of possession and privation (ὡς στέρησις καὶ ἕξις), and (*d*) of affirmation and negation (ὡς κατάφασις καὶ ἀπόφασις).[16] The first one has no direct bearing on our discussion and is presented only incidentally. Therefore, our analysis is confined to the last three kinds of opposition.

So far, contraries appear to be a species of opposition. But, as it will become evident from the subsequent discussion, the arrangement of concepts in accordance with contrariety is used interchangeably with *oppositional* arrangement, and also seems in certain cases to be identical with opposition. For example, while in the above passage from the *Categories*, the contraries appear to be a species of opposition, the third case of opposition, i.e. possession and privation, is in fact a *contrariety* and as such it is employed in both the *Physics* and the *Metaphysics*. The difference is that in both the *Physics* and the *Metaphysics*, the contrariety of privation-possession is introduced as a fundamental generality for metaphysical analysis, while in the *Categories* the contraries are treated primarily from a linguistic point of view. The entire discussion of *opposition*, *contrariety*, and *difference* is not altogether clearly stated, perhaps on account of the lack of adequate and precisely fixed terminology, or of the suggestiveness of the preposition ἀντί, which is the first part of the word ἀντικεῖσθαι, a preposition which always implies opposition of two terms, or entities.

It seems that Aristotle was aware of the extraordinary difficulties of this complex and rather confusing interchanging of meanings and uses of terms. This material came to him in a fashion which indicated a free, loose, and poetically vague and unfixed employment of terms. The unfixed terminology concerning *opposition*, *contrariety*, and *difference* is obvious in all the pre-Aristotelian thinkers.

A. *Contraries.*

The contraries are considered to be an instance of opposition, and unlike the correlatives which are explained by reference to

[16] *Cat.*, ch. 10; 11b 15–24.

each other,[17] they cannot be understood by reference to each other but only as the counter extremity of one another.

'Pairs of opposites which are contraries are not in any way understood in terms of being dependent upon each other, but are said to be contrary to one another. Thus, the good cannot be referred to as the good *of* the bad, nor is the white spoken of as the white *of* the black. Consequently, these two kinds of oppositions (i.e. correlatives and contraries) are entirely different.'[18]

The uses of the contraries have already been presented in chapter 4 under sections 1 and 2 and there is no need to repeat them. The contraries are meaningful terms not by reference to each other, but solely by virtue of a substance. A detailed examination of the impossibility of the simultaneous co-existence of the terms of a given contrariety led Aristotle to a more refined distinction between two types of contraries:[19] (*a*) direct contraries, and (*b*) contraries with intermediates.

Direct contraries: These are related to a given locus in either of the following two ways: (*a*) either they are 'naturally' present[20] in it, or (*b*) they are predicated of it.[21] But in both cases of direct contraries the connection existing between them and the locus is such that *either* one of the two contrary terms is possessed in a given instance but never both, or a third, intermediary term. To state the same relation the other way around, there can be no subject-in-process which does not possess at a given instant an identifiable term which is the extremity of some function, activity, operation or change expressible through a contrariety.

Contraries with intermediates: This type of contraries does not necessarily require the possession of one and only one of the two contraries, but allows for the presence in a locus of an intermediate stage of a change that is determined by two extremities.

'Blackness and whiteness are naturally present in the body, but it is not necessary that either the one or the other should be present in the body, inasmuch as it is not true to say that everybody must

[17] *Cat.* 11b 25-34. [18] *Cat.* 11b 35-40 (translation mine).
[19] *Cat.* 12a 1-25.
[20] An instance of a direct contrary (*a*) is *health* and *disease*. The example is drawn from his biological observations. *Ibid.*
[21] The illustration of direct contraries (*b*) is taken from the mathematical sciences, *odd* and *even*. *Ibid.*

be white or black. Badness and goodness, again, are predicated of man, and of many other things, but it is not necessary that either the one quality or the other should be present in that of which they are predicated; it is not true to say that everything that may be good or bad must be either good or bad.'[22]

In the case of colours, black and white form the extreme terms in a series of homogeneous qualities, and hence they are the *most* contrary in a series. The same seems to apply in the case of good and bad, which are taken in this connection as terms for certain qualities standing at the extremities of a given series of moral situations; hence they are the *most* contrary in the series. Thus, it is safe to infer that contraries with intermediates are found in qualitative situations and processes that taken together form a given quality, e.g. *colour* or *morality*. In such cases contraries with intermediates are distinguishable, because here not only are extremities admissible, but there are also possible variations of degree and gradual passage from positive to negative and *vice versa*.

B. *Possession and Privation*

We have stated already that the third type of opposition, namely that between privation and possession, is the 'primary contrariety'. In the *Categories*, Aristotle brings into the discussion the similarity and difference between these two kinds of opposition, i.e. that between contraries and that between privation and possession. We shall briefly state this point before passing on to the relation between truth and contraries. There are three distinct ways in which the difference can be presented:

1. The two forms of opposition, namely, direct contraries and the opposition of privation-possession, are not necessarily the same, because whether a direct contrary is in a subject-in-process or is predicated of it, that contrary is *constantly* there; in other words, while both direct contraries belong to the subject by *nature*, in the case of privation-possession, only 'possession' belongs *by nature* to the subject.

2. In *intermediary* contraries, neither of the extremities need necessarily be there. Yet when one of the two contraries is a constitutive property of the subject-in-process, it is necessary that *one* of the two contraries, but not the *one or the other*, should be

[22] *Cat.* 12a 10–18.

Contrariety in the Theory of Opposition in Language

present. Therefore, the nature of the subject decides which of the contraries must be present.[23] But in the opposition between possession and privation, neither of the two foregoing cases, i.e. of direct and intermediary contraries, holds.

'... For it is not necessary that a subject as a locus of such opposition should always have either the one or the other; that which has not yet advanced to the state when sight is natural is not said either to be blind or to see. Thus privation-possession does not belong to the kind of opposition of *direct contraries*. On the other hand, privation-possession does not belong to the class of *intermediary contraries*. For under certain conditions it is necessary that either the one or the other should form a part of the constitution of every locus.'[24]

In *Metaphysics*, Iota, chapter 7, Aristotle states that the intermediates must belong to the same genus where their containing contraries belong. Thus, within a given genus an intermediate 'a' is contrary not only to the contrary boundaries, but also to any incidental intermediates. Take the case of the colours: white ... black. The colour red is contrary to both white and black as well as to any other intermediate colour. Again, the intermediates, unlike the contraries, are not principles, for they partake of both extremes. Summarily: 'The intermediates then are (*a*) all in the same genus, (*b*) intermediate between contraries, and (*c*) all compounded out of the contraries.'[25]

3. The difference between the opposition between *contraries* and that between *possession and privation* becomes more precise when it is seen in the light of the concept of change. What sets off the *contrary* opposition from the other types of opposition is that the *contrary* terms embrace functions and activities by setting their limits. The unfolding of a process entails a transition from either contrary term to the other, while the subject-in-process, which is the locus, retains its identity.[26] But in the case of privation-

---

[23] *Cat.* 12b 26; 13a 3. ἀεὶ τῷ δεκτικῷ ...

[24] *Cat.* 13a 3–8 (translation mine).   [25] *Met.* 1057b 32–4.

[26] It is interesting to see that in the above connection Aristotle gives biological examples. The only exception to the rule which demands the identity of the subject during the change from contrary to contrary is the case of a subject in which a contrary is also its fundamental constitutive property, as *heat* is to *fire*. Here, the change of the contrary into its opposite necessitates change in the constitution of the subject and causes substantial change. *Cf. De Gen. et Corr.*

Contrariety in the Theory of Opposition in Language

possession the process of change between the terms designated by a contrariety is *always a one-way process* where privation always presupposes possession.

'In the case of privation-possession, change in both directions is impossible. There may be a change from possession to privation but not from privation to possession. The man who has become blind does not regain his sight; the man who has become bald does not regain his hair; the man who has lost his teeth does not grow a new set.'[27]

C. *Affirmation and Negation*

We are now able to pass over to the relation between truth and contrariety, which links the contrary opposition to that between *affirmation and negation*.

Affirmation-negation is a distinct type of opposition, for it is in reference to this opposition exclusively that truth and falsity can be judged to belong either to affirmation or to negation as *two opposing statements*. Since truth and falsity belong exclusively to statements, then, contraries are neither true nor false. This is also valid for the other types of opposition, correlativity and privation-possession, because they, like the contraries, consist only of simple terms.[28] Further it is shown that the properties of truth and falsity belong more characteristically to those combinations of words which include contrary terms and statements containing privation-possession terms.

'... Where there is no sort of combination of words, truth and falsity have no place, and all the opposites we have mentioned so far consist of simple words.

'At the same time, when the words which enter into opposed statements are contraries, these, more than any other set of opposites, would seem to claim this characteristic.'[29]

The fundamental idea which seems to underlie Aristotle's conception of the affirmation-negation opposition, especially its relation to contrariety, is that all statements are necessarily either

---

[27] *Cat.* 13a 31–6.

[28] *Cat.*, ch. 2. While *correlativity, contraries* and *privation-negation* consist only of simple terms, the *affirmation-negation* opposition alone is never found apart from statements.

[29] *Cat.* 13b 10–14; *Met.* E 1027b 25; *De Int.*, ch. 1, 5; compare *De An.* III, ch. 4, 430a 26.

affirmations, where a predicate is affirmed of a subject, or *negations* where a predicate is denied of a subject. No third type is possible because of all four types of opposition the one of 'affirmation and negation' excludes intermediates.

'... of opposites only contradictories admit of no intermediate terms (for contradiction is that kind of opposition in which either of its two terms could be present in anything whatever); and this opposition clearly has not intermediates.'[30]

Since truth is a property of statements and since statements are either affirmations or negations, the principle of contrariety is related to truth in the sense that it states the conditions that any statement has to meet in order to be meaningful. That is, language affords only two ways of combining words into statements, positively or negatively. Furthermore, contrariety is related to truth in that it requires that any pair of contrary terms which enters the linguistic situation of communication as terms in statements must satisfy the conditions for being *either true or false*. Contrary statements can accordingly be (*a*) either affirmative or negative, and (*b*) either true or false.

The above remarks taken together with the position that the subject-in-process is the ultimate point of reference of statements, enable us to understand the following rules concerning the logical relations of contrary statements in respect to truth and falsity:

1. Statements are not contrary because they have contrary subjects, but because they are connected with contrary effects.[31]
2. Those statements should be termed contrary to true statements, in which error is present. These are those that are concerned with the starting points of generation, and generation is the passing from one extreme to its opposite, therefore error is like transition.[32]
3. Contrary statements are those which state contrary conditions, and contrary conditions cannot subsist at one and the same time in the same subject.[33]
4. Consequently, contrary conclusions cannot be deduced from a single syllogism. The assumption of opposite premises in a single syllogism yields a contradiction of the original

---

[30] *Met.* 1057a 33–6 (translation mine).
[31] *De Int.* 23b 6–7.
[32] *Ibid.*, 23b 11–14.
[33] *Ibid.*, 24b 8–10.

hypothesis. There is no way in which the assumptions of a single syllogism can be truly contrary.[34]

5. Two contrary statements cannot be both true at the same time with reference to the same subject (while their subcontraries may).[35]
6. In particular statements, if the affirmative is false, the contrary is true;[36] in universal propositions, if the affirmative is false, the contradictory (its negation) is true.[37]
7. The 'affirmation and negation' opposition is such that it does not permit transitions from one type of statement to another. There is no process from affirmation to negation.[38]

4. LANGUAGE AND THE SUBJECT-IN-PROCESS

In the light of the theory of opposition, we may now present what seems to comprise a feasible Aristotelian philosophy of language in its relation to process. Truth and falsity are necessarily connected with the linguistic situation where statements are expressed. The forms of all possible statements are only two, affirmation or negation, and this condition is given by the principle of contrariety. Contrariety governs the linguistic situation in so far as language states intelligibly the connections between two terms, a subject and a predicate, a noun and an adjective, a particular and a universal. Language in so far as it is 'proposition' either *affirms* or *denies, tertium non datur*. Further, significant language contains terms which, when taken separately, are significant and their meaning is agreed upon. The constituents of a statement *must* be meaningful by agreement, i.e. significant

[34] *An. Pr.* 64b 17–28; 63b 33.
[35] *De Int.* 20a 17–18; 17b 20; also 23b 37; 24b 6.
[36] Because the contrary of an affirmative statement (susceptible of contrary) is not by necessity a negative statement.
[37] *De Int.* 20a 23 ff.
[38] In *Met.* Iota, 1057a 26–8, Aristotle states explicitly that there is no process or transition from the process distinguished within one categorical contrariety to that of another category, except in an accidental sense. There is only one exception to this rule in so far as reference is made to 'opposition'. Since in opposition we include that of 'negation and affirmation' or contradiction, we must be careful to exclude contradiction from the forms of opposition in which process or change is delineated. The reason for excluding it is that either term of the 'negation and affirmation' opposition applies to anything whatever, and it does not possess intermediates.

and communicative. Significant terms, *qua* terms, are not themselves statements that affirm or deny.[39] But simple terms do not become *subjects* unless something has been affirmed or denied of them. If propositions are to communicate truth and falsity,[40] they must in every case contain a *subject*. But it is not always the case that the subject of a sentence is also a subject-in-process. Consequently, affirmations and negations may be true or false in cases where the subject is not a subject-in-process, as in mathematical statements.

It is very important to observe that while not all true or false statements are limited to subjects-in-process alone, since the grammatical subject may be either a particular or a universal, statements concerning particulars are always either true or false. Again, one cannot but observe that the possible subjects are of only *two kinds*, either particulars or universals, *tertium non datur*. Language is such an activity that by virtue of its abstractions it enlarges the concept of subject. Apart from this all-too-important trait no scientific knowledge would be possible; only the perception of particulars.[41] In turn, the nature of things is such that it makes scientific knowledge possible because there is a community of traits. There are structural similarities which can be stated in the linguistic situation as universals, as generic traits, as characters of particulars and their activities. If knowledge, in Aristotle's view, is the subsumption of the particular under the universal, such cognitive activity is possible only in the linguistic situation, where universals, predicates and generic concepts are possible and where they can function as subjects of judgments.[42] Knowledge as the cognition of the structure of the particular is knowledge of its determinate predicates that render intelligible all its functional particularities. The universal determinations of a subject's structure constitute its formal cause.

[39] *De Int.*, chs. 4, 5, 6, 7.
[40] Yet there are sentences which are neither true nor false. 'Every sentence has meaning, not as being the natural means by which a physical faculty is realized, but, as we have said, by convention. Yet every sentence is not a proposition; only such are propositions as have in them either truth or falsity. Thus a prayer is a sentence, but is neither true nor false.' *De Int.* 17a, 1–5.
[41] See Appendix: ch. 6, note 3.
[42] *Met.* 1053b 17–20. No universal can be a first substance, but is only a predicate. There is an exception concerning the 'what-it-was-to-be' notion. See ch. 1, sect. 2, 'subject-in-process', p. 11.

Contrariety in the Theory of Opposition in Language

The form and essence of a subject-in-process can be stated in its definition, which is a linguistic articulation of its structural character. However, the demands of knowledge go further, for knowledge must be extended to cover the efficient aspects of a subject in its entirety. To bring under universals the efficient factors in the developmental character of a particular is the most difficult task that scientific inquiry has to perform. The subsumption of a subject-in-process under a universal must include the subsumptions of its functions, for a subject-in-process is understood in terms of its *telos*. In this respect, the linguistic situation is faced with all sorts of problems because the execution of these demands requires the most careful scrutiny. The curious fact about the linguistic situation with regard to its subject is that while *logos* has enlarged the extension of 'subject' through the use of the grammatical subject, on the other hand the subject-in-process is not necessarily exhausted in the linguistic situation.

The fact that language, prior to a careful and detailed examination and observation of the subject-in-process, does not exhaust the field of metaphysics is what makes *inquiry* necessary. Inquiry is not limited to linguistic possibilities at all. The linguistic situation is itself a particular type of process which is characteristic of a particular type of being. Only particular human beings (not the concept of man or the predicate) are the subjects of the linguistic situation. Since language is a process, and (though not always) language itself can be an intelligible activity, it must accept the conditions that are set by the criterion of process.

The difference between language as a process and the other processes of the human subject is that while all activities can be understood through the *criterion of process*, language itself can *alone* articulate the principle of contrariety.

Therefore, language in its functioning capacity does not fall outside the orbit of the principle of contrariety. This can be demonstrated as follows: (1) when it forms statements, language moves within the limits of *the opposition of truth and falsity*; (2) the subjects of its statements must be within the opposition whose terms are the *subject as concretion* and the *subject as abstraction*; (3) all statements constitute pairs of opposition with the following species: (*a*) affirmation-negation, (*b*) correlatives, (*c*) possession-privation, and (*d*) contraries; (4) its most comprehensive principle

Contrariety in the Theory of Opposition in Language

of significance is the principle of non-contradiction,[43] which is the *sine qua non* of the process of inquiry, and is patterned after the demand of the principle of contrariety. Significant language as a particular function of the cognizing individual subject-in-process, i.e. man, obeys the formal demand of contrariety and has the unique ability to articulate it.

5. CONTRARIETY AND THE LAW OF NON-CONTRADICTION

There remains but one more *aporia* before this chapter is brought to its end. It has been stated that in the Aristotelian scheme of inquiry the principle of contrariety is a necessary condition for scientific knowledge. Although contrariety is not a cause, nevertheless it is the condition for the intelligibility of cause, and though it is not an ontological entity, it is ontologically supported by the nature of processes which affords and displays determinations. That contrariety is related to the law of non-contradiction has been sufficiently suggested in the previous chapters. Again, the law of non-contradiction is the *logical formulation of the principle of contrariety*. The law states the ultimate conditions that rational discussion about subjects-in-process has to satisfy in order to secure meaningfulness and knowledge.

The law refers to a plurality of individual natures that possess, as loci, at least two characters: (*a*) a subject-matter which displays change toward the completion of its pertinent structural configuration, and (*b*) a set of determinations that mark the boundaries of its process, affording thus the grounds for a generic contrariety, the metaphysical contrariety, which in turn sustains the law of non-contradiction. But did Aristotle have to prove that contrariety is the criterion of the intelligibility of process? He says:

'In what way can there be a *science* of first principles? For we are aware even now what each of them in fact is (at least even other sciences use them as familiar); but if there is a demonstrative science which deals with them, there will have to be an underlying kind, and some of them must be demonstrable attributes and others must be axioms (for it is impossible that there should be demonstration about all of them); for the demonstration must start from certain premisses and be about a certain subject and prove certain attributes. Therefore it follows that all attributes

[43] *Met.* 1005b 7–34; 1011b 13.

Contrariety in the Theory of Opposition in Language

that are proved must belong to a single class; for all demonstrative sciences use the axioms.'[44]

The argument here is that if there is a science of axioms this science must be able to define or demonstrate them. It must also, then, be able to define or demonstrate the principle of contrariety. Could such a science prove the principles as well as contrariety, then it would automatically turn them into middle terms. But metaphysics is the science or the inquiry concerning principles, and principles as *archai* are by definition undemonstrable. First philosophy is not like geometry or any other special science, though it is equally rational and scientific. Metaphysics does not try to 'prove' contrariety; it only seeks to study and understand its nature. Knowledge of the metaphysical contrariety is not the same as knowledge about specific contraries. The principle of contrariety is the object of metaphysical study because it is a generic trait of being; it constitutes, with substance, the foundations for the logical articulation of the law of non-contradiction, apart from which no sound thinking is possible and no intelligibility is conceivable. If contrariety were provable it would have to fulfil the demand of proof: *all that can be demonstrated must belong to one genus*. Then, in order for the axioms to be demonstrable, they would have to belong to the same genus.

'We cannot in demonstrating pass from one genus to another. We cannot, for instance, prove geometrical truths by arithmetic. For there are three elements in demonstration: (1) what is proved, the conclusion—an attribute inhering essentially in a genus; (2) the axioms, i.e. axioms which are premisses of demonstration; (3) the subject-genus whose attributes, i.e. essential properties, are revealed by the demonstration.'[45]

But as was said, the genus of the subject-in-process is ontological and the genus of contrariety is contingent upon the existence of loci; their 'principle-ness', however, is indisputable. To conclude:

1. With reference to 'being', contrariety is a first principle; in so far as it is the ground for the formulation of the law of non-contradiction, it is equally *unassumed* or non-hypothetical.[46]

[44] *Met.* B 997a 2-11.   [45] *An. Post.* 75a 37-75b 2.
[46] *Met.* 1005b 13-15; *An. Post.* 71b 20-3. See also Appendix: ch. 6, note 4.

Contrariety in the Theory of Opposition in Language

2. The undemonstrability of first principles and contrariety enables Aristotle to avoid absurdities such as infinite regress or the reductionist fallacy of material principles to formal principles and *vice versa*. Since all principles collectively are principles of the understanding of being, they are the object of metaphysical inquiry, for it is metaphysics that aims at the knowledge of substance.

Chapter Seven

PROCESS AND THE PRINCIPLE OF SOUL

THE purpose of this chapter is to explore the connection between the principle of contrariety and Aristotle's theory of the soul. The main thesis defended here is that contrariety besides being a fact of nature and a principle of rendering process intelligible is also deeply rooted in the operations of the soul. But Aristotle's conception of the soul requires special attention. In building his scientific psychology, he found it necessary to free the problems of psychology from the various pre-Socratic and Platonic speculative associations and reconstruct them on the basis of his biological and methodological findings. Soul as redefined by Aristotle became the form of the unity of the activities of living beings. The activities of the soul are special cases of natural processes and as such they involve the principle of contrariety. Soul is both the first actuality of living organisms and the final cause of all behaviour; and equally so the source of the self-moving capacity of life. All natural existents display the contraries of generation and destruction, but organic beings in particular are delimited in addition by the contraries of growth and decay. The diversity which prevails in the various types of organic life is an indicator of the increasing complexity of the functions of the soul as inquiry passes from plants to animals to human beings. This complexity is accompanied by additional factors discoverable always which call attention to new contrary delimitations. Contrariety is thus fundamental in affirming the continuity from nature to man.

Process and the Principle of Soul

1. SCIENTIFIC FOUNDATIONS OF ARISTOTLE'S PSYCHOLOGY

Aristotle is not simply the founder of psychology, but is indeed the first to found psychology on a scientific basis. We might disagree with him on both matters of theory and scientific detail, but there is no reason why we should blind ourselves to his lasting contributions. His original scientific work here is connected with three philosophical principles that loom largely in the background of his psychology.

(*a*) The methodological principle that psychology as a science cannot ignore the general canons of inquiry, the logic of investigatory procedure: that it cannot reach satisfactory answers apart from the objective study of empirical fact. In this sense, Aristotle is a naturalist in his methodology and an empiricist.

(*b*) The principle of the irreducibility of the subject matter of psychology. This means that the phenomena of life and awareness constitute a domain of their own, continuous with other domains of inquiry. Psychology is not a chapter of physics, of logic, of mathematics, or of theology. Its principles and assumptions are relative to the subject matter. His teleology, for example, as a necessary postulate in his theory of organism and growth, is a modification of the more general principle of form, and is unique and irreducible, indubitably necessary for the phenomena it purports to explain; it is related to the other inquiries through a generalized theory of first principles which is part of his science of metaphysics. Here Aristotle is a functionalist since he tries to understand this subject matter in terms of the particular functions its 'substances' manifest, the factors and powers involved, and the purposes it pursues. His pluralism with respect to the subject matter of cognitive behaviour and his teleology in psychology go hand in hand, and are empirically warranted.

(*c*) The principle of the inter-relatedness of subject matters and inquiries. It is unfortunate that the critics of his metaphysics missed this aspect of his thought—probably because their anti-speculative predilections prevented them from seeing in Aristotle his sober analysis of the generic traits of being, its pervasive principles, and comprehensive distinctions applicable to all possible and discoverable subject matters. His modern critics especially deemed it best to attack his science of metaphysics in its entirety just because some speculation in it—almost inevitable yet so sweet to philosophers—became the core for further speculation by subsequent thinkers, for which they came to claim, rather unabashedly, philosophical supremacy.

The synthetic experiment in Aristotle's metaphysics need not obfuscate the distinctive merits of the categories, the theory of causation, the science of first principles, the laws of logic, the doctrine of the elements and the levels of being. And it should be mentioned here that Aristotle, unlike most contemporary psychologists, made a bold attempt to relate the subject matter of psychology to the other sciences through a general theory of existence. He also constructed a view in which the soul as the principle of growth and behaviour on the plant, animal and human level is, as the explanatory principle of the dynamics of organic beings, in a serious sense fully intelligible in the light of a philosophy of process. The soul itself is both the principle of understanding and the originative source of a special type of process.

The principle of the inter-relatedness of inquiries is a cornerstone in his psychology; for he knew that psychology, though irreducible to biology, presupposes it, and biology in turn works closely with a theory of elements—what we call chemistry today. This is exactly what physiological psychology, biology, histology, plant and animal anatomy, organic and inorganic chemistry, biochemistry, physics and astronomy are doing today in a highly specialized fashion and with the aid of the mathematico-experimental technique of controlled inquiry. Aristotle's conception of psychology also points to the other direction, that of the formal and social sciences. The nature of man as living and thinking organism connects the subject matter of psychology to a theory of knowledge and perception, logic, method, and intelligent conduct, that is moral and political conduct. And this in fact is what the social sciences, in their increasing variety, are doing today. And those scientists do it best who can discuss the psychological foundations of a given branch of the social sciences without reducing or deriving their *archai* from other domains, viz. psychology.

Aristotle's pluralism of subject matters is consistent with his ontology of being, where being is distributively understood. Where the context of inquiry changes, there the new set of assumptions and principles become the 'theses', and the general

Process and the Principle of Soul

pervasive traits are sufficiently amplified and redefined to provide these concepts with interpretive broadness to satisfy the principle of inter-relatedness. Herein, it seems to me, lies the chief value of Aristotle's metaphysics: in being the science of generalities and inclusive connectives as principles of understanding any subject matter whatever.

Considering the vagueness that characterized the entirety of pre-Aristotelian theories on the nature of the soul and its processes, the contribution of Aristotle in this field of knowledge is without exaggeration a scientific revolution. The psychological treatises, particularly the *De Anima*, constitute on the whole epoch-making works which for the first time in history placed psychological inquiry on a scientific basis. The impact of his biological and other empirical studies on his psychology is the main reason for the abandonment of the views he inherited from the speculative influences of his early years in the Platonic Academy as expressed in the *Protrepticus*, the *Eudemian Ethics*, and the other early works. The process toward the formulation of his new theory was undoubtedly slow and cumbersome. Even at the end of his journey, as the third book of the *De Anima* reveals, his psychological position was not completely free from speculative notions, namely the doctrine of *nous*,[1] which had become dear to his heart.

The maturity of his psychological views is marked with a radically new approach, the psycho-physical theory. This new element emerged almost inevitably from his logical investigations, methodological refinements, biological inquiries, and his own ontology of distributive being. In his new ontology,

[1] That the doctrine of *nous* in the *De Anima* and the other works was carefully preserved by Aristotle should be of no surprise to the student of his thought. Jaeger has observed correctly that it is 'a traditional element inherited from Plato' (*Aristotle*, p. 332). That which is really difficult to explain, however, is the place in which the doctrine appears in the economy of the composition of the *De Anima*. Peculiarly enough, the last book of this work, which is expected to be the most carefully worked out part of the treatise, is apparently the least scientific and most speculative one. There is sufficient evidence that Aristotle remained fond of the concept of *nous*. We have no evidence that he tried to reconstruct this concept in the light of his mature ontological position. Thus, what *nous* without Platonism must have been for Aristotle is open to interpretation. But the fact that it appears in the last part of the *De Anima* is no small token of the place he wished to assign to this inclusive philosophical concept.

Process and the Principle of Soul

concerning the nature of beings on the sublunary level, the organic existents are seen as composite wholes displaying an integrated unity of form and matter, where form and matter are pervasive traits of being and limiting concepts grounded in the nature of reality. Yet the tradition within which Aristotle worked had contributed in no small measure to his formulation of what became the most sound interpretation of life phenomena in antiquity. The accumulation of historical material on the subject, his classification and keen analysis of the views his predecessors expressed on the nature of the soul, had been valuable in guiding his research and formulating the crucial questions pertinent to this subject matter.[2]

A serious problem, however, arises from the mode of his criticism and his manner in presenting the views of his predecessors and making explicit the inherent difficulties in these views. Preliminarily it must be said that Aristotle derived a double gain from his historico-critical enterprise. Negatively, he removed one by one the inadequacies he saw in his predecessors and brought into the open the limitations and discrepancies in their logic. But positively, he came to understand a great variety of answers,[3] their background and presuppositions as well as their place in a system. Yet it does no justice to his genius to say that he distorted his predecessors' views in order to make them suit his purposes and the particular course he gave to psychological inquiry. Undoubtedly a case may be made against Aristotle's manner of handling the historical material, but one must also remember that an objective summary or exposition of historical material certainly was not his main purpose. A decisive factor that seems to have determined his way of treating the historical part of psychological theory was the nature of the material itself. With all due appreciation of pre-Aristotelian theories of the soul the fact remains that they can hardly be called scientific in spite of whatever empirical elements they contain.[4]

---

[2] *De An.* 403b 20-4. The concluding chapter of Book I contains a list of the questions he proposes to answer.

[3] See E. E. Spicer, *Aristotle's Conception of the Soul* (University of London Press, 1934), pp. 7-28.

[4] For suggestive criticism of this point see J. I. Beare, *Greek Theories of Elementary Cognition* (Oxford, 1906), pp. 3-8; Zeller, *Aristotle*, I, p. 443, English translation.

Process and the Principle of Soul

Aristotle is not only a scientist with regard to his attitude toward the subject matter of psychology as such: he equally assumed a similar position towards the historical part he inherited. What stands out from his treatment of his predecessors is not simply the critical analysis of whatever theories he chose to discuss, but the very fact that he is willing to admit these theories as though they were serious hypotheses scientifically constructed to bear upon the question of the soul as explanatory hypothesis of behaviour. It is with this attitude that he proceeded to examine these theories for what truth they might disclose and to draw the theoretical consequences entailed in their assumptions. But the picture of Aristotle's criticism becomes complete only when one considers the additional fact that (*a*) it is done from the particular standpoint of his own theory, and (*b*) he reformulated these theories in order to give them the appearance of plausible psychological hypotheses. Actually, however, in most of the cases the re-rendering is done in a terminology not consistently faithful to that of the original.

In his criticism he has made ample use of the *reductio ad absurdum* method. Here he showed, with impressive mastery of the analytic technique, what contradictions and impossibilities result from his predecessors' theories when viewed in the light of all the problems a more adequate psychology must face. By doing so he derived considerable wisdom in theoretical preparation which, in addition to his methodological and empirical work accomplished independently, became the basis for the newly founded scientific psychology.

In the light of our previous discussion then it is not impertinent to state that the appreciative reader will do well to bear in mind the following three considerations, basic in understanding the historico-critical part of the *De Anima*: (1) the pre-Aristotelian theories have been reformulated by Aristotle on the assumption that they might be regarded as tenable psychological hypotheses and then are criticized for the purpose of discovering not so much the discrepancies as for the valuable questions they raised and which no complete theory on the soul could afford to neglect to answer; (2) the particular views held by Aristotle himself which grew out of the investigatory stage of his post-Platonic period and were constructed according to his methodology of the physical and biological inquiries; (3) knowledge of the Aristotelian

Process and the Principle of Soul

qualitative chemistry on which the theory of elements is based, which, as it will be shown, throws considerable light not only on the physical foundations of a theory of perception and the physiology of the senses but also provides an explanation for his epistemological realism in which things *are* what they are said to be.[5]

The Aristotelian treatises that contain most of the relevant material for our inquiry are the *De Anima*, *De Sensu* and *De Memoria*.[6] This chapter, however, is in no way a recount of the material of the works mentioned,[7] for detailed expositions abound both in general works on Aristotle and on special aspects of his philosophical system. Only those passages have been selected here that bear on the argument that contrariety is a central principle in Aristotle's theory of the soul as viewed within the framework of his philosophy of process. While the whole of nature is divided between inanimate and animate phenomena, all animate nature is encompassed between the following contraries: (*a*) youth and age; and (*b*) life and death.[8]

---

[5] Aristotle's epistemological realism is in a serious way connected with his view that language and its structure share in the stability of the universe. The fact of linguistic development, i.e. language in its historical setting, was not suspected by Aristotle. To him the Greek language was the perfect instrument for the articulation of the order of processes. The rationality of the universe and the *logos* of man are not dissimilar; both are permanent and alike in form though not co-extensive as actualities. See H. G. Alexander's suggestive article 'Language and Hypostatization', *Proceedings of the XIth International Congress of Philosophy*, V (August, 1953), pp. 185-90.

[6] The procedure that Aristotle followed in these treatises is not uniform and could, therefore, serve as a point of contrast between them. In the *De Anima*, for example, the procedure is from the universal to the particular, specifically, from the general definition of the soul to its particular faculties. In the *De Sensu* and the *De Memoria* the inductive, not the deductive, method is followed. Here the inquiry proceeds from the specific, manifest faculties to the general notion of the principle of soul.

[7] The chief psychological works of Aristotle are the *De Anima* and the collection of essays entitled *Parva Naturalia*, which contains the following: (i) *De Sensu et Sensibilibus*, (ii) *De Memoria et de Reminiscentia*, (iii) *De Somno*, (iv) *De Imsomniis*, (v) *De Divinatione per Somnum*, (vi) *De Longitudine et Brevitate Vitae*, (vii) *De Vitae et Morte* (incomplete), (viii) *De Respiratione*, and (ix) *De Spiritus* (a spurious work).

[8] In the *De Sensu* these contraries are referred to as two of the four pairs of correlatives, which are: waking and sleep, youth and age, the inhalation and expulsion of breath, and life and death. Only youth and age, and life and death are true of all organisms. All four are particularly true of animals. 436a 13–16.

Process and the Principle of Soul

It is then clear that the use of the principle of contrariety in Aristotle's psychology is necessitated by the admission of the notion that here we are dealing again with a unique type of determinate processes occurring in an organic locus. The particular activities of the soul are processes and consequently delimited by the appropriate specific contraries marking the *termini* which delineate the range of possible operative efficacy of the relative powers. Another reason for introducing contrariety as a necessary principle in the theory of both nutrition and sensation and, therefore, cognition, is the general background of the physiology of the senses. The senses, as it will become clear, especially in the next chapter, are due to their physiology connected with a theory of elements. Each sense in particular is materially derived from either one or more elements. In view of this doctrine, it is not difficult to see what is meant by the notion that the sense organ is potentially what the sensible object is actually. Both perception as a psychological process and the physiology of the perceptive organs in general point directly to the centrality of the concept of contrariety.

The role of this principle is further appreciated by taking into consideration the fact that the function of perception is ultimately conditioned by the chemical constitution of the nature of the basic elements. The theory of the elements, which is presented in a previous chapter, must be remembered here because it is essential to the problems of perception. In Aristotle's view, perception has its foundations in the nature of the elements which in turn are subject to the inter-elemental change discussed in the appropriate parts of the *De Generatione et Corruptione*. The phenomenon of inter-elemental change is finally based on a theory of the properties of the ultimate contrary qualities: hot and cold, wet and dry. It follows that we perceive because the universe is perceivable, and we understand it because it is intelligible. Nature and human nature are continuous.

In the case of cognition, again, it so happens that this activity, being a psychological process, moves within its own contraries. In its linguistic setting as discourse it is delimited by the law of contradiction. Here thought employs contrariety to know all determinate processes, including its own. And the mind attains knowledge of both nature and the principles of the intelligibility of all processes, which is a distinctive mark of human wisdom.

Process and the Principle of Soul

2. PROCESS AND ORGANIC NATURE

Negatively, there are two notions that must not be taken as constituting contraries or forming *termini* of processes in Aristotle's psychology, namely body and soul. They are in no way contraries or distinct parts of an organism, but distinguishable *aspects* of the same organism found in analysis.[9] As a consequence of this position it will be shown that Aristotle demonstrated again in the special case of psychology that contrariety as such is neither an elemental principle nor an operative factor to be found in the organic type of qualitative change. The role of contrariety in both the physical and the psychical processes is the same because the processes in the soul are but more subtle and more elaborate ones than those found in the field of physics. The soul is the principle of a unique type of movement but is not a movement itself,[10] for the soul is not a separate substance completely independent and existing in itself.

It follows that since body and soul are not contraries there is no need to assume a third principle, a substratum, a new substance, of which body and soul are the delimiting extremities. With the removal of the body-soul opposition, the theory of the soul is in complete agreement with the demands of the principle of contrariety in its logical and physical setting. In his psychology, apart from the criticisms of his predecessors and the attempts at a definition of the soul which occupy a substantial portion of the

[9] Again the sensible and the intelligible are not contraries but *correlative opposites*. This is further supported by the view that contrariety and privation demand that the presence of the one contrary excludes or demands the destruction of the other. The sensible does not negate the intelligible. In fact the function of perception presupposes the sensible and makes actual the intelligible.

[10] The relation between movement and soul is discussed in *De An.*, Book I, chs. 3, 4. The theories that regard soul as something in motion or a self-moving number are rejected. He bases his position on the notion that 'it is not necessary that that which produces motion should itself move', 406a 2. He is critical here of the inability of his predecessors to view the soul in its organic setting. The error in these theories is due to a bifurcation of the organism which then leads to a soul wholly separable from the total organic situation. To put the matter differently, Aristotle refutes theories that have turned into hypostases the terms of a particular distinction, namely, body and soul. Consequently, such theories, as he points out, leave much to be desired.

Process and the Principle of Soul

De Anima, Aristotle is basically building his case by viewing the organism as the subject-in-process, the locus in which other processes or qualitative changes take place.

These processes within the organism are determinate and contained within contraries. Their limits, as specific contraries, are the *termini* of psychic movements and are, therefore, typically subject to the same principle of analysis as the total process of the entire locus or organism in which they occur. The characteristic of having contraries is shared by all specific functions of the organism, and it is in this sense that contrariety is a generic trait of psychic processes. Understanding these processes, then, calls for the employment of contrariety as a metaphysical and logical principle and as one of the preconditions of the intelligibility of all change. We may then say that Aristotle has no real or apparent psycho-physical dualism,[11] nor is there in his philosophy of nature, and organism in particular, a monism of speculative cosmology. In his ontology he remains an empirical pluralist, and in his analysis of being he is consistent within the limitations and principles of his methodology. The application of the principle of contrariety in his approach to all types of process in the sublunary level bears witness to this.

The events and processes of psychology, the organic phenomena, are special cases of physical facts. They exist and constitute a pluralistic physical universe. By things natural, *physica*, we understand that realm of existence which encompasses all entities called corporeal substances. They fall within the contrariety of motion and rest. This movement is mechanical change in place. But there are also other entities, equally natural, that

[11] Jaeger observes a basic difference between the early and later views of Aristotle on the nature of the soul. He states 'what distinguishes Aristotle's early view of the soul is in fact that the soul is not yet the form *of something*, but a form in itself . . .' *Aristotle*, p. 45. In his later view, Aristotle, according to Jaeger, 'held that the essential problem of psychology was the connection between the soul and the bodily organism, and he claims to have been the first to recognize the psycho-physical nature of mental phenomena. The first result of the discovery of these psychological relations was inevitably to undermine the Platonic belief in the permanence of the individual soul, and the only part of his original conviction that Aristotle could retain was the belief that pure *nous* is independent of the body. All other functions of the soul, such as reflection, love and hate, fear, anger, and memory, involve the psycho-physical unity as their substratum and disappear together with it.' *Ibid.*, p. 49.

Process and the Principle of Soul

contain within themselves their own principle of motion. This principle, the internal originating source of movement, is the defining characteristic of organic entities. The inherent principle of self-movement, of autonomous motion, in life is soul. The individual organism in movement or process is related to the totality of beings, animate and inanimate, the environment at large, and between the two a continuous interaction takes place. Two kinds of change are caused by the action of the environment upon the organism: (*a*) the process of mechanical change, and (*b*) the process of qualitative change.

All life is comprehended between the contrariety whose extremes are *growth* and *decay*. All organic beings exemplify the linear process of life between generation and destruction. Fundamental, therefore, to all forms of animate life is the nutritive function, which is universally distributed to everything alive. The universal principle of life is differentiated. Aristotle does not give a speculative or genetic account of the differentiation of the principle of life; he accepts it as a fact to be dealt with and understood.

Aristotle, the student of natural forms of life, the empirical seeker of knowledge, proceeds to enumerate the types of differentiation found in the process of scientific investigation. Here we shall look in vain for a story of evolution or emergence of the species. But this attitude did not prevent him from assuming the eternality of the species. To turn to the principle of life, soul, it permeates every type of organism, plants and animals, and renders impossible an absolute distinction between them. The transition from plants to animals is not presented in evolutionary terms but is done in the light of factorial analysis. Animal life is found to be more complex than the plant life and inclusive of the characteristics of the latter. The absence of absolute distinctions is equally evident in the conception of the relation between inorganic and organic processes. Factorial analysis again shows that the difference is one of degree of complexity.

'Nature proceeds little by little from things lifeless to animal life in such a way that it is impossible to determine the exact line of demarcation, nor on which side thereof an intermediate form should lie. Thus, next after lifeless things in the upward scale comes the plant, and of plants one will differ from another as to its amount of apparent vitality; and, in a word, the whole genus

Process and the Principle of Soul

of plants, whilst it is devoid of life as compared with an animal, is endowed with life as compared with other corporeal entities. Indeed, as we just remarked there is observed in plants a continuous scale of ascent towards the animal.'[12]

Natural processes in their inclusive consideration display a continuity, at least to the scientist who goes to his subject matter relatively free from speculative preconceptions and appreciably equipped with an understanding of the methodological principle of the continuity of analysis. And in Aristotle's case his approach to natural processes is based on continuity of method and factorial analysis; i.e. an analysis in terms of factors discovered during and through an inquiry continuously and consistently applied.

3. THE SOUL AS THE PRINCIPLE OF ORGANIC UNITY

The subjects-in-process that are animate beings are in possession of certain unique vital functions or life:

'By life we mean the power of self-nourishment and of independent growth and decay. Consequently every natural body possessed of life must be substance, and substance of the composite order. And since in fact we have here body with a certain attribute, namely the possession of life, the body will not be the soul: for the body is not an attribute of a subject, it stands rather for a subject of attributes, that is, matter. It must follow then, that soul is substance in the sense that it is the form of a natural body

---

[12] *Hist. of Anim.* 588b 4–12. See also *De Part. Anim.* 681a 12. G. Sarton makes the following remark: 'Note that the Aristotelian *scala naturae* does not necessarily imply evolution, for the *scala* might be conceived as static and the idea of the fixity of series is not incompatible with it. The *scala* appealed to medieval imagination, especially in the Muslim world. Arabic men of science often spoke of it, and those who were mystically minded liked to think of a continual scale or chain of being leading from minerals to plants, from plants to animals, from animals to men, and from men to God. The *scala naturae* was a means of illustrating the fundamental unity and order of nature.' *A History of Science* (Harvard University Press, 1952), pp. 534–5. See also G. Sarton's *Introduction to the History of Science*, III, 211–13, 1170.

The hierarchy of being became one of the most cherished notions in Thomistic natural theology. See *Summa Theologica*, Part I, qu. 47, art. 2. The influence of Neoplatonism on the prevalence of ontological hierarchies in medieval philosophy as well as Byzantine thought cannot be over-emphasized.

Process and the Principle of Soul

having in it the capacity of life. Such substance is actuality. The soul, therefore, is the actuality of the body above described.'[13]

And further down:

'Soul is the first actuality of a natural body having in it the capacity for life. And a body which is possessed of organs answers to this description.... If, then, we have to make a general statement touching the soul in all its forms, the soul will be the first actuality of a natural body furnished with organs.'[14]

Soul with Aristotle is no longer a thing, a hypostasis, or number, or harmony of parts, or any of the notions with which it had been identified by the various pre-Aristotelian thinkers. As the given quotations from the *De Anima* make evident, soul is now viewed as the determined configuration of the functions and activities of each organism and it is the principle that makes an animate being what it is. Here Aristotle has gradually overcome the difficulties in the formulation of his doctrine through an inductive definition of the soul in which soul is now stated as the essential character of animate life.

As the form of the unity of the activities of living beings soul is no longer a self-existing hypostasis but a principle found in all types of living matter and is in turn used as a general explanatory concept to understand the phenomena of the organic level of being. Nor is soul a self-abiding universal, for what is encountered is always determinate souls which are plant-souls, animal-souls, and finally human-souls. The types of life manifest modifications of the principle of soul and in each case the degree of complexity and continuous enrichment is also a fact of nature. Soul, again, is not identical with total life but rather the principle and the power of life, because life in its entirety involves an actualization of the inherent capacities of the soul and a complete fulfilment of its functions.

The soul, by being the form of a body endowed with life, is an actuality which makes the organism what it is, that is, a substance and individual existent. But every living organism is delineated between the inclusive contrarieties of generation and destruction, and growth and decay. Figuratively speaking, the 'distance' between these contraries is covered by the process of the development of the individual existent. This development is a purposive

[13] *De An.* II, 412a 14-21. [14] *De An.* II, 412a 27-412b 6.

Process and the Principle of Soul

one, a notion already suggested by the meaning of the term 'entelechy', which is Aristotle's own coinage. The soul is the first actuality in the sense that it is both the principle of the structural configuration of the organism and the principle of developmental efficiency and purposiveness. Thus the total life process of existents is a career contained between two *termini*: (1) the first actuality which from the outset renders an existent a determinate subject-in-process of the organic type, and (2) the final stage of actuality which stands for the fulfilment of form and the complete actualization of the appropriate powers-in-operation.

This is undoubtedly a fundamental distinction in Aristotle's psychology which plays a more general role in both his philosophy of knowledge and theory of ethics. However, it is not proper to apply to the two actualities the term 'contraries'. In both actualities we are dealing with the same thing: the soul of the living bodies as the form, but as the form in two different stages of the organism's process of actualization. But there again it is not free from ambiguity to say that the form changes; because the form, being what it is, cannot change. And yet a development, in fact, takes place. The soul as form does not change[15] because here the soul is not a 'this', a subject-in-process, but the principle of structure, the unique unity of the functions and activities of an organic being. As such, the unity of powers in operation remains unalterable throughout the life of an existent, and whatever change occurs happens to the whole organism which develops as a unit.

Change does not affect the principle of structural unity but occurs as a function of a co-ordinated system of powers in response to the purposive possibilities inherent in the organism as a whole. This development is a dual operation of adaptation to both the external conditions of the environment and the internal limits of functional integration. The infant, for example, possesses form, and this is his first actuality. But it is only the fulfilment of the entelechy that will make his life complete. In the complete man the unity of the powers in operation as determinate functions reaches the stage of fulfilment in the attainment of excellence in rationality. Reason, then, is not an actuality of body with soul. It is the formal cause consummated as final cause, as completed entelechy. Seen as rational fulfilment, the soul is not just the

---

[15] See Appendix: ch. 7, note 1.

Process and the Principle of Soul

unity of purposive activities in operation but primarily the structural unity[16] of fulfilled activities operating as completely actualized or virtuous. And what is in process is not the soul as unity, but the operative powers of the organism whose actualization makes possible the consummation of the inherent purposiveness.

The principle of the unity of the soul is central to Aristotle's psychology. But prior to any discussion of the unity of the soul's special activities and functions, the notion of the psycho-physical unity of the organism must be made clear,[17] for both body and soul are but aspects of the same composite concrete existent and are distinguishable only in discourse. Then, it follows that the purposive development effected by the actualization of the determinate powers of the organism should be predicated of the organism as a whole and not simply of the soul; for the soul *qua* form is not affected. Indeed, the soul is the final cause of the entire purposive fulfilment and the particular actualizations. Aristotle makes this point explicit when he informs us that 'the soul is incapable of motion; and if it is not moved at all, clearly it does not move itself'.[18]

The composite nature of the living organism seen as a psychophysical unity guided Aristotle to avoid the error of predicating

---

[16] To view the soul as an additive organic whole rather than a principle of understanding organic wholes is not strictly in line with Aristotle's position. Such an additive view is taken by Stuart who says that the soul 'is the totality of the functions of the body'. *Notes on the Nic. Ethics.* See note on 1102a, 30, I, 163.

[17] *De An.* 412b 4–9. In *Met.* 1075b 34, he points out that his predecessors have been unable to offer any explanation for the grounds of this unity. See also *Met.* 1045a 7–b23.

[18] *De An.* 408 b31–2. Cherniss puts the matter correctly when he writes that 'Aristotle does seem to recognize that one might ascribe motion to the soul without meaning locomotion. At any rate, after showing that the soul cannot move locally except accidentally and before concluding generally that it is incapable of motion he had considered the argument that the soul is said to grieve, rejoice, be emboldened, fear, grow angry, perceive, and think and that all these are movements. To this his answer was that, even if these processes are movements and movement is caused by the soul, it does not follow that the soul is in motion, for the subject of the processes is the individual composite of soul and body, the soul being the origin or terminus of the movements which are not in it or of it but are logical motions or alterations of the bodily organs.' *Aristotle's Criticism of Plato and the Academy,* p. 402. See also *De Anima* 408a 34–b30.

Process and the Principle of Soul

movement not only of the soul but also of the body. The soul is not in motion except in an accidental sense;[19] and the body as such does not move itself. Whatever motion it has, *qua* organic, cannot be resolved ultimately into the type of process particularly true of its constitutive elements. In discussing the whole organism, however, we are dealing with a subject-in-process irreducible to its material components and to be understood only in its unique structural configuration as a composite whole endowed with life. The foregoing analysis makes clear that the nature of the organism is such that it imposes upon our inquiry certain new ways of approaching its processes and, consequently, of relating them to the principle of contrariety.

(*a*) Contrariety when applied to the body as such is irrelevant to the new context of organic whole, in which case the discussion is relegated to the categorical contrariety of place. (*b*) Contrariety does not apply to the 'motion of the soul' because the soul is not in process but is the final cause of the actualization of the particular activities of the living subject-in-process. (*c*) Contrariety does not apply to the unity of body and soul, which is the whole organism, because this existent is a first substance and as such it has no contrary to it. But this does not by any means imply that there is a discrepancy between the metaphysical use of contrariety and the inapplicability of this principle on the biological level. What is suggested here is that while the metaphysical contrariety of form-privation is a generic trait of being distributively understood, it does not hold true in the case of the *terms* of a particular type of analysis, for the terms or limiting principles and not the actual existents. Indeed, body and soul are not *per se* existents but the limiting principles of the understanding of biological existents and their processes.

Organic beings, plants and animals, from the point of view of process and identity, present the following three aspects:

(i) Each organism remains what it is by maintaining its formal identity throughout its lineal process between generation and destruction. Its formal individuality makes it an independent substance.

(ii) Each individual organic existent is also a subject-in-process, but what changes is neither the soul nor the body as such but the

[19] *De An.*, Book I, ch. 3.

total organism whose purposive development aims at the completion of the unified powers-in-operation. The analysis of the organic subject-in-process from the standpoint of the four causes may be introduced at this point. The body is the material cause. The soul is in turn the efficient, formal, and final cause, and, collectively, an *arche*, a principle for understanding the living body in three senses: as the efficient cause of movement, as the essence and formal principle of the whole living body, and as the end, the best use and consummation or final principle of such bodies.

'Now the soul is cause and origin of the living body. But cause and origin are terms used in various senses: accordingly soul is cause in the three senses of the word already determined. For the soul is the cause of animate bodies as being in itself the origin of motion, as final cause and as substance. Clearly it is so as substance, substance being the cause of all existence. And for living things existence means life, and it is the soul which is the cause and origin of life. Furthermore, actuality is the notion or form of that which has potential existence. Manifestly too, the soul is final cause. For nature, like intelligence, acts for a purpose, and this purpose is for an end. Such an end the soul is in animals, and this in the order of nature, for all the natural bodies are instruments of soul: and this is as true of the bodies of plants as of those of animals, showing that all are means to the soul as end; where end has two senses, the purpose for which and the person for whom. Moreover, the soul is also the origin of motion from place to place, but not all living things have this power of locomotion. Qualitative change and growth are due to the soul. For sensation is supposed to be a sort of qualitative change, and nothing devoid of soul has sensation. The same holds true of growth and decay. For nothing undergoes natural decay or growth except it be nourished, and nothing is nourished unless it shares in life.'[20]

Another way of denying the opposition between body and soul is to say that there is not such a thing as a contrariety whose extremities are the formal cause and the material cause, for both are *archai*, principles of understanding, generic traits of organic being and not *termini* of changes and activities of subjects-in-process. It is only with the introduction of the contrariety of potentiality and actuality that the material and formal aspects of

[20] *De An.* 415b 8–28.

Process and the Principle of Soul

beings take on new meanings due to their re-definition in developmental terms. In the light of Aristotle's theory of process, form and matter are ultimately identified with the extremities of the metaphysical contrariety of form-privation. The re-definition of the terms is possible because the notion of form is the explanatory principle of change, implying both efficiency and purposiveness, function and uses.[21]

(iii) The subject-in-process is at the same time a locus of processes. They are the activities and powers-in-operation as determinate developments and purposive actualizations, faculties undergoing qualitative modifications, and like all other processes, encompassed within *termini* of appropriate contrarieties.

Summarizing the main thesis concerning the relationship between soul and process, it is evident that since the soul is not in process but the unity of the purposive functions of a locus of process, contrariety applies not to the soul itself but to the understanding of developments characteristic of the powers-in-operation of animate substances.

4. THE NUTRITIVE SOUL AND CONTRARIETY

Animate life is divided into two types: plants and animals. Growth and decay are characteristic of plants or the nutritive type of life. On the animal level life is manifested through the power of growth and decay *plus* the powers of locomotion, sensation, and in the case of the human animal, *plus* rationality. The transition from plant to man is one of increasing degree of complexity in structure and faculties.[22] As the principle of life becomes more and more complex it must be remembered that the more complex souls include and presuppose the functions manifested in the less complex souls.

'The types of soul resemble the series of figures. For, alike in figures and in things animate, the earlier form exists potentially in the later, as, for instance, the triangle potentially in the quadrilateral, and the nutritive faculty in that which has sensation. So we must examine in each case separately, what is the soul of plant, of man or of beast. Why they are related in this order of succession remains to be considered. There is no sensitive faculty apart from

[21] *De An.* 412a 6–19; 412b 26–413a 10.   [22] See Appendix: ch. 7, note 2.

nutritive: and yet the latter exists without the former in plants. Again, none of the other senses is found apart from touch; while touch is found apart from the others, many animals having neither sight nor hearing nor sense of smell. Also of those which possess sensation, some can move from place to place, others cannot. Lastly and most rarely they have the reasoning faculty and thought. For those perishable creatures which possess reason are endowed with all the other species of soul, but not all of those which possess each of the other faculties have reason. Indeed, some of them have not even imagination, while others live by imagination alone. As for the speculative intellect, it is a theme that calls for a separate discussion. Meanwhile it is clear that an account of the several faculties is at the same time the most appropriate account of soul.'[23]

The principle of life becomes increasingly complex as the context shifts from plants to men. The degree of complexity, however, in no way affects the unity of the functional configuration of the organism. Another point that must be remembered is that the more complex souls include and presuppose the functions manifested in less complex types of life.[24] There is no discontinuity in life, no absolute breaks in nature. Consequently the science of human life and behaviour calls for an understanding of the other types of life, less complex, of course, but not dissimilar in what they have in common. The structural and functional similarities and differentiations found in the various types of living organisms provide the basis for classification, a theory of classes—reflected in Aristotle's logic of classes—and the notion of logical *differentia* of the biological genera and species.[25]

The contrariety of growth and decay permeates all animate beings but is especially characteristic of plants. The distinctive principle of this type of life is nutrition[26] and propagation. Therefore, the contrariety of growth and decay is denotatively the most inclusive one because it encompasses the entire organic realm. The function of the nutritive faculty, Aristotle states, is

[23] *De An.* 414b 20–415a 13.   [24] *De An.* 415a 1–11.

[25] It is questionable whether one is justified in attributing to Aristotle a theory of hierarchy of faculties especially when the inquiry is about the principle of life. See Appendix: ch. 7, note 3.

[26] The predominant element in plants is earth, which accounts for the absence of sensation. Aristotle did not attribute sensation to plants, unlike modern botany.

Process and the Principle of Soul

the absorption of food.[27] The process of nourishment is a qualitative change occurring in a substance to be explained in two ways: (*a*) contraries are nourished by contraries, and (*b*) like is nourished by like. We must now turn to the examination of these two possibilities.

(*a*) Contraries are nourished by contraries. Aristotle observes that according to the theory of elements this cannot possibly happen universally because 'while water serves to feed fire, fire is not nutriment to water'.[28] If contraries are nourished by contraries, the argument implies, the law should operate both ways. But he continues further down to say that 'It would seem, then, that it is in the simple bodies above all that of two contraries one is nutriment and the other is nourished.'[29] Here Aristotle makes an unnecessary concession and misleads the student by confusing organic growth with what we termed in his theory of elements the doctrine of elemental transformation,[30] according to which the four elements are capable of changing into one another. It can hardly be said that Aristotle has refuted the theory that contraries are nourished by contraries because his own view of elements contains a basic incompatibility. Ultimately fire and water are not contraries, though he holds this view elsewhere.[31] Only the qualities, which are not identical with the elements, are contraries; the hot is contrary to the cold, and the wet is contrary to the dry.[32] We cannot, consequently, speak of contrary elements, but only of contrary qualities. The relations between elements and qualities could be represented by the following diagram:

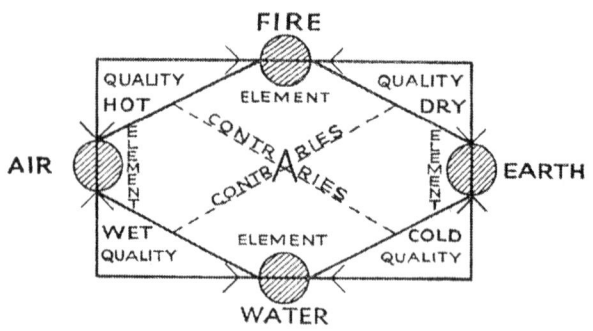

---

[27] *De An.* 416a 19–21. [28] *De An.* 416a 26–7. [29] *De An.* 416a 27–9.
[30] See ch. 3, pp. 45–6. [31] *Mag. Mor.* 121a 16.
[32] It was Empedocles who held the view that the elements are contraries.

Process and the Principle of Soul

What follows from the foregoing discussion is that Aristotle has not refuted the explanation of the process of nutrition since his argument is essentially irrelevant to the question raised and, what is more, it is based on an untenable view.

(*b*) Like is nourished by like. It is Empedocles again who supported this view.[33] Nourishment occurs because like attracts like.[34] Now Aristotle refrains from advancing arguments against this view but proceeds to state his own position. His explanation is one which brings the two views together by keeping the discussion strictly on the biological level. He finds that there is some truth in both positions. Before the assimilation of food, the organism and the food are unlike. It is the process of digestion that turns the food into nourishment and makes it become like the body. This process of qualitative change through nutrition is a precondition for quantiative change, called growth.

'It is impossible that there should be increase without the previous occurrence of alteration: for that which is increased, although in a sense it is increased by what is like itself, is in a sense increased by what is unlike itself: thus it is said that contrary is nourishment to contrary: but growth is effected only by things becoming like to like. There must be alteration, then, in that there is change from contrary to contrary. But the fact that a thing is altered requires that there should be something that alters it, something, e.g. that makes the potentially hot into the actually hot.'[35]

In this passage, he places the problem in its proper context by reminding the reader that a solution can be found only by relating growth to alteration which is a process that takes place in subjects-in-process capable of growth. Finally, the process of alteration is seen as another manifestation of the first contrariety of relative privation and form. In this case it is between potentially hot and actually hot.

In this respect, Aristotle is closer to Anaxagoras than he is, as it is commonly believed, to Empedocles; because not the four elements, but the qualities are contrary pairs.

[33] Diels, *Die Frag. der Vors.* (Empedocles), frag. B 62 and B 90. Apparently Democritus held similar convictions though for different reasons. See *De Gen. et Corr.* I, 7, 323b 3 sqq.

[34] *De An.* 416a 29–31.   [35] *Phys.* 260a 29–260b 2.

Process and the Principle of Soul

In the *De Anima*, he states:

'But it makes a difference whether by nutriment we mean the final, or the primary, form of what is added. If both are nutriment, the one as undigested, the other as digested, it will be possible to use the term nutriment in conformity with both theories. For, in so far as it is undigested, contrary is nourished by contrary: and, in so far as it is digested, like by like. So that clearly both sides are in a manner partly right and partly wrong. But since nothing is nourished unless it possesses life, that which is nourished must be the animate body as such: so that nutriment also is relative to the animate being which it nourishes: and this is not incidentally merely.'[36]

In diagram form the solution is something like the following:

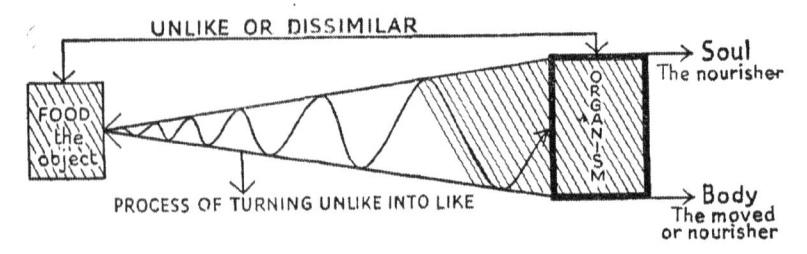

[Diagram: UNLIKE OR DISSIMILAR — FOOD the object → ORGANISM → Soul, The nourisher; PROCESS OF TURNING UNLIKE INTO LIKE → Body, The moved or nourisher]

5. ON THE NATURE OF SENSATION

With the appearance of mental phenomena, the study of psychology directs its attention to beings of greater complexity than that found in plants. Not merely the psychology of plants, but in more general terms, the science of biology must precede that of animal and human psychology. A fundamental idea in Aristotle's theory of sensitive soul and its powers of sensation is the conviction that (*a*) there is a qualitative identity between the sensing organ and the medium in which the quality to be perceived is originated, and (*b*) this identity is the outcome of a special process by which the organ is adjusted to the qualitative actualities of the particular objects of sensation. Sensation thus is a process of assimilation, like nutrition, but it is unlike nutrition in that it is not food or material bodies that are assimilated.[37] Sensation must be contrasted with the usual notion of alteration as nutritive assimilation, because in sensation we are dealing

---

[36] *De An.* 416b 2–11.   [37] *De An.* 425b 22.

Process and the Principle of Soul

primarily with a process of actualization or a movement toward actuality.[38] Yet when we say that sensation takes place it must be remembered that what perceives is not merely the instrument of sensation, the organ, but the whole soul[39] because it is the soul as form that gives unity to the entire sensitive organism for the sake of which all processes of sense-actualizations happen. In sensation the organism is both affected and active; active as an actualized locus, affected as a purposive individual entity moving toward fulfilment through the particular and co-ordinated operations of its powers. But to this topic we will return later.

The organ, in order to assimilate, must possess powers that enable it to undergo such changes as to respond to the dynamic configuration of the sensible objects. It must, consequently, undergo processes which are internally qualitative and at the same time delimited by a pair of contraries, or a contrary and an intermediate. Both the sensing organ and the sensible object have qualitative properties; or to put the matter differently, the qualities exist in both the object and the knower. The object, however, is in a given moment what it happens to be; and its qualitative state is determinate at the time it is sensed. Then, it is not the object but the perceiving organism that has to make the response and produce within itself by means of the process of sensation a situation which in its structural and formal determinateness will be identical in kind with the stimulus.[40] Sensation then, by virtue of being a process—in this case, producing a formal similarity to an actual external determinate structure of qualities—is bounded by the principle of contrariety. In fact, contrariety is a permeating feature characteristic of all the particular senses of animals and the corresponding sense organs. The very capability and range of perceptibility of each of the senses is determined by the operational efficacy allowed by such contraries.

The nature of the process of sensation is fully understood when seen as a double actualization of two inter-related movements: (a) The actualization or purposive development that all subjects-in-process exhibit as concrete individuals which in their totality constitute the subject matter of sensation in general. And here,

[38] *De An.* 417a 2–16. This thought is more fully developed in 424a 5; 424a 32–618; see also *An. Post.* 99b 35 sqq.
[39] *De An.* 414a 12 sqq.; also 408b 13–18.
[40] See Appendix: ch. 3, note 4.

again, Aristotle raises no doubts concerning the existence of an external world, for the subject matter of sensation is itself a principle, an indubitable 'beginning' for philosophical reflection on the phenomenon of life and knowing, which reflection and inquiry are in fact the very content of his psychological treatises, and the *De Anima* in particular. But we must emphasize the notion that the actualizations of subjects-in-process are fulfilments and developments of whole entities. (*b*) The internal movement which is the actualization of a power-in-operation and of sensing organs which in turn involve the entire faculty of sensation. But in this case it is operations of special organs that are in process and not the whole organism except in so far as the exercise of a faculty contributes its share toward the development of the whole organism. However, for the purpose of analysis we may be justified in distinguishing between the two different actualizations that together account for the occurrence of sensation. The two actualizations or processes coincide in the act of sensation and as actualities they become alike.[41] This is possible by what Aristotle calls the 'inception of form'. The fact of sensation as the inseparable intertwining of the two actualizations forms the foundation for what could be called his epistemological realism, which in turn guarantees the existence of external processes and entities and the continuity from universe to man.

The factorial analysis of the phenomenon of sensation, by virtue of which we may call Aristotle an epistemological realist, makes it clear that no complete account of the process of sensation can be given unless three components are taken into consideration: (i) the faculty as power-in-operation, (ii) the organ used, and (iii) the sensible object. Aristotle insists that the objects of sensation exist separately and independently of the knowing organism not simply because they possess a material substratum but equally

[41] *De An.* 425b 26 sqq. Perceiver and perceived are relative to each other. In *Met.* 1010b 30–1011a 2, Aristotle states: 'In general, if only the sensible exists, there would be nothing if animate things were not; for there would be no faculty of sense. Now the view that neither the sensible qualities nor the sensations would exist is doubtless true (for they are affections of the perceiver), but that the substrata which cause the sensation should not exist even apart from sensation is impossible. For sensation is surely not the sensation of itself, but there is something beyond the sensation, which must be prior in nature to that which is moved, and if they are correlative terms, this is no less the case.' Compare also the passage from *Cat.*, ch. 7, 7b 25–8a 14.

because of their being, their actuality and *energeia*—ultimately, their form. And it is this form that the organism inceives. Hence, it is only informed matter that is 'inceived'. The possibility of unstructured substratum having actual existence cannot be regarded as a serious philosophical problem because such 'prime matter' is both non-existing and 'unnatural', it cannot be in process, and as such it is to be rejected on psychological grounds. Unstructured objects can never be given in experience. Form is a precondition for the activity of sensation.

The foregoing analysis allows us now to restate a basic principle in the Aristotelian theory of sensation *qua* process; namely, while sensation is a process of actualization it is also a qualitative change ranging between contrary determinations in accordance with the organic constitution of the sense organ and assimilating such structural possibilities of the external world that fall within the limits of perceivability. The qualitative change occurring in the knower happens *via* the organic constitution of the organ of sensation. It is therefore clear that no change is observed in the inceived form, because form does not undergo change of any kind.[42] Now sensation not as process but as a completed mental act, is identical in form with the structural determinateness of its object. What differentiates one from the other is their particularity, their distinct separate existences.[43] Sensation is potentially what the sensible objects are actually.

Sensation as a faculty is capable of inceiving an indefinite variety of structural configurations of substances, quantities, qualities, relations and others implied by the types of predication. All inceived forms ultimately presuppose the fundamental category of *ousia* as 'being' in its distributive meaning. Thus sensation inceives all sorts of forms, structural configurations related to all types of predication, and is thereby a faculty of both *inception* and *discrimination*. The unity which characterizes sensation as an act of consciousness secures the co-ordinate function of both inceiving and discriminating.[44] A conscious act of perception discriminates elements (i) belonging to the same sense, in which case we speak of *contrary qualities*,[45] like black and white, and

[42] *De An.* 416b 35; 417a 18–20; 418a 3–6.   [43] *De An.* 425b 26–426a 20.
[44] *De An.* 426b 17 sqq. This theme is fully developed in the next chapter.
[45] *De Sensu*, ch. 7, 447a 27. G. R. T. Ross in *Aristotle, De Sensu and de Memoria* gives the following suggestive explanation of apperception of both

Process and the Principle of Soul

(ii) belonging to different senses, and here we deal with *otherness*, i.e. 'other' qualities, viz. sweet and white.[46] The physiological make-up of the faculty of sensation is such that its flexibility and swift responsiveness secures the assimilation of the multiplicity of natural forms, the differentiations of being, and the diverse transitions in development and qualitative changes manifested in the processes of individual actualizations. Sensation thus becomes for Aristotle the faculty which supplies the soul with its experiential content which has, by virtue of its source, an objective principle of formal unity, a *logos* of structural integrity belonging also to the object to which the soul responds and is capable of recapitulating in form.[47] Nature, then, is neither wholly unknown nor does it disguise its secrets to reveal itself only through appearances. Intelligibility and rationality, for Aristotle, are undeniably present in the elementary acts of sense perception.

---

contraries and *different* qualities. 'Opposed qualities ... though existing in different parts of the same total object must (if between them they cover the whole extent of the ground) meet in a common indivisible point if they are still to be ascribed to the same object, and diverse characters ... like white and sweet, which do not exist in different parts of the substance, must be deemed (as long as substance has those qualities) to belong equally to its minutest parts, i.e. to be held together in a unity which, like the point, is absolutely indivisible' (pp. 32-3).

[46] *De Sensu*, ch. 7, 447b 23; 447b 9. The various applications of the term 'different' are given in *Met.*, Book V, 1018a 9-15 and 1054b 14-23; see also *Met.* 1018a 38-67 for 'different in species' and 1024b 9-16 for 'different in genus'. For the distinction between 'difference' and 'otherness' see *Met.*, Book X, ch. 3, 1054b 13 sqq. The finer discriminations in the differences in meaning between 'otherness' and 'difference' are discussed in the next chapter. By 'other' qualities he refers to qualities not related to the same sense, viz. qualities of smell and qualities of sight.

[47] Aristotle would disagree on this epistemological issue with Kant who insisted that all principles of unification of experience are properties of the knowing and perceiving mind. The unity in nature for Kant is an inference from a fact of the mind. This is not the case in the Aristotelian conception of being, for the perceiver is not unlike the perceived, or rather, the perceiver is both like and unlike the perceived. The permeating metaphysical principles of unity and diversity (the age-old distinction between the one and the many) are both subjective factors and objective features. Nature and intelligence are continuous: to put it in Aristotelian language, intelligence, in the form of sensation, is potentially what nature is actually. Furthermore, human *nous* is potentially what universal rationality is actually. To achieve in form the ideal rationality of the universe by means of human intelligence is the aim of all science.

Process and the Principle of Soul

The content of experience is received by the faculty of sensation through the five senses: touch, taste, smell, hearing, and sight. A limited number of qualities are perceivable by each of the senses, as it will be shown in the following chapter. All qualities can be arranged in linear series, the extremes of which determine the range of sensibility. However, it must not be inferred that the qualities form a continuum; for example, there is no necessary qualitative transition[48] from olfactory qualities to visual qualities and the like, because the qualities are distinct and require distinctive organs to be perceived. The objective locus of the qualities is the individual subject-in-process and the subjective focus of their inception is in the knowing subject. The link between the two, the locus and focus, is provided by the sciences of psychology and physiology.[49] The irreducibility of perceptible qualities and the differentiation of the senses are correlated facts.

The particular senses, however, are 'neutral' to the particular perceptual possibilities of the objects; they are, as it were, balanced between the binding, delimiting qualitative contraries. 'The sense is a kind of mean between the opposite extremes in the sensibles.[50] This is why it passes judgment on the things of sense. For the mean is capable of judging, becoming to each extreme in turn its opposite.'[51] The sense responds thus to the external stimulus and becomes 'active' by producing a similar *ratio* as that residing in the sensed features, properties, relations and the like in the object or event; provided, of course, that this *ratio* is within the range of the organ and its physiological constitution.[52] We perceive the

---

[48] *De Sensu*, especially ch. 7; see also *De An.*, Book III, ch. 2.

[49] The simple special qualities form the extremes. The other qualities are intermediates between the extremes, their position depending on the prevailing element in the quality under consideration. *De Sensu*, ch. 6, 445b 24 sqq.

[50] A literal translation of the text is 'of the contrariety in the sensibles'.

[51] *De An.* 424a 2–7.

[52] *De An.* 426a 28–68. He states here that 'The due proportion constitutes the sense, while objects in excess give pain or cause destruction.' This due proportion is the *logos*, the ratio, between the extremes. It might not be altogether unsafe to conjecture that the doctrine of the mean in the ethical writings has its antecedents in the physiological basis of his psychological theory. One could mention here for further support the remarks made in the *Nic. Ethics* about the virtuous and intelligent statesman who is expected to ground his political wisdom on a sound knowledge of human psychology, which science, in Aristotle's view, cannot be seen apart from biological and physiological considerations. See *Nic. Ethics*, Book I, ch. 13, 1102a 12 sqq. In

Process and the Principle of Soul

ratio of qualities in the objects, that is their *form*, by virtue of a reproduction in the sense organ of the same *ratio* or identical form because the organ possesses the same qualities in a passively neutral ratio, a *mesotes*. The flexibility of the organ in reproducing ratios enables us to discriminate between different configurations of beings and their properties. Sensation, thus viewed, is both a capacity for change of ratios and an activity effecting configurations.[53]

Aristotle's theory of sensation in general casts additional light on what has been termed his epistemological realism[54] through the answer he gave to the question of identity-difference[55] in the complex perceptual relation which involves the three factors —object, organ, activity. In traditional terminology it is the problem of the 'like and unlike' in perception. In what sense can

---

the same passage, line 26, Aristotle states explicitly that the nature of the soul has already been dealt with in previous studies. This admission in addition to the fact that the passage occurs in the first book of the *Nic. Ethics* increases the degree of probability of the above contention. Independently of the question of which is prior to what, the important thing here is that the doctrine of the mean is given scientific support and as a hypothesis, at least, it is founded on the principle of contrariety. For the development of Aristotle's psychology, see F. Nuyens, *L'Evolution de la Psychologie d'Aristote* (French translation, Louvain, Paris, 1948).

[53] Just as excesses in moral life prevent man from developing and maintaining virtuous conduct, similarly in psychological behaviour stimuli beyond the range of perception cause either pain or destruction. De An. 426b 3–7; compare 429b 14–16; 432a 2 sqq. One might raise at this point the question concerning Aristotle's implicit trust in the senses, or the normalcy of perception. It did not occur to the ancients that controlled continuous refinement of instruments which increase the range of sensation and reveal unsuspected details, prevents damage of the natural sense organ and, methodologically speaking, brings forth new philosophical problems as well as demands the re-examination of concepts derived from trust in the 'ultimacy' of gross experience. Perhaps this acceptance of the ratio of the sense organ as the indicator of normalcy prevented Aristotelian science from probing into the direction of experimental science which was destined to become one of the most effective innovations of modern man. With the rise of modern science and the revolution in method, man has opened new vistas to the ancient philosophy of *logos*. *Logos* is no longer limited to what teleology has determined but extends its effectiveness into the new spheres and opportunities brought about through *techne*.

[54] W. D. Ross, in his *Aristotle* (Oxford, 1949), p. 132, surprisingly enough calls him 'a naïve realist'.

[55] This point is examined more closely in the next chapter.

Process and the Principle of Soul

it be said that the knower, who is 'other than' the known environment, i.e. the objects in their permanence and changing aspects, stabilities and invariant relations, comes to cognize and hence effect an act of *assimilation*. The fundamental role of the *formal principle* in his theory of knowledge can be readily seen. Form is shared by both external object and sensing organism.

But sensation is not only the coinciding of the inceived form of an external object and the achieved structural configuration in the sensitive faculty, but is equally an actualization and a culmination whereby the knower and the known, in a sense 'other', have become, through a process, formally 'like'. The complexity of sensation as a process received special attention in Aristotle's psychology; and as a consequence of such careful consideration, the principle of contrariety was reconstructed to suit his scientific investigations. In line with the theory of contraries, then, is the thesis that subjects-in-process are not contrary to each other, especially when the two subjects-in-process are the sensing organism and the sensed object or event. Therefore, the delimiting extremes in the act of sensation must be found in sensation as a process located in the knower. This notion is essential in order to see why Aristotle insists that prior to the act of sensation the organ is both 'like' and 'unlike' the object and its properties, but never contrary to it.

Aristotle provided a solution for the problem of 'like' and 'unlike' in sensation by combining physiology with a theory of elements[56] and the related doctrine of contrariety. Closely knitted to his answer is the historico-critical approach to his predecessors'

[56] The modern reader can easily detect numerous inconsistencies which resulted from Aristotle's attempt to connect the physiology of the senses with what is, for us, a totally inadequate theory of elements which was constructed along lines imposed by his trust in gross experience. These inconsistencies are not discussed here. A satisfactory account would be found in G. R. T. Ross's *Aristotle's De Sensu and De Memoria*, Introduction, pp. 9–14, Section V, 'Physiology and the Special Senses'. Ross states there characteristically the following: 'The above inconsistencies only show the enormous difficulty in giving any coherent account of the process of sense stimulation in terms of ancient physics. They in no way detract from the value of the central principle involved—that the organ is of a nature capable of manifesting in itself the contrary determinations which characterize the objective qualities falling under any one specific sense; that apart from stimulation by an object the organ is perfectly neutral as regards these determinations, and hence may in certain cases (touch at any rate) be regarded as a μεσότης for the

doctrines of sensation. It would be better for the purposes of the present discussion to deal briefly first with the historico-critical aspects of his solution. The two main pre-Aristotelian views concerning the nature of sensation are (*a*) the theory that sensation occurs because like acts upon like, a position held by Empedocles, and (*b*) the theory that sensation involves a knower and a sensed object both being unlike, a view shared by Heraclitus and Anaxagoras. Just as he did in the case of nutrition, Aristotle synthesized the two theories by maintaining only that portion that seemed true to him. He did for the faculty of sensation exactly what he effected in his answer to the problem of nutrition. His answer is aptly stated in the following:

'The sensitive faculty is potentially such as the sensible object is in actuality. While it is being acted upon, it is not yet similar but, when once it has been acted upon, it is assimilated and has the same character as the sensible object.'[57]

---

mean is neutral as regards opposite determinations and hence is κριτικόν· (pp. 13–14).

[57] *De An.* 418a 3–6; also 416b 35 and 417a 18–20. In Book I, ch. 2, of the *De An.*, Aristotle advances his criticisms of his predecessors' theories of the soul and its relation, as a principle, to the elements. In order to account for the cognitive nature of the soul, some thinkers found it convenient to view the soul either as an element in itself or a product of the elements. Empedocles for example, who adhered to the 'like is known by like' interpretation, considered the soul to be a compound of all the elements. The reduction of the principle of the soul to something material is criticized by Aristotle not because of what it might entail for moral ideals or religious objectives, but primarily for its inherent difficulties as an explanatory hypothesis for psychological phenomena. Anaxagoras' position is mentioned in rather favourable terms since Anaxagoras was the only pre-Socratic philosopher to propound the independence or aloofness of the soul (*nous* it is called) as a separate and irreducible principle upon which the universe depends for its process and intelligibility. In another passage, 405b 10–23, Aristotle uses the terms 'psyche' and 'nous' synonymously, and the passage deals with 'elemental' theories of the soul, including the Anaxagorean. Aristotle is not interested there in tracing the history of psychology; he is rather making a critical survey of alternative theories and exploring their implications for a scientific inquiry into the principle of the soul. In the case of Anaxagoras, the aloofness of *nous*, though suggestive and fertile, is still entangled with cosmological stoichiologies and remains, at best, only an assumption from which human *nous* is deduced, or more accurately, produced. Other pre-Socratics sought the beginnings of the soul not simply in the elements but in their contrary arrangements. 405b 23–30.

Process and the Principle of Soul

The following diagram shows the Aristotelian solution which combines both the 'like' and the 'unlike' aspects in the act of sensation:

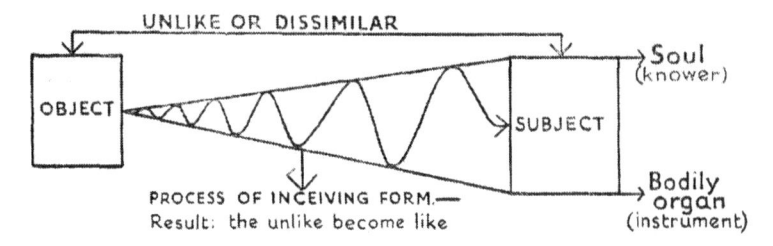

```
         UNLIKE OR DISSIMILAR
    ┌──────────────────────────────┐
    │                              │     → Soul
    │                              ↓        (knower)
 ┌──────┐                      ┌────────┐
 │OBJECT│◄─────VVVVVVVV───────►│SUBJECT │
 └──────┘                      └────────┘
    │                              │     → Bodily
    ↓                              │       organ
    PROCESS OF INCEIVING FORM.—          (instrument)
    Result: the unlike become like
```

The principle of contrariety is fundamental to understanding the entire process of sensation, because it is present in both the object and the subject. Now, with respect to the object, contrariety is involved (*a*) in the material cause of the subject-in-process *qua* sensible, as being ultimately composed by the four elements which in turn depend upon the ultimate contrary qualities; (*b*) in the developmental aspect of the object, which points to the metaphysical contrariety of form-privation; and (*c*) in the special qualitative changes of the object viewed either (i) *statically* as given ratios of such changes or (ii) *dynamically* as completed special actualizations enclosed within potentiality and actuality. Again, contrariety is equally important with regard to the subject, because (*a*) the sensing organ is composed of the same elements that all natural beings are composed of and the elemental contrarieties are consequently present in the knower; (*b*) the change caused in the organ is an activity, the range and intelligibility of which depends on the subject's capacity to effect ratios identical in form with the structural arrangements of the sensed realities; and (*c*) the operation of the sense organ is in its own terms a determinate process whose span of activity must be judged not simply as correlative to particular responses to given stimuli, but equally as functions inseparably intertwined with the other senses, the faculties, and the total teleological behaviour of the organism.

Sensation, then, must not be itemized into instantaneous acts but should be seen, functionally, as a co-ordinated and continuous process manifested either as a power (*dynamis*) or an activity and power-in-operation (*energeia*). In both its manifestations, sensation involves contrariety. And thus, once again, Aristotle

Process and the Principle of Soul

is consistent in the application of this principle as a permeating feature in all types of being—elemental, biological, and psychological: it is also a general notion in understanding being in both its distributive setting and its aspects of change. With the general remarks above on the problem of sensation, we may now turn to the place of contrariety in the particular senses.

Chapter Eight

BEING AND THE RANGE OF KNOWLEDGE

Before the place of contrariety in the sensitive soul can be fully appreciated, a careful examination of the common features of the particular senses must be conducted. It is shown that each sense is functional and subordinate to the central end of the organism; it is the source of a kind of knowledge; it is a power subject to development for which it depends upon the presence of external stimuli; it possesses an initial state of neutrality, a *mesotis*, which enables it to respond to a wide range of sensible qualities contained between contraries; and finally this *mesotis* is the basis for discrimination and judgment. *Mesotis* is not limited to the special senses but is also an essential characteristic of the common sense. Notably common sense possesses a *mesotis* which determines the operative range of sensibility with respect to the common sensibles. While qualities are sensed directly by the special senses, common sense is the basis of experiencing the properties of objects, common sensibles, which constitute the empirical grounds for a psychological theory of the origin of Aristotle's doctrine of the categories which is defended in this work. The contrariety detected in the faculty of common sense leads to the threshold of intelligence. The operations of the faculty of intellecting are again special processes and like all others point to the presence of contraries. The contraries here are soul as form and as actuality. The metaphysical contrariety finds in the development of intelligence its highest expression because *nous* comprehends all forms and all principles of its own operations, including contrariety.

1. COMMON FEATURES OF THE PARTICULAR SENSES

(a) From the discussion on the general nature of the soul it will now become clear that the same principle of purposiveness that pervades the behaviour of organic bodies *in toto* is equally useful in explaining the structure and function of the particular senses. The teleological operation of each avenue of sensibility is not isolated from the over-all purpose of the organism. Aristotle's physiological psychology defends exactly this view: that all faculties of sensibility and cognition are co-operative *and* purposive *and* subordinate not to each other but to the specified entelechy of the organism under consideration.

'As every instrument and every bodily member subserves some partial end, that is to say, some special action, so the whole body must be destined to minister some plenary sphere of action. Thus the saw is made for sawing, for sawing is a function, and not sawing for the saw. Similarly, the body too must somehow or other be made for the soul, and each part of it for some subordinate function, to which it is adopted.'[1]

(b) Next to this principle of purposiveness which runs through each particular sense is the essential characteristic that all senses are the physiological starting points of cognition, because each and every one of them possesses the power to inceive the form or ratio of the external object's experiencible[2] properties without the material substratum.

(c) Each particular sense viewed from its products is a kind of knowledge,[3] *gnosis*, and its deprecation as such is without justification. Yet sensation in its barest performance inceives the form but is not capable of yielding what will become the mental object

---

[1] *Part. An.* 645b 14-20.

[2] The term 'experiencible' does not necessarily imply that there are other properties which are not given to experience at all and are therefore destined to remain utterly unknown. Aristotle is clear on this point and what he excludes from the range of sensation are those *ratios* or features of the objects that exceed the limits of human psychological capacity, e.g. extremely bright colours and high sounds the intensity of which endangers the sensible organ and its performance.

[3] *De An.* 432a 2-9; *De Somn.* 458b 2; *Gen. An.* 731a 33.

of the contemplative and deliberative intelligence, i.e. the 'intelligible', *noeton*, the universal. The universal concept is a subsequent product of the inner life, but impossible without the inceived forms.[4] The operations of the particular senses differ from those of the intellect in that the first depend upon the presence of external stimuli, the correlative objects of the entire event of sensation, whereas the latter works with the intelligible material supplied through sensation and stored in the psyche by retention to make up our world of experience.[5]

[4] Aristotle has no separate terms such as 'sensation' and 'perception'. The latter term has a wider meaning in modern philosophical psychology; it includes sheer sensation and in another application it stands for apprehending with the mind, cognizing intuitively, or through judgment, activities which extend from mere awareness of sensations to thinking ideas and 'perceiving' mathematical axioms. Locke, for example, held the view that having ideas and perception amount to the same thing. Philosophical tradition has not observed terminological fixedness with respect to this and other terms. 'Sensation', 'perception', 'sense-perception', have been used interchangeably; and application varies with the context of the ideas presented by various modern philosophers. In cases of translation of philosophical works from one language to another, the lack of linguistic isomorphism has caused numerous mishandlings in rendering the original thought with precision. The various translations of Aristotle's works are not exceptions to this almost inevitable error. Aristotle's term for both sensation and perception is *aisthesis*. This faculty or power manifests itself in a variety of functions and is related directly or indirectly to the entire gamut of our psychological operations. The faculty of sensation stands for the following five psychological processes: (i) the inception of forms-ratios through the particular senses; (ii) awareness of the common sensibles through the operation of the 'common sense'; (iii) the discriminative activity which detects different sense-eventuations; (iv) consciousness of the process of sensation; and (v) inferential discrimination by which an object X, e.g. Socrates, is identified by way of an accidental property, viz. his nose. Aristotle groups these processes into (a) sensation of particulars and (b) sensation of common sensibles. From another standpoint of analysis, sensation as a faculty, in the broadest meaning, includes or involves operations like judging, relating, imagining, retaining, recollecting and, perhaps, abstracting. Intellecting frequently operates co-operatively.

[5] It is scientific knowledge that is concerned with universalized ratios of sensation. Science as an operation then lies within the volition of the individual (*De An.* 417 b 24) because the intelligibles are achieved actualities and exclusive possessions of the soul, unlike sensation which does not operate independently of natural processes. However, science, when all factors are considered, is impossible without sensation, and possible because there is a universe which is cognizable.

(*d*) Sensation, hypothetically isolated and viewed developmentally prior to any operational manifestation and apart from the excitement caused by the external correlative object, is a mere power, a faculty, abstractable only in analysis. Being a mere power, it is inactive and therefore incapable of self-awareness. The turning of a power into an operative faculty requires the negation of this hypothetical subjectivity as well as the effective presence of a stimulus. This source of excitement is external to the sensing organism: it is our environment which as such includes our bodily existence, since our own bodies can set the senses going. It is not untrue then to say that Aristotle's empiricism points to the notion that it is sensing our environment that makes us what we are. It is here that we find the source of intelligible matter and the beginning of the actualization of intelligence in man.

The other distinctively cognitive faculties in their operative efficacy are contingent upon the complex event which, when present, causes sensation to change from a faculty into a power-in-operation—from a factor, distinguishable only in analysis, into a determinate process whose primary function is the co-ordination of the organism and its environment through immediate, unmistakable acquaintance by means of the inception of forms. Yet the cognitive faculties are fully excited only after the inceived forms have reached the stage of mental productivity lying beyond the level of mere ratios, i.e. after the ratios have been sufficiently universalized. The story of intelligence and the psychological antecedents of scientific, syllogistic reasoning is the actualization of the inceived forms, their passage from potential to actual universals. The analysis of the faculty of particular sensations does not bear directly upon the making of universals. The latter process begins with common sense and, as a discovery, it is done by intellecting. The individual senses are restricted to particulars,[6] but universality begins with common sense; the mental products of both are images, or *phantasmata*. How universality is implicit in the faculty of common sense and how its operations make possible the inception of features of natural processes which are existentially ascertainable permeating traits of all subjects-in-process will be treated in a later part of this chapter.

(*e*) Each particular sense in its operative aspect is a process, a

[6] *De An.* 417b 27–8.

qualitative change, but not in the physical and elemental way. Here we are dealing with psycho-physiological changes. The understanding of such processes requires the introduction of a special meaning of the permeative contrariety of potentiality-actuality[7] interpreted in the light of the power *to suffer* or *to be acted upon*.[8] The change that occurs here is that whereby a power, itself an entelechy, becomes an active operation, a psychological fulfilment. The particular sense potentially like its object becomes actually like its object through the accomplishment of a form identical with that of the external stimulus. This change or psychological response is possible because each particular sense, as a power, is a *mesotis*, a notion which constitutes the key that connects the psychological theory to the principle of contrariety.[9]

(*f*) While the qualitative processes of the world of concrete individual substances are delimited by contrary extremities, the physiology of the senses is such that it permits an amazing adaptability on the part of the experiencer to inceive the continuity of change by an adjustment of the sense organ to the given ratio of a configuration in the object. This theory is doubtless an ingenious explanation which Aristotle owes to his biological investigations. He declares that each sense, by virtue of the constitution of the sense organ, is a *mesotis*, a mean state between a pair of contraries or a system of pairs of contraries that mark the limits of objective processes. As such, the *mesotis* of each particular sense is indifferent to the contraries; and this indifference exists only before an actual sensation occurs. But when the sense organ is activated through a determinate stimulus, the sense becomes identical *in form* with the quality sensed by an active

[7] *De An.* 417a 21.

[8] *De An.* 417b 2–418a 4. In this passage Aristotle's account is not a direct treatment of the nature of this unique qualitative change. His explanation is based on an analogy, the capacity for wisdom and the actual possession of wisdom. The treatment obviously leaves much to be desired since what should be given here is a direct explanation of this type of process based on scientific finding. But since Aristotle knew nothing about physiological chemistry and the biochemical transformations in phenomena of sensation such an attempt would amount to mere speculation. Had he done the latter he would end in the same camp of theorization he was out to criticize, the materialism of Democritus. Yet the basic difficulty is not removed. The problem of the passage from physiological biochemistry to psychology is still a problem for us today. Its definitive answer is yet to be discovered.

[9] See Appendix: ch. 8, note 1.

response that produces within the sense organ the same *ratio*, *logos*, that prevails in the outside object.

Contrariety, consequently, shows that, as far as the intelligibility of the world as a system of processes goes, there is a continuity between nature and human nature in both the physical and the psychological modes. The original 'indifference', the *mesotis* of sensation, becomes in turn the initial point of responsiveness and provides the basis for the discriminative powers of the senses, which collectively taken comprise the beginning of *judgment* (which Aristotle discusses in connection with the common sense). Now judgment as a power is warranted by the nature of the senses and is the work of both sensibility and intelligence.[10] The awareness of differences and the inception of determinate ratios of qualitative processes make sensation a kind of knowledge. And since there are ratios that exceed the range of sensation, we must admit that the universe, in its rich and vast variety of processes, is more than we can experience and at least what we inceive immediately through the senses[11]—yet not untrue, not an illusion. In Aristotle's naturalistic philosophy, psychology testifies to the existence of a plurality of natural orders and the intelligibility of the cosmos, because contrariety is continuous and permeative both existentially and cognitively.

2. CONTRARIETY AND THE PARTICULAR SENSES

Aristotle, in spite of his significant contributions to psychology and to the physiology of the senses, had no conception of the function of the nervous system and its relation to phenomena of sensation. But this is no reason why we should discard his acute

---

[10] *De An.* 432a 16.

[11] Sensation, on the whole, is a highly complex faculty. Its analysis presupposes a discussion of the faculty of nutrition. Though the nutritive principle precedes the sensitive in order of analysis, it would be false to say that a given animal literally possesses a nutritive and a sensitive soul, because the soul, as a principle of understanding behaviour and as the principle of the psycho-physical unity of the organism, is one. On the human level, the operation of the senses necessarily precedes the use of the other faculties, and in the order of the uses of the senses, touch precedes the others. The sequence, either in operation or analysis, must not be turned into a basis for a hierarchy of the senses. Such a hierarchical scale betrays an ethical attitude rather than a psychological and biological finding. See Appendix: ch. 8, note 2.

Being and the Range of Knowledge

observations and frequently ingenious solutions to problems extremely subtle and difficult.[12] It is not the details of the physiology of the particular senses that are discussed here but the natural grounds of sensation that make the inception of particular ratios possible, and how in each particular sense contrariety is present as a necessary condition for the intelligibility of natural processes.[13]

(a) The sense of touch

According to the general principle of sensation, the organ of touch which senses tangible qualities is potentially what the experienced objects are actually as the *loci* of sensible qualities. The response of the organ to a determinate ratio of the object is a qualitative change of an internal kind by which the organ achieves a similar ratio as the result of a corresponding qualitative state of its material constituents identical with those of the stimuli. This is true for touch as well as the other particular senses. The organ of touch, prior to its response, is a *mesotis*, an organic equilibrium or neutral combination of the materials constituting the sensible qualities. The organ of touch is related to flesh; but flesh is, strictly speaking, the medium, while the real organ is identified as the heart. The material composition of the heart is that of a compound made of all the basic elements, but in its largest portion, of earth.[14]

Apparently, Aristotle conceived of touch as being a compound sense, unlike sight. Touch is a response to the stimuli of two different, though not dissimilar, areas: temperature and resistance. As a *mesotis*, touch can respond simultaneously to two types of ratios. As a power, it is the commensurable and neutral point of departure for sensing a range of possibilities contained between the contraries which delimit temperature and resistance. Touch as

---

[12] E. G. Boring, an authority in the history of psychology, has made some rather hasty criticisms of Aristotle's psychological position. Boring attributes to Aristotle a dualism which is not there—mainly because Boring failed to see that the distinction between form and matter is not one of dichotomy in nature, but is rather a principle for understanding any subject matter including, or rather particularly, that of the organic level of nature. See Appendix: ch. 8, note 3.

[13] See *De An.*, Book II, chs. 7-11, for the special objects, media and fields of the particular senses; also, the treatise on *De Sensu*.

[14] *De Sensu* 439a 1-2; *Part. An.* 647a 19 sqq., 653b 29, 656a 29.

a *mesotis* lies, figuratively speaking, at the intersection of temperature and resistance. The sensitive capacity of touch does not necessarily spread over the entire range of natural temperatures, because high temperatures evidently destroy both the organ of sensation and the organism. It is nevertheless capable of covering such possibilities as lie within the limits of survivability, and as such its reports are true to the demands of gross experience.[15]

Touch, by comprising two areas of tactual stimuli, is not operative within the physiological limits of one pair of contraries, but a number of them,[16] which are upon analysis reducible to two: hot and cold, fluid and solid.[17] It is here then that we must look for the empirical background of Aristotle's postulated theory of elements.[18] Yet his theory of touch, as related to the theory of elements,[19] presents the same difficulty as the latter, for it shows no generic contrariety under which all pairs of tangible contraries could be satisfactorily arranged as, for example, in the case of

[15] It is curious to note that the ancients were aware of the physiological limitations and the far greater range of natural powers, yet they made no remarkable strides in the direction of refining the instruments that would enable them to extend safely the limits of observation. Whether they could have achieved significant accomplishments in this field without the parallel development in experimental science carried on as the institutionalized practice of modern times is a question for the historian of science and culture to answer. However, there is no doubt that the Greek thinkers were aware of the fact that nature is more than our sensibilities allow us to experience but not dissimilar to our sensations. It seems that it is here that their natural philosophy failed. The fruits of the explorations of modern science are not so much the results of distrusting the senses or natural reason, but willingness to work with intellectual schemes and contrived instrumentalities which yield new and more satisfactory interpretations of nature.

[16] *De An.* 422b 25–7; *Part. An.* 647a 16–20.

[17] *De Gen. et Corr.* 330a 25–9. These ultimate contraries are never experienced in their pure state. They are inferred, not sensed.

[18] *De Gen. et Corr.* 330b 3.

[19] In this respect Aristotle is closer to Anaxagoras than he is to Empedocles as it is commonly believed. Not the elements (*rizomata*) of Empedocles but the qualities are what Aristotle accepts, except that he reduced the indefinite number of Anaxagorean element-qualities to only two contrary pairs. Curiously enough, Aristotle took over from Anaxagoras not only his elemental ultimates but also the concept of *nous*, which he re-interpreted in the light of his teleology. The antecedents of teleology are Socratic and Platonic, but Aristotle re-interpreted this concept again by relating its moral intent to his scientific and biological philosophy.

Being and the Range of Knowledge

sound.[20] Consequently, the sense of touch is ultimately analysable into two senses, never named by Aristotle, but evidently united through a common medium and organ. And the contraries are present in both the sensible processes and the sensing organ. Every particular sensation of touch is the eventuation of an inner ratio of the organism's contraries corresponding to the determinate ratio of the external stimulus. The awareness of this inner event of rational adjustment—which is inevitable since the index or original *mesotis* has moved—resolves itself in a *krisis*, or judgment. A sensation is then complete as an actuality.

(b) *The sense of taste*

Taste could be regarded as a special case of touch though not reducible to the latter, because here the stimulus is contacted immediately and, unlike touch, it serves a particularly vital function necessary for the preservation of the organism. It serves nutrition by making tactual discriminations of those properties of objects that are termed nutritive means,[21] and consequently it senses the contrary qualities as constituents of nutriment. In the human situation, both touch and taste are essential to man *qua* animal, but the other senses, especially sight and hearing, are morally significant as instrumentalities for the good life. Because of its nutritive aspects taste is a psychological process co-ordinately operating with the power of desire, the discriminative pursuit of the pleasant.

'For it is taste which discriminates between pleasant and unpleasant in food, so that the one is avoided and the other pursued, and speaking generally, flavour is an affection of the nutritive part of the soul.'[22]

The nature of this sense is such that it requires no medium because its organ, the tongue, serves exactly this purpose. The tongue is capable of becoming what its object is actually on the condition that the tastable properties are mixed with moisture. Strictly speaking, the tongue tastes these properties as converted

---

[20] *De An.* 422b 32.
[21] *De Sensu*, ch. 4; also G. R. T. Ross, *Aristotle's De Sensu et Mem.*, p. 13, and comment, p. 129, l. 436b 16. That the object of taste is also an object of touch, *De An.* 422a 8.
[22] *De Sensu* 436b 17–19. The final cause of taste is nutrition, 436a 15 (Loeb translation).

into sap, for the elements as such are neither tactual nor tastable. Moisture is a property also residing in the tongue, but the tongue has its own *mesotis*, its power to act in either direction of contrary determinations.[23] Literally, the objects of taste are either tasteful or tasteless. But in so far as objects can be tasted, the tongue can discriminate only those determinate variations or ratios which range between the contraries of sweet, which is positive and pleasant, and bitter, which is negative and unpleasant. Between these contrary extremities Aristotle places the succulent (a variety of sweet), the harsh, the pungent, the astringent, the acid and the saline.[24] Any ratio that exceeds this range and its relative degrees of sweetness, harshness and the like, remains beyond our discriminatory powers.

(*c*) *The sense of smell*

Aristotle's account of this sense is doubtless incomplete, unsatisfactory on the whole, and frequently conjectural. He pictures it as a kind of intermediate sense or transitional between touch and taste on the one hand, and hearing and sight on the other.[25] Though it seems to be the least perfect of all senses,[26] it serves both the need for maintaining health and recognizing pleasing food; it is also enjoyable in itself, a feature peculiar to man, somehow anticipating what is true to a greater degree of hearing and sight. The object of smell is actually what the organ is potentially. The odour possessed by the object reaches the organ of sense through a medium 'inhabiting', as it were, either air or water, which Aristotle calls 'pneuma'; it is of the same nature as the transparent or *diaphanes* that makes seeing possible.

Through this medium the odour of the object reaches the sense organ and causes a movement, a qualitative change[27] in the organ or, what it amounts to, a disturbance of the *mesotis* of the sense of smell, activating the organ and causing it to effect a corresponding ratio.[28] Though he admits that there are pervasive contrarieties for the particular senses, there is no explicit reference to the contrariety of smell. Instead, he speaks of it as analogous to that of taste.

[23] *De An.* 422a 34 sqq.   [24] *De An.* 422a 8–b 16; 414b 1–16.
[25] *De Sensu* 445a 5–10.   [26] *De An.* 421a 7–20.   [27] *De An.* 434b 27 sqq.
[28] For the operation of smelling see *Gen. An.* 744a 3 sqq.; *De An.*, Book II, ch. 9.

'And smells must be analogous to flavours. Moreover this certainly happens in some cases; for smells like flavours are pungent, sweet, harsh, astringent and rich, and one could call the fetid analogous to the bitter. So as these flavours are unpleasant to drink, so are the fetid unpleasant to inhale.'

And further down:

'There are two kinds of objects smelt; for it is untrue to say, as some do,[29] that there are not different kinds of objects smelt. But we must define in what sense there are and in what sense there are not (kinds of smells). There is one kind of odour which may be placed in the same category as flavours, as we have said, and to these the terms sweet and bitter belong incidentally; for because they are affections of the nutritive faculty, these smells are pleasant when animals desire them, but when they are sated and do not need them they are not pleasant, nor is the smell pleasant to those animals to whom the food having the smell is unpleasant.'[30]

It is clear that Aristotle suggests a range of olfactory ratios from pleasant or sweet to unpleasant or fetid, with intermediates contained between these extremities. But his terminology here is primitive and awkward.

(d) The sense of hearing

Sound is divided into two kinds, ordinary noise and voice or articulate sound.[31] The production of sound and its final inception by the sense of hearing as a determinate ratio is a complex process involving a number of factors which centre around two actualizations: of sound and of hearing. But the distinctive factors are three: (a) the external object which because of its nature is capable of producing sound; (b) the medium which connects the sounding object with the receiving subject; and (c) the particular sense the physiological peculiarity of which enables it to adjust itself, through the organ, to the determinate external ratio.[32] Therefore, sound and hearing are indistinguishable in the act of sensation and analysable only in the study of this phenomenon.

---

[29] The reference is to Plato, *Timaeus* 66D–67A. In this passage Plato states that smells are incapable of division and subdivision into genera and species, the only classification possible is that of pleasant and unpleasant.

[30] *De Sensu* 443b 8–24. In the same chapter he points to a distinction between purposive smells and intrinsically pleasant smells (Loeb translation).

[31] *De An.* 419b 3–8.   [32] *De An.* 419a 32; 420b 14.

Being and the Range of Knowledge

Sound is a potential feature of certain types of objects and it may occur even in the absence of an actual hearer. In itself it is apparently a kind of movement, but it does not cause actual hearing, *akousis*, unless it produces a qualitative change in the organ of the receptive subject. On the other hand, a hearer who possesses the faculty of inceiving sound ratios has only potential *akousis*, which becomes actual only in the presence of a stimulus. The medium which carries the actualized sound and causes the responsive actualization of the hearer is air, which in itself is free from sound though capable of transmitting it and resides in the organ as a necessary constituent of its nature.[33] A locomotion, therefore, occurs here: a *fora*, by which the activated air which surrounds the stimulus reaches the organ; because the medium is ultimately a *continuum*, extending from the physical boundaries of the sounding object to the 'connatural' air residing within the organ.[34]

The sounds produced by objects are contained between a contrariety whose extremities are the sharp and the grave. Within this range other features are distinguishable, such as the high and the low, the loud and the faint, the soft and the harsh. The internal or connatural air within the ear is a *mesotis*, a mean condition neutral to both extremes. In the presence of a stimulus whose sound ratio differs from the *mesotis* of the organ, a motion or inner qualitative change is produced and the connatural air abandons its neutrality to effect a ratio identical in form with that of the stimulus. Actual hearing, then, is perpetual production of corresponding ratios of objects ranging between the audible limits of sharp and grave sounds. And there are natural audible limits to the ear beyond which it cannot experience and discriminate. If the sharpness exceeds the maximum capacity of the hearing organ its destruction follows; if the sound is below the limits of the other extreme, then hearing does not occur. 'Excesses in the sensible objects destroy the sense organs.'[35] And elsewhere: 'hearing is destroyed by either excess, whether of high pitch or of low.'[36] The sounds the ear senses belong to neither extreme, but to mixtures of the two; audible sounds are ratios of which there is an indefinite variety.[37]

---

[33] *De An.* 420a 18 sqq. See also *Part. An.* 656b 13–16.
[34] *De An.* 419b 5–420a 4.   [35] *De An.* 424a 29–30.   [36] *De An.* 426a 30–1.
[37] Concords are special cases of mixture, which in comparison to the immense variety of possible sounds, are few. Concords are numerically expressible ratios. See *Met.* 1043a 10; *De Sensu* 448a 9; 439b 31–440a 2.

Being and the Range of Knowledge

Even if the range of natural sounds exceeds the range of the sensible capacity of the organ as determined by the contrariety within the organ, hearing occurs as the accomplishment of inner actualities which are in form identical with the *logoi* of audible stimuli. Natural processes and psychological events of sensation are homologous.

(e) *The sense of sight*

The whole operation we call seeing is a highly complex one, and Aristotle's account of it is by no means easily comprehensible. What is of interest here is the fact that the analysis of sight shows that contrariety has been employed, and perhaps to a far greater extent here than in the other senses, because there are three actualizations contributing to the final sensation of seeing. They are the actualizations of (*a*) colour, (*b*) medium, and (*c*) organ. Colour and medium are so closely intertwined that it is extremely difficult to discuss the one without continuous reference to the other.

What the organ sees is coloured bodies, but, in a more strict sense, colour. In two passages, one in the *Physics* and another in the *Metaphysics*,[38] Aristotle insists that the object of sight and the quality of colour are not altogether identical. His case rests on the distinction between the sensible and its surface extremities on the one hand, and the medium, the *transparent* (*diaphanes*) and its properties, on the other. Furthermore, colour is not dependent on the eye because sight, being a determinate capacity, has a delimited range of responsiveness.[39] There are colours which admittedly exceed the seeing power of the eye; and, therefore, the world of coloured objects is far greater than that disclosed to the sense of sight. What is seen then is relative to our capacity in two ways: in comparison to (i) total darkness, and (ii) total brightness. The term 'invisible' thus has two meanings.[40] But what is invisible is not necessarily colourless.

Since colour as an actuality presupposes the theory of its medium, it is better to start with the latter. This medium is a distinctive element, the *transparent*, found in celestial objects,[41]

---

[38] *Phys.* 201b 4; *Met.* 1065b 32.　　[39] *De An.* 429b 3.
[40] *Met.* 1022b 34; also *De An.* 421b 3 and 422a 20-2.
[41] *Meter.* I, 3, 340b 6; *De Caelo* 286a 11.

and though not a constitutive element of the material existence of the objects on the sublunary level, it penetrates all objects.[42] The penetrating characteristic of the transparent makes it (i) a necessary condition for colour, (ii) the vehicle[43] or medium of light, and (iii) an indispensable component of the eye. The explanation of the sense of sight requires the application of the contrariety of actuality-potentiality to the transparent element.[44] As potentiality it is darkness and as actuality it is light. The process from darkness to light is an actualization caused by the presence of fire (sublunary or celestial).

With the transparent, actualized as light by fire, and the fact that every subject-in-process is also permeated by it, the phenomenon called colour inevitably follows. In spite of the fact that the transparent is diffused throughout the substances, colour occurs only on their external boundaries, namely, the surface.[45] This being the case, colour can be identified neither with the substance itself nor with the transparent as such.[46] Colour is defined as 'the limit of transparence in a limited body'.[47] There is no such thing as colour *per se*, but coloured objects. Particular colours happen because there are particular objects which have surfaces, external boundaries due to their discreteness; and because these surfaces effect modifications[48] to the extremities of the transparent permeating each body when the transparent is actualized by fire. Colour is the qualitative change which the surface of the body causes on its co-extended and actualized transparent. Light, which is the actuality of the transparent, actualizes in turn the structure of the bodily surfaces.

The sensation of coloured objects necessitates the simultaneous awareness of surface and external shape. As a property of bodies, colour is but a power which they have to produce modifications in the co-extended transparent; in the presence of light, it will become coloured surface. What is finally inceived by the organ is

---

[42] *De Sensu* 439b 9.

[43] *De Sensu* 438b 3. Because of the distance between the object and the organ of sight some movement is necessary for seeing to take place. The object, when placed directly upon the eye, cannot be seen. *De An.* 419a 12.

[44] Light and darkness are neither substances nor elements. They are contraries, delimiting extremities of the transparent element. See *De An.* 418b 18; also *Met.* 1057b 8; *Top.* 119a 30.

[45] *De An.* 418a 29–30. [46] *De Sensu* 439a 34 sqq.
[47] *De Sensu* 439b 12. [48] *De An.* 418a 31.

never pure light—there could be no such thing—but the determinate movement that particular surfaces of objects have caused in the actualized transparent.[49] Colours as determinate movements are ratios ranging between white and black which as contraries never co-exist simultaneously in the same object, except in the sense of potentiality and actuality of the transparent. The species of colour, the intermediates, are to be explained as continuous ratios and combinations of black and white.[50] The transition from the one contrary to the other is one of actualization of the transparent from privation to possession of light.

The intermediates between black and white are golden-yellow, crimson, violet, green, and blue. These and their intensities are what the eye perceives. But the objective actualization of colour is not sufficient to explain the act of seeing. Seeing a colour is explained by Aristotle as the consummation of another process, namely the adjustment of the organ to the actuality of the stimulus. The organ, itself a bodily part of an organic substance, is equally permeated by the transparent element. The pupil of the eye consists essentially of water which itself is transparent,[51] and the brain supplies the necessary moisture for the making of the eye.[52] The physiology of the eye, then, shows that this organ contains the very element which makes the colours of objects possible, except that *mere* possession of the transparent by the eye entails only the capacity of inceiving colours and not the actual possession of colours. Sensation occurs through a process[53] whereby the colour, actuality, reaches the eye, acts as a stimulus, and causes an inner process in the seeing organ. The neutrality of

---

[49] Light as modified by the surface of bodies raises the question of the colours of the four elements. Fire—hot and dry—is white at its best; air—hot and moist—is mostly white; water—moist and cold—is deep black because it contains no fire; and earth—cold and dry—is only less black than water.

[50] *De Sensu* 440b 15 sqq.; *Phys.* 188a 3–188b 21; *Met.* 1057a 23; *De An.* 426b 8 sqq. and 422b 19 sqq.

[51] *De Sensu* 438a 15–b16; also *De Gen. An.* 779b 15–28, 780a 4. Water and air also contain the transparent, a feature due to the presence of the unchangeable element (aither) in them. *De An.* 418b 7–9.

[52] *De Sensu* 438b 30; *De Gen. An.* 744a 5 sqq.

[53] The transmission of light, Aristotle insists, requires no time because the transparent as a medium does not travel in space. No satisfactory explanation is given for the peculiarity of this medium so much unlike the media of sound and odour which involve both time and place. *De Sensu* 446a 20–b30; *De An.* 434b 25–435a 10.

the colourlessness of the organ is abandoned and a response is initiated which culminates in the sensation. The response is a new actuality: it is an inceived form, an inner adjustment to an external determined structure. The eye, initially capable of undergoing changes, becomes what the object was actually prior to the response.

Contrariety, therefore, is present in all three components of the complex phenomenon of sight. In the medium it points to the transparent as mere power or darkness and as actuality or light; in the correlative object it denotes the range of the modifications the object effects on its own transparent as diffused over the surface. Collectively, these modifications give the varieties of colour contained between the contrary extremities of black and white; in the sensing subject contrariety delimits the range of the seeing capacity of the organ as this power is physiologically constituted. Each sensation of sight is the achievement of a ratio identical in form to natural consummations. The contrariety of the range of seeing is contained within the contrariety that marks the range of physical events. Nature is at least what is sensed.

3. THE FACULTY OF COMMON SENSE

Common sense (κοινὴ αἴσθησις) as a function of sensibility is a highly specialized topic and is therefore not considered here in its various details but only as a psychological operation closely knit to the principle of contrariety. As a power common sense emerges efficaciously together with responses of the particular senses. Simultaneously with the inception of the determinate ratios, the faculty of common sense does the necessary distinguishing and comparing. With the sensations of the particular qualities and the awareness of the common sensibles, the organism goes beyond what is immediately disclosed to the senses to reach the threshold of self-awareness. Common sense is that psychological function which, among other services, enables the organism (i.e. those organisms that possess it) to become aware of itself as a psychological centre of activity.

(a) Discriminating and comparing

In *De An.* 426b 12–427a 16, Aristotle shows that the fact that we are able to discriminate between a white ratio and a sweet ratio, which are not contraries but *different* qualities, calls for an explanation; because apparently the respective senses sensing these qualities are distinctive. The power in which this discriminative ability resides must be one which is different from all the particular senses, and its discriminating ability goes beyond the qualitative range of the senses. This problem points to the inter-relations of the senses. The solution is given in his analysis of the faculty of common sense as simultaneously co-operative and discriminative with and through the exercise of the special senses.[54] The total act of sensation, to begin with, is more than a passive inception of ratios.

Aristotle tries to understand the complex act of sensation by bringing into the open the multiplicity of factors discoverable in its effects. The sequence of these factors as presented in his analysis must not be interpreted as a basis from which one could infer a natural series, or a separateness of faculties, or a sensationalistic atomism. Instead, the co-operative simultaneity of special senses and common sense is what Aristotle starts with as part of his subject matter. The investigation of the complex nature of sensation will then show how the content of awareness acquired through the senses points to an environment which warrants the principles of unity and plurality, difference and contrariety. It is with the faculty of common sense that these principles and generic traits of being are first brought into the limelight of self-consciousness.

The notion of *difference* which the faculty of common sense brings to our attention is contrasted with that of *identity*.[55] An explanation is needed here. Let us examine the following two cases: (*a*) A given object X is sensed. The eye inceives its determinate whiteness, the ear, its determinate sharpness, the tongue, its sweetness, and so on with the other senses. These ratios are *differences* belonging to the same object X as their locus. Therefore, predicating these qualitative ratios of object X implies that the identity and substantial unity of X is accepted as a matter of fact while the sensation of these discrete qualities occurs. Then if during a given period of time the object X would lose its sweetness and acquire a quality of bitterness, its identity as a concrete

[54] The defective operation of common sense as a discriminatory faculty gives rise to error. See Appendix: ch. 8, note 4.
[55] *De An.*, Book III, chs. 1, 2.

individual is equally maintained throughout the qualitative change from a given feature to its contrary. Identity, then, is given with sensations just as difference, plurality, and contrariety are. (b) Suppose we examine next two different objects belonging to two different genera, viz. a piece of ice and a sheet of paper, both of which are white. Here the same sense, through two discrete acts of inception, senses the white colours and if their ratios are the same or approximately the same, the objects are pronounced identical in a certain respect. We then speak of identity of colour; but in spite of the fact that both objects are 'seen' by the same sense, and are identical in their whiteness, common sense in its discriminatory function will proclaim the objects different. The identity of the knower is assumed in both cases.

In case (a) the differences observed were due to differences in quality in the locus, but the discovery would never have occurred were it not for the differentiations in the sensing apparatus of the organism, i.e. the special senses. In case (b) the different experiences were originated in the pluralistic nature of the environment, the discreteness of being. And the act of sensation, including special sense and common sense, testifies to the fact that identity and difference are both subjective outcomes and objective realities. In this sense, identity and difference point to unity and plurality. In the language of the *Metaphysics* the answer is stated as follows:

'Since the term "unity" is used like the term "being", and the substance of that which is one is one, and things whose substance is numerically one are numerically one, evidently neither unity nor being can be the substance of things, just as being an element or a principle cannot be the substance, but we ask what, then, the principle is, that we may reduce the thing to something more knowable. Now of these concepts "being" and "unity" are more substantial than "principle" or "element" or "cause", but not even the former are substance, since in general nothing that is common is substance; for substance does not belong to anything but to itself and to that which has it, of which it is the substance. Further, that which is one cannot be in many places at the same time, but that which is common is present in many places at the same time; so that clearly no universal exists apart from its individuals.'[56]

[56] *Met.* 1040b 15–28.

Being and the Range of Knowledge

Identity as the persisting formal unity of an individual substance must not be confused, as the passage quoted implies, with identity as a 'common notion' which is a mental product reached through a series of sensations. Since identity and difference, unity and plurality, have meanings which are both subjective and objective, some confusion seems inevitable. It happens when reflection fails to screen the content of these terms, particularly in the light of the psychology of common sense which is the faculty of effecting discriminations and unifications in the manifold of experience. Not infrequently have comprehensive unities, based on identity, been thrown back to nature and regarded as reality itself. Thales had called it *water*, Parmenides *being*, Anaximenes *air*, and the last of the Greek philosophers, Plotinus, the *one*. In this type of philosophical error, a 'unity', reached through a psychological process, has come to take the place of reality, that plurality of substances with which all inquiry starts. As an aid to sound philosophizing, psychology must have been of invaluable help to Aristotle's own original conception of metaphysics, not merely in the sense of avoiding the cosmological preoccupations of his predecessors but primarily in the sense of understanding the nature of principles by tracing their limits and natural history through psychology.

(b) Common sense as a 'mesotis'

Both unity and plurality feature in the common sense. This faculty has 'oneness' as the power of discriminating and judging; it is also 'many' in that it manifests itself simultaneously and in co-ordination with each of the special senses. To put the matter differently, the power of discriminative judgment is a unified faculty while its actual manifestations are many judgments implicit in every sensation and rendered explicit in articulate discourse.[57] Just as each particular sense, prior to any given sensation, is a *mesotis* between the contraries which determine the operative range of sensibility, so it is with common sense as a co-operative and permeative power. The *mesotis* of common sense is a neutrality with regard to the range of responsiveness to those sensibles which are disclosed to awareness simultaneously with the special sensibles but never alone.

[57] *De An.* 427a 3; *De Sensu* 447b 17 sqq.

Being and the Range of Knowledge

By common sensibles Aristotle means certain properties present in individual substances, never perceivable in themselves through any special sense, but always given as simultaneous accompaniments with the special sensibles—colours, odours, sound and the like. They are, to quote, given 'incidentally by every sense',[58] and are motion, rest, figure, magnitude, number, and unity.[59] But the *mesotis* of common sense raises a difficult question because it is not like that of the special senses, and as such it has no special organ. Yet to assign a special organ to this faculty would mean that it is no longer common, in which case two serious problems arise: (i) A sixth sense becomes necessary and the 'common' sensibles should be sensed directly. As a consequence, motion, rest, magnitude, figure, and the rest would acquire the same status of accidental properties the special sensibles have, which means they would no longer be regarded as generic traits of subjects-in-process. (ii) Common sense could no longer serve as the faculty of discriminative judgment due to which statements like 'this white object is sweet' are possible, especially when the sweetness of the object is predicted solely through the sensation of its whiteness (viz. a lump of sugar).

Aristotle avoids both difficulties by defining the faculty of common sense as both discriminatory and operating simultaneously through the acts of special senses. This position is

[58] For a summary of the various interpretations of this difficult passage, *De An.* 425a 15, see E. E. Spicer's *Aristotle's Conception of the Soul* (London, 1934), pp. 77-81. Though some of the answers are to be commended for their ingenuity, it appears that the crux of the problem lies elsewhere. A definitive answer cannot be given apart from what Aristotle could have said had he written a treatise on developmental psychology. The question of the relation between the sensation of special sensibles and awareness of common sensibles is by no means peculiar to Aristotle; it became a central theme in British empiricism and modern epistemology. Had Aristotle written on developmental psychology, it would then become clear to his readers how he conceived of sensation, imagination and thought, as operations, developing during the span of life. His ethical theory demands the maturity of the powers as the necessary psychological conditions for the good life; yet we have no scientific treatise stating the laws that explain their development.

[59] These sensibles are called common because they are so either for all the senses or at least two. The common sensibles stated in the various passages, taken together, are: unity, movement and rest, number, magnitude, figure, the rough and the smooth, the sharp and the blunt (as found in solid bodies alone). *De An.* 418a 6-25; *Phys.* 225a 15; *De Sensu* 442b 5.

Being and the Range of Knowledge

fortified by a demonstration of the impossibility of a sixth sense. In the opening chapter of Book III of the *De Anima*, Aristotle tries to prove his case through an appeal to his theory of elements.

'Of the elements air and water are the only two of which sense organs are composed. For the pupil of the eye is of water, and the ear is of air, and the organ of smell is of one or the other, while fire, if present anywhere, enters into all, since nothing can be sentient without warmth. Earth, again, belongs to none of the sense-organs, or, at most is a constituent peculiar to touch. It follows then that outside water and air there is no sense organ. Now sense organs composed of air and water certain animals do, in fact, possess. We may infer, then, that all the senses are possessed by those animals which are fully developed and are not crippled: even the mole is found to have eyes beneath its skin. And thus, unless there exists some unknown body or some property different from any possessed by any of the bodies within our experience, there can be no sixth sense which we lack.'[60]

After rejecting the possibility of a sixth sense, which is only an indirect answer to the problem, he offers a direct answer:

'Nor again, can there by any special sense organ for the common sensibles, which we perceive incidentally by every sense; for example motion, rest, figure, magnitude, number, unity. For all these we perceive by motion. Thus it is by motion that we perceive magnitude, and consequently figure, figure being one variety of magnitude, while that which is at rest we perceive by the fact that it is not moved. Number we perceive by the negation of continuity and by the special senses also: for each sensation has a single object. Clearly, then, it is impossible that there should be a special sense for any one of those; for example, motion: for it is the case that we should perceive them in the same way as we now perceive sweetness by sight (and this we do because we have a sense which perceives both); and by this we actually apprehend

---

[60] *De An.* 425a 3-13. The concluding sentence is introduced to secure his position, which Aristotle apparently considered impregnable. On the other hand it is indicative of his cautiousness and his unwillingness to close the door completely to future discoveries of elements that would entail and necessitate the emergence of more senses. The weakness of the argument lies primarily in the crude empiricism which underlies his physiological chemistry. It is questionable, however, whether Aristotle could have envisaged a scientific revolution in chemistry which would overthrow so fundamental a doctrine in ancient science as the theory of elements.

the two simultaneously when they occur in conjunction. Otherwise we should never have more than an incidental perception of them.'[61]

What the special senses inceive is not the total form or the whole structure of the object, but only ratios within their appropriate qualitative range. The senses then experience determinate 'passions' of objects, and the objects only *per accidens*.[62] Teleologically speaking, the special senses function for the sake of the cognition of the common sensibles which do not share in the flux and instability of the sensible qualities, and for this reason are more important for science and demonstrable knowledge. Psychologically, the common sensibles are wider than the special ones; for example, whereas colour is the object of one sense alone, magnitude and unity are given coincidentally through all the special senses, affording thus more objective grounds for their experience. The faculty of sensibility in its entirety discloses to experience individual existents which have unity, magnitude, shape, motion, location and are *loci* of particular affections, qualities, i.e. 'passions' in continuous change.

4. THE 'MESOTIS' OF COMMON SENSE AND THE EMPIRICAL GROUNDS OF THE CATEGORIES

By not making the common sense one of the special senses Aristotle has been able to avoid certain crucial difficulties in his theory of sensation. But there still remains the problem of the *mesotis* of common sense, because the notion of *mesotis* necessitates the presence of another factor, the sensing organ, which as mentioned in the previous section, common sense does not possess. Aristotle has an answer to this problem but it cannot be adequately discussed without an examination of the nature of the objects of common sense, the common sensibles, and their relation to a theory of contraries.

The common sensibles, compared to the special sensibles, are more fundamental in the sense that they are indispensable to the existence of particular objects, necessary, and more stable. Yet,

[61] *De An.* 425a 14–25.

[62] In *Met.* 1010b 2–26, Aristotle distinguishes sensibles, both special and common, from substances.

in another sense, the special sensible qualities are equally basic because they are the occasions for the inception of the common sensibles. Furthermore, since all qualities regardless of their rate of changeability are distinctive aspects of subjects-in-process and no subject-in-process is absolutely quality-less, it is essential to know that quality—sensed always distributively, and differentiated —is as fundamental a notion as that of the common sensibles. This is why quality, one way or another, is always predicated of substance and never itself a substance.

Quality as a generic characteristic of objects is not more fundamental than quantity. The difference, from the point of view of sensation, lies in their manner of inception. Quantity is sensed 'directly', i.e. without a special organ, a fact which classifies it as a common sensible. Viewed in the theory of predication, quality is not, again, more fundamental than quantity. While quality is given through all five senses, the common sensibles, quantity being one of them, are given simultaneously with each particular sensation of quality in the special senses, or at least two. Here is perhaps the psychological origin of Aristotle's theory of predication which provides the empirical grounds for the doctrine of the categories.

It is in the epistemological realism of his psychology that an explanation of the nature, scope and origin of the types of predication may be found and not the other way round, namely, in a conjectured hypothesis based on the idea of an Aristotelian analysis of the ultimate parts of speech of the Greek language.[63]

[63] This view, i.e. the grammatical origin of Aristotle's list of categories, was vigorously defended by A. Trendelenburg in his work, *Geschichte der Kategorienlehre* (Berlin, 1846), p. 209, and was advanced earlier in the seventeenth century by A. Geulincx, a Cartesian philosopher. G. Grote, in his *Aristotle* (London, 1880), pp. 99–100, shows great sympathy with Trendelenburg's explanation. J. S. Mill in his *System of Logic* wrote in a similar vein: 'It is a mere catalogue of the distinctions orderly marked out by the language of the familiar life, with little or no attempt to penetrate, by philosophic analysis, to the *rationale* even of those common distinctions. Such an analysis would have shewn the enumeration to be both redundant and defective. Some objects are omitted and others repeated several times under different heads' (Book I, ch. 3). Windelband, in his *History of Philosophy* (London, 1901; translated by Tufts), p. 142, supports the same view; and so does E. P. Papanoutsos in his recent work, *Gnosiologia* (Athens, Greece, 1954), pp. 150–1; Papanoutsos argues that Kant's criticism of Aristotle's categories is irrelevant today because the real problem in the Aristotelian view of the

Being and the Range of Knowledge

It is more plausible to say that Aristotle's psychological investigations led him to the view that since things *are* what they can be said to be, then the ways of saying are the ways of experiencing the world. The physiology of the senses warrants the ontological correspondence and isomorphism between *cosmos* and *logos*, being and predication.

Of the categories, substance, quantity, relation, place, time, position, state, action, affection, are warranted by the common sensibles, whereas quality, a generic term for all the qualitative modifications of the objects, is inceived through the organs of the special senses. Even when this list is limited to the four categories of substance, quantity, place and quality, it is not difficult to see how the first three are associated with the common sensibles and the fourth with the special senses.[64] Each act of sensation is, then, not a simple but a complex psychological event. What we sense is not simple isolated qualities but with them we become aware of other objective properties as well which are the ontological counterparts of the ultimate ways of referring to our acquaintance with distributive being.

The physiological theory of the faculty of sensibility throws new light on the relation between reality and discourse. The categories, the elemental ways of predication, have a natural history and a natural cause rooted not in some rational principle native to the mind, but present in the experienced world to which sensation refers; dynamic features to which the mental faculties of the human organism are adapted in order to assimilate its cognizable aspects and processes. In all given occasions of interaction between organism and environment, sensation, special and common, and discrimination operate concurrently. Qualitative

---

categories is not so much Aristotle's failure to deduce them from a single principle like Kant, as the difficulty in the naïve realistic conception of the theory of categories that they are both ways of thought and types of being. Papanoutsos is right in questioning the epistemological efficacy of Aristotle's categories for contemporary science, but is mistaken in siding with those who suggest the 'grammar' theory. E. Kapp has a more flexible and suggestive view, and points out that much could be gained if one could start with the *Topics*, an early Aristotelian work, and follow the making of the theory from there. See Kapp's *Greek Foundations of Traditional Logic* (N.Y., 1942), pp. 39-42. Obviously none of these writers tried to find a connection between the categories and the Aristotelian biological psychology.

[64] See Appendix: ch. 8, note 5.

determinations and common sensibles evoke the ultimate types of linguistic reference and predication, i.e. the categories. Implicit discrimination as a natural operation of human psychology brings forth under certain circumstances a corresponding articulateness in man in the form of judgment. Inherent in every sensation is a potential judgment. Discrimination, when completely actualized, becomes rational articulation.

Ultimately, awareness of process or movement[65] is given with every particular act of sensation and every act is necessarily a disclosure of some quality.[66] Since every particular sensation is due to some process,'[67] change, modification occurring in substances and to effected processes or changes in the cognizing subject, then with each sensation there emerges the experience of process. This permeative characteristic of process as a subjective and objective event gives it, as a common sensible, universality and makes it a generic principle of sensibility. Besides having qualitative processes, individual existents—some of them—are also capable of locomotion, in which case a distinction can be made between motion and rest, rest as privation of motion.[68] Reference to such features is done in accordance with the category of rest; and through rest, number is experienced which is due to the negation of continuity in process. Under no circumstances is it then possible to have a particular sensation without an implicit concurrence of the common sensibles of either movement or rest. The category of place has its psychological origin in common sense through which the organism becomes aware of pervasive traits of the subjects-in-process.

Discreteness as unity and individuality is given concurrently with the special sensations and is judged through common sense. Unity is implicit in each particular psychological actualization because of the separateness of the senses and the oneness of the

---

[65] *De An.* 425a 16.

[66] Sensation of particulars is unmistakable or true; to put it differently, particular sensations are false in the least degree. *De An.* 428b 18; *De Sensu* 422b 8; *Met.* 1010b 2-26.

[67] It is not necessary to read this use of process in connection with a passage from *Phys.* IV, ch. ii, 219a 12 sqq., as Hicks does (*De Anima*, commentary, p. 428), simply because Aristotle is not interested in deducing all common sensibles either from movement or from unity. Hicks's interpretation appears confused at this point.

[68] *Phys.* 226b 10-16; 239a 13-14; 264a 27-8; *De An.* 425a 18.

stimulus. Each sense has operative distinctiveness which is actualized upon the inception of a determinate ratio. Yet it is with common sense that unity and discreteness, otherwise potentially in the special senses, are apprehended. Not only each sense is discrete but also each inceived ratio and each substance of which it is a feature.[69] Common sense, further, makes explicit unity and plurality as the matter for the science of arithmetic.[70] Awareness of number and magnitude leads to the category of quantity; they are the object of mathematical inquiry.[71] Finally, by bringing together substance and unity in a metaphysics of distributive being, Aristotle is justified in making quantity a category dependent upon the priority of the category of substance.[72]

It now becomes evident that common sense cannot be a *mesotis* in the same way the special senses are. Common sensibles, as such, are not contained between contrary determinations. Quantity, for example, does not admit of more or less, but the notions of greater or smaller are meaningful only as the outcomes of comparative judgments. Common sense as the faculty of comparisons is neutral to both 'great' and 'less', but judges quantities as related. It is here then that the category of relation enters as a factor in the making of comparative judgments. Given magnitudes, taken in themselves, are neither greater nor smaller. 'Great', 'small', 'much', 'little', are contraries only in a derivative sense, i.e. when related through comparisons and regarded as terms of relations. Quantities have a stability due to which they do not admit absolutely of 'more' or 'less'.[73] Therefore, there can be no absolutely great or absolutely small quantity.

[69] Awareness of the number *one* comes by seeing an object, hearing a sound, feeling a tap on the hand and the like. The same can be said for the number two, three, etc. Every sensible object has a number (*De An.* 449a 20). Sensation points to the universality of number, magnitude, and to the other common sensibles, time, figure, etc.

[70] Aristotle's philosophy of mathematics bears witness to his realism. Unity is psychologically subjective and ontologically objective, it is in the act of consciousness and the facts of nature; both are natural events. There is no room for dualism here. Aristotle, unlike Kant, for whom unity is *a priori*, made it both a common sensible and an attribute of substance. Every sensible is a magnitude. *De Sensu* 449a 20.

[71] See Appendix: ch. 8, note 6.

[72] The relation between quantity and contrariety has been presented in ch. 4, pp. 64-5.   [73] *Cat.* 6a 20.

Being and the Range of Knowledge

With the common sensibles we do not sense contraries,[74] but the grounds for correlatives.[75] This peculiarity does not imply that relations are not intelligible. Relations are given in sensation only implicitly but not inceived as determinate ratios by the organs of the special senses. They are given with the multiplicity of sensations. It is, therefore, the faculty of common sense that explicates relations and renders them intelligible through connective and comparative judgments of (i) particular sensibles or (ii) particular common sensibles. Correlatives come into existence together.[76] Awareness of relations requires conjunction and comparison of sensed discriminations. Exception to this is the relation between sensible externality and sensing knower which is basic, and in a sense presupposed by all acts of sensation and cognition. All knowledge is ultimately dependent upon the relation between knowing subject and object known, which is, like all relations, true and due to the pluralistic character of all reality. The category of relation points to a pervasive characteristic of all being and is given with the very origin of sensation and the operation of common sense.

This is the reason, then, why we can speak about 'x' being sweeter than 'y', 'a' whiter than 'b', 'p' larger than 'q', or 't' not bigger than 's'. Relations are discoverable everywhere; they are universally present in the objective events and acts of awareness. The only way to obliterate relations is to limit experience to one and only one psychological act—necessarily inwardly directed.[77] Yet relation, in comparison to the other categories based on the common sensibles, is the least substantial.

'What is relative is least of all things a kind of entity or substance,

---

[74] In *Cat.* 6b 15, Aristotle admits that relatives sometimes have contraries, for example, virtue being contrary to vice. This, however, is a special case taken from the processes of moral life. This problem is more fully treated in the next chapter.

[75] *Cat.* 7a 23. He states here that 'All relatives are referred to their correlates provided they are rightly defined.' Also, *Cat.* 5a 12 sqq.

[76] *Cat.* 7a 15.

[77] This is the ideal of the mystic, who is therefore forced in the pursuit of his final vision to negate all externality and rational discriminations. Mysticism and ineffability are consequently synonymous terms. Whatever knowledge the mystic claims cannot be knowledge in the philosophical and scientific use of the word. For Aristotle all knowledge is fundamentally relational. Knowledge which negates relation is an impossibility.

and is posterior to quality and quantity; and the relative is an accident of quantity, as was said, not its matter, since something of a distinct nature of its own must serve as matter both to the relative in general and to its parts and kinds. For there is nothing either great or small, many or few, or, in general, relative to something else, which without having a nature of its own is many or few, great or small, or relative to something else. A sign that the relative is least of all a substance and a real thing is the fact that it alone has no proper generation or destruction or movement, as in respect of quantity there is increase and diminution, in respect of quality alteration, in respect of place locomotion, in respect of substance simple generation and destruction. In respect of relation there is no proper change.'[78]

Change in relations is contingent upon more fundamental processes: substantial, qualitative, quantitative, and spatio-temporal. What is challenged in the above quotation is not the ubiquity and universality of relation but its significance as a standard of reference and its degree of being.

Finally, common sense is a *mesotis* with regard to activity and passivity. In itself and prior to given acts of sensation it is neither active nor 'suffering' but a power, and therefore, neutral, which can operate in both directions. As a factor in sensation, it can be acted upon; and as awareness it can view passivity as present in all psychological processes as 'passions' of the soul. As a discriminatory operation it works with the inceived ratios and becomes active; through self-reflection it apprehends activity itself. The *mesotis* of the common sense lies in the fact that it is both capable of activity and passivity and of attaining consciousness of its own operations. And since every act of sensation is such that calls into play both activity and passivity by energizing the total faculty of sensibility, the universality of action and passion is grounded in psychology and in the nature of things. Here, again, is where to look for the empirical grounds of the categories of action and passion. They are predicated of all subjects-in-process

---

[78] *Met.* 1088a 22–34. The modern scientific temper differs radically with the Aristotelian position regarding the controllability of relations. The introduction of mathematical quantifications in investigating relation in order to discover patterns of invariability opened new frontiers in physics, astronomy, and the social sciences. Herein lies the significance of the mathematico-experimental method. Yet the accidental character of relations is still not disproved.

Being and the Range of Knowledge

and all the movements of the soul, including the highest manifestations of intelligence, the operations of *nous*. They form the background of the comprehensive contrariety of form-privation, or actuality-potentiality.

5. THE THRESHOLD OF INTELLIGENCE

With the operations of the cognitive faculties we deal only with actualities, intelligent content, forms, universals. The faculty of sensibility, common sense and the special senses, have provided the organism with the elements of knowledge, the ratios.[79] Common sense, in a way, forms the bridge between the power of sensing through particular organs and the power of intellecting; it does so by sensing the common sensibles without the aid of organs, and by initiating the inner processes of discriminating, retaining and recollecting ratios and images. We may use the term 'intelligence' to designate the operations of cognition. The activities of intelligence are qualitative affections. As processes they undergo change, alteration;[80] as manifestations of cognition they are both operations and *energeiae*, actualizations and actualities. Their movement is not one of adjustment but one of fulfilment.

The activities of the powers of intelligence should not be regarded as physical qualitative processes whereby a certain bright red surface changes to a dark red as the presence of light diminishes. Basic to these powers is their continuity in fulfilment, which when carefully and patiently directed leads to excellence of habit or virtue. Here then, we encounter activities of the soul to which the contrariety of potentiality-actuality finds its supreme application; since, as it will become increasingly clear, both terms of the distinction are *energeia*. It is fair, then, to speak of intelligence and its processes as purposive activities characterized by their uniqueness to pass from the stage of first actuality to an ideal fulfilment. Herein lies their moral significance as well. The fulfilment of intelligence will become *form*. Prior to its operations on the content of sensibility, intelligence is but a power. Experience is the necessary condition for the actualization of intelligence; it is its material cause, as it were.

A distinguishing characteristic of intelligence is that its identity

[79] Intelligence is receptive of intelligible form, whereas sense is receptive of sensible form. *De An.* III, ch. 4.   [80] *Cat.* 9b 34.

remains unalterable, so that whatever modifications it undergoes during its development, in so far as it can be said to be in process, are such that they participate in the eventuation of its fulfilment. The consummation of intelligence is not, therefore, a contrary *terminus* in a determinate process, whose presence negates the initial contrary. Apparently, we have here a special type of process and a special case of contrariety. The explanation is to be found in the application of the principle of passivity to the processes of psychology.

'To suffer or be acted upon, too, is a term of more than one meaning. Sometimes it means a sort of destruction by the contrary, sometimes it is rather a preservation of what is potentially existent by what is actually existent and like it, so far as likeness holds of potentiality when compared with actuality. For it is by exercise of knowledge that the possessor of knowledge becomes such in actuality: and this is no qualitative change (for the thing develops into its own nature and actuality), or else is qualitative change of a different sort. Hence, it is not right to say that that which thinks undergoes change when it thinks any more than the builder undergoes change when he builds.'[81]

What is true about the faculties of nutrition and sensation as psychological processes, namely, that they are determinate, purposive, and their range of efficacy is contained within a contrariety whose extremities are the soul as the principle of form and soul as the fulfilment of the form, i.e. first entelechy and its consummation, is also true of the faculty of cognition. The soul of man is differentiated by the possession of intelligence. It must be acted upon through the exercise of knowledge to become explicitly what it is implicitly. Apparently, then we can speak of a legitimate contrariety here, just as we do in all cases of process except that the transition from one contrary to the other does not indicate an incompatibility between the two but a progressive actualization of intelligence. What we start with is actualities; what we end up with is their intelligible integration in a system of first principles.

The contrariety which marks the process of intelligence is one whose terms are (i) possession of the power of intelligence and (ii) the actual and continuous exercise of this power, which is *nous*

[81] *De An.* 417b 2–9.

Being and the Range of Knowledge

at its best. The range of intelligence is then between passive and active *nous*. The final cause of cognition is the active possession of all psychological actualities. The ratios organized in the light of universals are the atomic constituents of cognition which through intelligence are integrated and reflected upon. *Nous* as accomplished intelligence is the *locus* of the principles of logic and the organization of forms. It is both the principles of scientific knowledge and the unity of intelligible essences. The principle of contradiction is cognized through *nous* because the nature of intelligence is such that by being a process and the culmination of awareness it understands all determinate movement as it occurs in both the nature of things and the powers of the soul.

The transition from passive to active *nous* is the natural history of the actualization of intelligence. The inception of determinate ratios or forms necessarily involves the cognitive faculty to a certain degree and acts upon it, or causes movement in it. The beginning of the actualization of intelligence is found in the faculty of sensibility. There man begins to assimilate the knowable aspects of his intricate and dynamic environment with the inception of tactual and other special sensible ratios which are determinate manifestations of properties residing in the individual substances. With sensibility man knows particulars, individuals, concrete existents and their qualitative ratios.[82] The emergence of universals is a subsequent development in the process of intelligence. And by means of cognition of universals the fulfilment of intelligence becomes the transition from *episteme* to *theoria*.[83] The inceived forms give rise to universal notions which in their totality constitute the intelligible matter for all cognition. The matter is now internal, not external.

Intelligence is actualized with the conversion of a system of ratios as articulate descriptive statements into a formalized system of scientific demonstration. The postulates of this system are in themselves undemonstrable, yet not innate, and established through an intuitive grasp and an inductive leap from the data of organized experience. The aim of intelligence is to attain the unified

---

[82] *De An.* 417b 19 sqq. The universal is sensed only indirectly and accidentally. *An. Post.* 81b 19 sqq.; 100a 17; *Met.* 1087a 19 sqq.

[83] The objects and tools of knowledge are universals. *An. Post.* 87b 37–88a 16. On the question of how universals exist in the soul, see *De An.* 429a 22–31; 431b 20–432a 14.

pattern of the inter-relations of universals as formal actualities. Intelligence is human entelechy fulfilled through mental labour. It reaches its culmination as consciousness of the accomplished intelligent order of the most inclusive universals and *archai* of understanding. *Nous* is then clearly an achievement effected through constant labour which turns the soul from a fact of nature to a noble vision replete with self-consciousness and universality. The fulfilment of intelligence is possible because there is a pluralistic universe which is both dynamic and intelligible.

The actualization of intelligence as a process then requires for its understanding the metaphysical contrariety of potentiality-actuality. Prior to any activity intelligence is a mere power and, therefore, nothing but a formal capacity, ultimately devoid of content. Viewing intelligence as a process renders clear two essential features: (i) the developmental aspect according to which human beings born with the power of reason reach that stage of rationality which marks them as mature personalities; (ii) the virtuous aspect through which the relatively mature person who possesses wisdom, both practical and scientific, can exercise these virtues at will. This explains how man, while having wisdom, does not always manifest it—for example, when he sleeps or is preoccupied with concerns which do not require full display of cognitive behaviour. Hence, the philosopher need not philosophize continually though his wisdom is potentially there as an accomplished state of mind. The extraordinary thing about intelligence as a process is that as a going concern it matures and fulfils human beings through knowledge of the world and the acquisition of self-consciousness. Intelligence knows both its contents and its operations.[84]

The distinction between active and passive *nous* has caused much controversy in interpretation to the point where even an historical survey of the views expressed by the various commentators would require the length of a whole book. It is a distinction that must not be taken literally as a real one. Its suggestiveness lies in the fact that it points to the two basic aspects of intelligence, as a power in operation and as a fulfilled actuality. When *nous* or intelligence is seen apart from transcendentalisms and supernaturalisms it ceases being a mystery. The best way to

[84] *De An.* III, chs. 4, 5.

Being and the Range of Knowledge

understand it is to see it as a coin with two sides. Passive *nous* is the psychological faculty of cognition and understanding which like all other powers of the soul must undergo developments in order to reach its completion. Active *nous* is the achieved co-ordination of all reliable knowledge which gives a systematic set of principles as the distilled order of logic and a highly inclusive set of statements true of all subject matters and all types of inquiry. Both are called pervasive traits of being.

Intelligence as the final co-ordination of all reliable knowledge is an ideal open to all human beings and at the same time not subject to caprice or wishful thinking. The natural processes do not alter their intelligible features to suit the whims of men; they remain what they are and are disclosed to those who unhesitatingly proceed to think and inquire into the nature of things. Intelligence as an accomplishment, as active *nous*, becomes knowledge distilled, communicable, independent, universal; it is a good of the rarest kind, in fact it is the good. It is the intelligibility of the universe stated in the medium of human *logos*. Intelligence as a power is individual, distinct, a given capacity in individual human beings; it is mortal. But intelligence fulfilled becomes immortal as a vision of the principles of nature and logic; it is immortal in its communication of the permanence of nature and the eternality of its structures. Here man changes his psychological ego into philosophical universality. Not that man becomes eternal in reality; he comes to understand the meaning of eternality by making his intelligence what the universe is in actuality.

Whether pure *nous* as non-human intelligence exists or not is a question of a different order. At least this much can be said about it, namely, that it does not exist in the sense that subjects-in-process do. If its existence cannot be affirmed, it can be imaginatively envisaged as wisdom perfected, as pure thought thinking its own thoughts, immediately, statically, in an absolute act of eternal self-illumination. It is wisdom befitting only a god. It is God itself. The difference between God and man is a simple one, but only to the philosopher who knows what wisdom as a complete and simple vision is. In ideality, God has wisdom because it is the principle of all actualized intelligibility. As such it is perfect and nothing, that is, not like anything that exists in the sublunary level.[85]

[85] See Appendix: ch. 8, note 7.

Being and the Range of Knowledge

On the human level intelligence starts as a process, the actualization of a power of a particular kind. Wisdom is not given but pursued. The individual man, Socrates, Plato, Aristotle, Kant, Dewey, and every student of nature and human nature must acquire wisdom, and this not in order to get where God is, but to understand how God must be. And the philosopher like every other human being starts out as a rational animal in whom intelligence is a mere capacity, one among many other capacities. This he develops until it becomes a virtue, an excellence, handling its contents logically, continuously integrating it and ever expanding its range of inclusiveness. At the summit, all necessary premises are intuitively clear and all principles of demonstration undemonstrable. At least this is an ideal to be reached. This is faultless science. It is often approximated; but throughout its pursuit man is constantly aware of the limitations of his grasp and his inability to either exhaust the universe or to hold his accomplished intellectual vision permanently. Man is a *logical animal*.

The completion of philosophic wisdom is the ideal end of man but the demand for satisfactions of the animal urges can never be negated; urges can only be disciplined. The animal has a permanent stake in his life. And he must sleep, retire, gratify those demands that will keep the organism going, renew and refresh it for new conquests.

If the accomplishments of intelligence are what the universe is actually *qua* intelligibility, then it is not necessary to turn into riddles Aristotle's words that *nous* is separable.[86] The pervasive presence of intelligibility in natural processes could serve as testimony of its non-human distinctiveness. *Nous* as the outcome of research and intellectual labour is separable in the form of reliable knowledge. *Nous* active in this sense is not a psychological power but scientific objectivity, not a particular subjective possession but knowledge shared in the manner of crystallized experience, of nature understood. Aristotle's active *nous* is comparable to science institutionalized, to man's totality of warranted beliefs and clarified ideals that have endured the vicissitudes of history.

As personal wisdom, active *nous* is the recapitulation and beholding of the order of intelligible structures and their pattern of inter-relatedness. Nature possesses it implicitly, man turns it into

---
[86] *De An.* 429b 5.

the object of his pursuit of wisdom. The history of human wisdom is the struggle to understand the rationality of the universe through the accumulative effort of the community of minds. What is gained is separable; as such it becomes the eternal possession of man, his precious heritage. Apparently, for Aristotle, what man finds through the actualization of his intelligence, nature possesses in its continuity. The species are continuous, the elements are indestructible, the orbits of the stars mathematically set and the movements of the spheres permanent in their cyclical perfection. To see it all is life complete, is science integrated and fulfilled, like an admirable work of art.

Chapter Nine

CONTRARIETY AND THE RANGE OF CONDUCT

THIS final chapter aims at discussing the place of contrariety in Aristotle's ethics. He based ethics on psychology which enabled him to extend the concept of *mesotis* to the field of morality. In his view ethics should be neither an incidental chapter in cosmology nor depend for universalities on untenable theories of reason. His scientific inquiry into human behaviour provided natural foundations for *logos* and reason. The teleology of soul discloses the universal end, but it is ethical theory that must render explicit the best end for man and the means for its attainment. The problem of conduct is occasioned by the fact that while man by nature desires his own end he does not possess *fully* from the beginning the means to attain it. In addition, the human soul is complex and disparaged by its diverse appetites. The passions of the soul prior to action could become anything within a wide range of possible courses. The possibilities of action are contained between the contraries of excess and defect. There is always *one* right mean position, but the guide here could be only a *mesotis* comparable to the natural *mesotis* of sensibility. The pursuit of happiness demands that this *mesotis* be achieved; when the task is done virtue is accomplished. Thus moral *mesotis* provides the ideal grounds for moral decisions; but its development is contingent upon the actualization of intelligence, which makes man the locus of all contrarieties and moral life synonymous with intellectual excellence.

Contrariety and the Range of Conduct

1. ANTECEDENTS OF THE ARISTOTELIAN THEORY OF ETHICS

Aristotle's view on ethics though historically continuous with those of his predecessors is sharply contrasted with the two main pre-Aristotelian positions, namely, the pre-Socratic attempts to discuss some problems of human conduct through cosmologies and comprehensive visions of nature, and the radically new Socratic-Platonic orientation of moral inquiry in the direction of logic and reason. Aristotle, who worked with both traditions, aimed at bringing the two positions together by securing the continuity from nature to human rationality and establishing a new theory of ethics that could rest on both for support and validation. The pre-Socratic cosmological concern of nature became for Aristotle the subject matter to be investigated by and distributed among the special sciences, biology and psychology included. Even reason, the great theme of Plato's work, became in turn a natural phenomenon, a principle of understanding and a subject matter for inquiry. The psychology of reason thus became a discipline presupposed for a wider understanding of the place of rationality in ethics.

A special feature from the psychology of sensation which was reintroduced in the philosophy of ethics was the notion of *mesotis* which became a fundamental ingredient in Aristotle's new definition of virtue. It is here then that we will find the connection between the principle of contrariety and the function of rationality regarding decisions that lead to the pursuit of happiness. We witness here a transition from the psychological conception of *mesotis* to the ethical. *Mesotis* turns out to be an ideal guide for balance and harmony between contrary courses of action. But what was a fact of psychology and a natural condition in sensation must now be accomplished in intelligent conduct as virtue, as habit excellent and enlightened, to serve as the means through which fulfilment and self-realization are attainable in the state of *eudaemonia*.

To return to the antecedents of Aristotle's theory of ethics, pre-Socratic thought gives the picture of a series of daring intellectual attempts to construct convincing yet inclusive theories of nature. Within such broad views of nature, man, an outcome of natural processes and factors, moves, develops, acts and makes history. In all pre-Socratic speculation there is no distinctive science of human conduct, no separate inquiry into human affairs except in an incidental way, for man—and his problems—is seen primarily as a part of nature. Heraclitus and Empedocles for example, due to their social interests, reflected on ethical issues and concerned themselves rather intimately about moral matters but they never treated these questions either systematically or through an articulate and independent method. Though the pre-Socratics placed man in his proper context, their major contribution consists not in their casual moral sagacity but in the fact that they initiated a revolutionary mode of exploring man's environment and a way of constructing explanations resting on the power of human intelligence and not on myth, belief or tradition.

With the decline of the mythical conception of the universe and the invention of science together with the trust in human intelligence, next came the attempt to remove the mythical element from human moral affairs. It was both natural and convenient for the pre-Socratics to view conduct as a chapter of natural history. When the initial phase of ancient philosophy is viewed in retrospection then it appears that it was necessary for the human mind first to discover and become accustomed to the attitude of objective research in areas not so delicate and intricate as those of moral and political affairs. Man the investigator had to learn, as it were, his first lesson of objectivity by inquiring into the ethically neutral area of natural phenomena and by understanding their remoteness to human values. It was only after scientific curiosity was accepted and became institutionalized practice that the human mind was prepared to embark on the more sensitive project of conduct and values.

As an enterprise of critical thinking the removal of myths from comprehensive views of nature is equally difficult as is the task of clarifying moral problems. But criticism in the latter field, since it raises far-reaching questions about accepted systems of values in individual and public life touching vested interests and traditional codes of conduct, entails inevitable dangers. For this reason the objective investigation of moral themes was apparently delayed in the history of man and frequently brushed aside and discouraged. And though the intellectual climate of moral criticism was prepared by the new cosmologies of the pre-Socratics, it was only with the appearance of the sophists and their teachings that the new method was slowly extended over human affairs. The pre-Socratics did not create explicit moral theories nor does it seem possible that they could have done so. Whatever they propounded about morality was but a consequence of their more general theory of nature and man's place in it. Granted that social wisdom and expertness in advice are not the same as ethical criticism, it is easy to see why the pre-Socratics were not ready for a thorough-going criticism of moral ideals and phenomena. On the other hand, the public itself was not prepared to tolerate the objective treatment on a vast scale of the matters with which it was vitally concerned.

The citizens of ancient Greek city-states were conservative with regard to their system of values if for no other reason at least because they were aware that a healthy polity required stability in moral and political loyalties as well as firmness of character and a set of social ideals beyond dispute and doubt. Alternative theories of morality did not interest the average citizen of the Greek city-state who saw value only in those beliefs confirmed by tradition and successful leadership; but at the same time he tended to suspect, though with appreciable tolerance, criticism of accepted practice as a possible threat to social stability. The growth of pre-Socratic thought had produced evidence through cumulative criticism that a rich variety of systems of nature was not only possible and more accurate than rival mythical explanations still accepted in popular quarters but on the whole more useful and valuable for their effects. But the new pattern of thought and criticism of beliefs about the nature of the universe did not affect the average citizen except in so far as the inherent clash of myth and reason was made apparent in matters of worship or through demagoguery. Gradually the scientific detachedness with which the new cosmological systems were propounded became accepted practice and prepared the way for a similar approach to political and moral questions. Meanwhile the theoretical re-examination of individual and collective values was anticipated in the arena of political action through the demand for democratic solutions of pressing social and political problems. The great reforms of Cleisthenes came with the closing of the sixth century.

Cosmology not only acquainted the public mind with objectivity in natural investigations but also carried with it the implication that a similar pluralism of systems might be possible in social and moral organizations of beliefs. The decline of traditional monarchic governments and aristocracy, the fall of kings and their family connections with the Olympians and the rise of democracy in Athens through a series of social reforms had in a very profound measure, at least in social practice, removed much of the mythical element in human affairs.[1] Philosophical inquiry as love for wisdom was invited to look further into these problems and integrate articulately the demand for political, moral and intellectual freedom. Yet the expansion of inquiry and criticism was in no wise easy, uniform and systematic; its unfolding was marked with the taints of personal ambitions, the groping usually accompanying the launching of intellectual conquests and the meandering wanderings characteristic of novel explorative undertakings.

The coming of the sophists, continuous with the philosophical movement of the early period, was the admirable beginning of the new approach to moral values. It was daring and imaginative, critical and learned, cosmopolitan and liberal. The new movement had all the fine features of intellectual curiosity and confidence in human reason which were extensively practised during the cosmological period. If the personalities of Protagoras and Gorgias represent the rising tide of curiosity and search for immediate solutions to be offered to a generation eager for success and novelty, it is the mind of Socrates that mirrors the intellectual crisis of Greece. His thought, in his passionate concern over the human situation in a period of relativism and transition, reflects the anxiety that goes with the decline of accepted standards and the inefficacy of traditional social beliefs to answer the demand for an ideal and a truth beyond scepticism and relativism.[2]

It became increasingly apparent to Socrates that the current practice of virtue was wholly unsatisfactory, that the specific laws were alarmingly short of complete justice. However, above and beyond all visible virtue and law there was the realm of reason, lucid in all its dimensions and universal in its scope,

---

[1] The reader is reminded that the more inclusive historical picture of Greece during the sixth and fifth centuries should be kept in mind for a fuller appreciation of the radical changes which occurred in the economic, social, and political scene. These changes invited criticism of the basic practical problems and necessitated in particular a vigorous examination of the prevailing moral ideals. [2] *Charmides* 174 D.

Contrariety and the Range of Conduct

powerful and ever-questioning, which alone could enable man to envisage, if not to possess, what unconditional virtue and justice should be like. The empirical findings of the sophists were beyond challenge. But to Socrates, the discovered relativism was wholly inadequate when taken as the only point of departure for moral conduct. The results of the new teachings were most disastrous, for the possibility of agreement on objective judgment in ethics was totally excluded. The investigation of human affairs brought into the open the discrepancy between empirical relativism based on sociological and psychological facts and the demand for ideal reference as the permanent standard for evaluation. What the nature of diurnal ethical practice denied Socrates felt should be granted by the essence of ethical reason itself. The Socratic-Platonic movement in ethics is one which sought to establish the independence of ethics and the autonomy of morality apart from the inevitable relativism implicit in the descriptive statements of the special sciences.

Confidence in human reason in its logical permanence is the steady theme present in all the Platonic works. In the universality of rational knowledge man could now find justification of the philosophical life which as an ideal is the very vision of permanence itself. The realm of thought is ultimately identical with the realm of values. Socratic ethics is not simply the triumph of *logos* but also the assertion of the uniqueness of human morality as a realm separate from physical theories and social relativism. The instrument of rational knowledge could not and should not be turned into a primordial element to explain universal movement in mechanistic terms. This was in fact Plato's complaint against the promising start of Anaxagoras' philosophy so eloquently recorded in the *Phaedo* (97–9). Plato's disappointment in Anaxagoras' inability to see the moral significance of *nous* was as thorough as his impatience with the reputation cosmological thinking enjoyed in times when healthy contemplation was deeply needed to cure the social and intellectual crisis of the fifth and fourth centuries. Plato, for all moral purposes, used *nous* without cosmology. But it was Socrates who first urged thinkers, as Xenophon reports,[3] to give primacy to and concentrate on human problems, and only after these were settled to

---
[3] *Memorabilia* I, 11 sqq.

move on to examine physical phenomena. The new and radical Socratic emphasis on moral issues meant more than the admission of new subject matters into philosophy. It demanded priority for the human situation.

Plato, as the universality of his interests indicates clearly, was not against the pursuit of knowledge in matters natural, but was convinced that the removal of modes of mythical thinking must first and foremost begin in the field of politics and morals since the very survival of the state itself and the welfare of its citizens depended wholly upon the rediscovery of virtue and ideals. The fact that he deplored myth and used it at the same time is one of the deepest ironies of his philosophical genius. For while fighting unmitigatingly for logical clarity and inclusive definition, Plato resorted without any fear or reservations whatever to the literary qualities of myth itself. But his myths were no longer literal substitutes for reality or persuasive devices of demagoguery for the promotion of devious or selfish interests. The search for values required ultimate universals. But the undemonstrability of the latter had to be made apparent to the citizens whose philosophical training was lagging in scope. Their imagination needed the concreteness of the specific suggestion before it could begin to appreciate the impersonal field of logical permanence and mathematical stability. Plato did not discard myth but turned it into an instrument pointing to a reality beyond itself, to the absoluteness of reason, the universe of ideas, the grounds for all judgment of transient matters and all particularity. The new emphasis on reason kept Plato so preoccupied with the intricate problems it was called upon to solve that he never undertook the task of conducting a scientific inquiry into its natural foundations. Plato's error is not in what he trusted; it lies in what he neglected to do.

It was Aristotle the natural scientist, the philosopher without a speculative cosmology, and the social scientist without the sleepless zeal of the patriot and social reformer who brought the Platonic tradition in ethics to its natural conclusion. With Plato he agreed that ethics required reason for its autonomy and society for its context of practice, but reason itself had a natural history. To the delight of the scientist, reason as a natural event was found to be universally distributed as a fact of psychology. Aristotle brought together the pre-Socratic notion of nature and the Socratic conception of reason in his psycho-biological approach to human nature. The human *logos* turned out to be in the final analysis both the grounds of understanding nature and a natural fact to be studied through psychology. With Aristotle the humanistic ethic of the Greek world finds its consummation. Reason came to be viewed as a psycho-biological event. But as an ultimate in moral behaviour it became the ideal end of all human conduct. Between intelligence as a power and as a fulfilment there lies the entire range of conduct in all its dramatic and problematic setting.

The passage from fact to value concentratedly exhibited in the panorama of the Greek city-state is what Aristotle has masterfully explored in the *Nicomachean Ethics*. This work shows how he never doubted the limiting factors in human life and the pursuit of happiness. At the same time it demonstrates how his empiricism saved him from theorizing from the magnetic appeal of ultimate ends alone. What he did as a scientist and philosopher was to inquire into the complex nature of moral phenomena and to unravel the intricacies of the relations between means and ends, desires and ideals, opinion and knowledge, motivation and deliberate choice, apparent satisfaction and genuine fulfilment. And by seeking the permanent means for the ultimate good, happiness or *eudaemonia*, in its distributive and naturalistic setting, he arrived at his own philosophical conception of virtue. It is his new conception of virtue that convinced him that the Platonic position where all virtue and all knowledge are one, though a lofty ideal, is for all practical purposes an unattainable and untenable one. Practice shows that knowledge of the good does not impel one to do the good; therefore, the distinction between practical and intellectual virtues should finally be drawn. This is what basically separates the *Eudemian Ethics*, a work so Platonic in its conception and content, from his *Nicomachean Ethics*, his definitive statement on morality.

2. THE TELEOLOGY OF CONDUCT AND THE APPETITIVE PRINCIPLE

The analysis of the place of the principle of contrariety in the psychological processes points to a further connection between Aristotle's ethical theory and his philosophy of organism. The emphasis on the notion of activity enabled him to extend his generalized theory of process over to the characteristically human processes of moral development. But activity in ethics is viewed not merely as a psychological process in its teleological aspects but as re-directed process and as development defined with explicit reference to ideal completeness. The beginning of moral conduct and awareness of its range involve by necessity the faculty of intelligence as an initial, final, and formal factor, because activity as moral conduct is totally dependent upon the actualization of intelligence. Psychology, however, made it clear that intelligence, prior to the acquisition and reworking of sensible content and the constant activity of thinking, is but a sheer power. Then, the ideally intelligent life as the good life is not a necessary fact of nature but only a felicitous outcome achieved and sustained through considerable labour. Apart from the external conditions for the good life, virtue as the proper organization of personal energies is the most indispensable means to that effect; and since it is not given, it has to be acquired. Consequently, in this sense, ethics cannot be a demonstrable science but an art whose premises, as it were, are not given but arrived at through the gradual blossoming of human entelechy. Intelligence in ethics must become wisdom in action, *phronesis*. And he who possesses it understands fully how the good was always within the nature of man.

By basing the beginning of ethical life on the science of psychology Aristotle was able to work out a theoretically satisfactory answer to the demand for universality which Plato made the necessary condition for a sound theory of ethics. Intellectual history had convinced him that the answer to universality could not be derived from the study of the prevailing institutions, traditional codes of mores, accepted educational practices or speculative systems of nature. Plato had also demonstrated that the unstable opinions of men are in no way compatible with the ideals as universal standards for moral judgment. But neither could Plato's own theory of ideas produce convincing evidence as to its own truth. Aristotle went to the sciences for the universal principle he needed for his ethics and as a result he connected it with the conclusions of his psychological investigations and his empirical studies of organic processes. The nature of the human soul, he concluded, warrants the universal identity of intelligence. Reason is not a primitive force of nature but a faculty distributed to all members of the human species as a defining characteristic of the human type of life. This conception of the rational soul as first entelechy became the psychological point of departure for his ethical theory.

Man is not only an organism with a unique type of soul; he is also by nature a political animal. And the political environment is what allows him to turn intelligence into a determinate actuality. The political life is the proper context for all ethical and rational activities, and must be therefore presupposed if man is to become moral at all.[4] He stated in a celebrated passage that 'he who is unable to live in society or who has no need because he is sufficient for himself, must be either a beast or a god; he is no part of a state'.[5] The aim of the state in turn is not simply that men may live, but that they may live well.

'A social instinct is implanted in all men by nature, and yet he who first founded the state was the greatest of benefactors. For man, when perfected, is the best of animals, but when separated from law and justice, he is the worst of all; since armed injustice is the more dangerous, and he is equipped at birth with arms, meant to be used by intelligence and virtue, which he may use for the worst ends. Wherefore, if he have not virtue, he is the most unholy and the most savage of animals, and the most full of lust and gluttony. But justice is the bond of men in states, for the administration of justice, which is the determination of what is just, is the principle of order in political society.'[6]

The city is for the sake of human fulfilment and the end of the citizen is to become good and reach happiness through excellence. The happy man and the well-governed city are interdependent. Through ethics men develop their human uniqueness and through politics they perfect their state as the just and organic unity of its institutions. The individual citizen by actualizing his intelligence adds to the good of the state through active co-operation and personal example.[7] All citizens start out with the same entelechy, the same principle of intelligence, and they become good only through its fulfilment in practice and by means of habits at once excellent and praiseworthy. The psychological conditions for happiness are then distributed and so it is with the ideal good as

---

[4] *Politics*, Book I, chs. 1, 2.　　[5] *Pol.* 1253a 27-9.　　[6] *Pol.* 1253a 29-39.
[7] *Nic. Eth.* 1099b 30-3; 1102a 12-15. That the statesman must possess knowledge of psychology to administer his responsibilities, see 1102a 23-6.

happiness. The test of the just state is in the quality of its institutions and laws as well as the wisdom of its statesmen to promote those factors in community life that enable the citizens, initially endowed with the power of rationality to become morally complete. In this way, the moral good, while necessarily private as a possession of character, is at the same time public in its outward consequences. And since the good involves intelligence, the latter is universally present as a faculty and publicly shared as a social ideal. The psychological beginning and the ethical end are in this sense identical; they are man as rational power and intelligent fulfilment.

Yet there is still the problem of the apparent gap between psychological entelechy and moral actuality. A close study of the actions of men in society shows that while every individual human being is endowed with intelligence as a capacity not everyone arrives at ethical completeness. In order then to explain the transition from psychological teleology to moral autonomy, further inquiry had to be done into the principle responsible for initiating the process of human development, namely the faculty of appetency, *orexis*. Since the case here is clearly one of a process whose *termini* are soul as entelechy and as fulfilment, Aristotle had to offer in his psychology an analysis of *orexis*, that motive force that causes purposive process and action. We are told that 'every passion and every action is accompanied by pleasure and pain'.[8] Then, coexisting and co-operating with all the manifest processes of the complex faculty of sensation is the feeling of pleasure and pain, of desire and aversion. The connection between the two is clearly stated in another passage:

'Plants possess the nutritive faculty only: other things along with this have sensation; and if sensation, then also appetency: where under appetency we include desire, anger, and wish. But all animals have at least one sense, touch: and, where sensation is found, there is pleasure and pain, and that which causes pleasure and pain; and where these are, there is also desire, desire being appetite for what is pleasurable.'[9]

In the *De Anima*, Book III, ch. 9, Aristotle discusses this faculty in greater detail and advances his arguments in support of the

[8] *Nic. Eth.* 1103b 14.
[9] *De An.* 414a 32-b 5; also 431a 9. Cp. *De Somno* 454b 29.

Contrariety and the Range of Conduct

view that the distinctive moving principle is neither sensation nor intelligence, but appetency, which is completely teleological or purposive.[10] *Orexis*, being a faculty causing origination of movement, points to two other factors, as it is the case with the other operative powers of the soul: (i) the unmoved mover, which is 'the practical good', and (ii) the whole organism, which is the object that is moved.[11] Since *orexis* is a permeative factor present in every animal motion, in the case of man it is both a faculty and a modifying ingredient of practical intelligence;[12] but thought as calculated action causes motion not as intelligence but only when its starting point is a special object of appetency as desire. The multiplicity of faculties, then, in so far as each faculty operates simultaneously with *orexis*, causes a plurality of desires, many of which frequently conflict in their concurrence.[13] The explanation is given in the following passage:

'This occurs whenever reason and the appetites are opposed, that is in those animals which have a perception of time. For intelligence bids us resist because of the future, while appetite has regard only to the immediate present; for the pleasure of the moment appears absolutely pleasurable and absolutely good because we do not see the future. Therefore, while generically the moving cause will be one, namely the faculty of appetency, as such, and ultimately the object of appetency (which without being in motion itself, causes motion by the mere fact of being thought of or imagined), numerically there is a plurality of moving causes.'[14]

Since the defining faculty of the human soul is reason, it appears that conduct should be spontaneously ethical, that is, an automatic organization of behaviour that would render life a rectilinear progressive development in accordance with the demand that all impulses and desires be subordinate to the principle of intelligence. But we are told that:

'Appetency does not imply the deliberative faculty. But sometimes it overpowers rational wish and moves to action; at

---

[10] *De An.* 433a 15.
[11] *De An.* 433b 15-18; Cp. *Phys.* 250b 14. See also *De Gen. Anim.* 742a 22 sqq.   [12] *De An.* 433a 9-30.
[13] Appetites are never contraries. Appetite is contrary only to choice. *Nic. Eth.* 1111b 15-16.   [14] *De An.* 433b 5-15.

other times, the latter, rational wish, overpowers the former, appetency. Thus one appetency prevails over another appetency, like one sphere over another sphere, in the case where incontinence has supervened. But by nature the upper sphere always has the predominance and is a moving cause, so that the motion is actually the resultant of three orbits.'[15]

The discrepancy here is one between the ideal form of organization of desires and the spontaneous response to appealing stimuli apart from constant reference to the teleological distinctiveness of the human soul. An explanation is therefore needed to account for those interferences that obstruct the moral development of man according to which harmony between appetency and reason ought to prevail. The answer the Aristotelian writings suggest is to be found in the functional inter-relation of the faculties and their interdependent development. The faculty of appetency shares in the rational but in itself it is irrational. With regard to man's moral fulfilment then, it must either obey or disobey rationality.[16] But *orexis* as a faculty is distinctive only in discourse; as an operative power it manifests itself always in conjunction with particular psychological acts. Since *orexis* is never found alone, it is evident that imagination is, in this sense, always appetitive,[17] and this is equally true of practical intelligence.[18] Under ideal circumstances, an object judged to be good at all should at the same time be able to move all faculties at once, for all co-ordinate their movements with that which causes movement. But since *orexis* affects all faculties by turning them into

[15] *De An.* 434a 12–15. R. D. Hicks makes much of the concluding sentence and believes that the three orbits (*phorai*) refer to the celestial movements. He does the same thing with the explanation of the term 'spheres' (*De Anima*, Comm., p. 571). It is better not to exaggerate what might well have been an illustration and an image borrowed from geometry to point out that certain appetites must be subsumed under other higher intellectual powers. As for the appetitive movement being the resultant of three *phorai* ('orbits' is a misleading translation which obviously fits Hicks's interpretation), the explanation appears to be a much simpler one when no extra-psychological concepts are introduced. Since Aristotle is discussing the ideal stratification of desires, it is in agreement with the text to conclude that deliberate motion results from the proper co-ordination of three appetitive movements, i.e. appetitive nutrition, appetitive sensation, and appetitive intelligence. This again shows why man at his best is also a harmonious process of his whole being, i.e. a conscious unity of his teleological faculties.

[16] *Nic. Eth.* 1102b 16–30. [17] *De An.* 433b 28. [18] *De An.* 433a 23.

purposive processes, it happens frequently that the correlative objects of simultaneously stimulated faculties do not necessarily coincide, in which case the result might be that desires will conflict.

The overcoming of such conflicts and the cumulative maintenance of the harmony of the faculties are essential to moral development. The directive guide for such action is implicit in the teleological nature of man's *orexis* which is in turn instrumental to the soul as the final cause. The basic relation between *orexis* and intelligence is stated as follows:

'The moral purpose . . . may be defined as desiderative reason or intellectual desire, i.e. as reason qualified by desire or desire qualified by intelligence; and it is this originative faculty which makes a man.'[19]

Thus, it is *orexis* in its human setting, principally determined by intelligence, that prompts all action and makes the origination of moral life possible. But still this process is not an inherently progressive one. Yet it is this conception of *orexis* that runs through the immortal opening sentences of the *Metaphysics*: 'All men by nature desire to know,' and of the *Nicomachean Ethics*: 'Every art and every scientific investigation and similarly every action and intelligent choice seems to be desirous of some good.'[20] And again in the same work: 'Every knowledge and intelligent choice are appetitive of some good.'[21]

Obviously for the virtuous man there are no subjective difficulties because no real problem exists between appetence and reason.[22] However, the question still remains why men who are rational by nature do not become virtuous by the same rule. The answer can be worked out from Aristotle's psychology though not explicitly stated in the *De Anima*. All processes of sensation, imagination, of memory, reminiscence and cognition are appetitive and, consequently, all psychological life is permeatively teleological.[23] But moral life is actually living in accordance with *orexis* directed by and subordinated to the principle of intelligence. It is the task of reason, then, to eventuate through its

---

[19] *Nic. Eth.* 1139b 2–5 (translated by J. E. C. Welldon).
[20] Translation mine. The Greek term for the infinitive 'to be desirous' is ἐφίεσθαι.   [21] *Nic. Eth.* 1095a 14–15. Translation mine.
[22] *Nic. Eth.*, Book I, ch. 13.   [23] See Appendix: ch. 9, note 1.

deliberative processes such habits that enable the moral agent to accomplish the stable co-operation and subordination of the appetitive functions of the other faculties for the total harmonious actualization of the soul. What makes this task impossible at the beginning of a human being's life is the fact that the intellect is not fully present in early life. The meaning of moral struggle lies in the fact that the faculty of reason has a history, that it may grow, that prior to the acquisition of intelligible matter, mind is a mere power.

Intelligence fulfilled as the highest good of action is not the object of human *orexis* in the early stage of life because evidently it is not complete yet. As the intellect grows, the demand for more intelligent behaviour becomes increasingly clearer; and as intelligence as the end of all human life slowly emerges with age to that extent men are able to re-orient their activities and amplify the range of their objectives. The fact that sensation precedes developmentally the faculty of reason, the pleasures and pains associated with sensation are far more familiar and influential in making choices. With the gradual emergence of the intellect and the transition from biological behaviour to ethical conduct, the pleasures and pains of reason begin to acquire their appropriate significance, a process in which effort and training play a major role. Education as the art which brings about an awareness of the nature of intelligence and its works is the most effective way of eliminating the obstacles that stand in man's path to rationality.

Since each faculty has its own correlative objects, they, as inceived and cognized forms, become possessions of the mind. At the same time each object is also a 'good' because its correlative faculty is operating in co-ordination with the appetitive principle. Intelligence similarly in its teleological aspect has its own correlative object which is for that reason a 'good'.[24] Consequently, the objects of intelligence are not merely the basic and highest principles of demonstrative knowledge but also the most excellent goods. Intelligence, fully developed, as the *locus* of scientific knowledge, the seat and origin of all self-awareness is itself the supreme good. In moral life, it turns out, the measure of all goods is reason as a good. Evidently then the philosophical type of life which is the highest degree of self-consciousness is the most valuable and

[24] This is the basis for the distinction between apparent good and the good. *De An.* 433a 25–30; *Nic. Eth.* 1113a 15-b 6; *Eud. Eth.* 1235b 25.

practical type of life. Here action and theory coincide. But to see, appreciate, and pursue this ideal is part of man's moral struggle, because like all ideals, intelligence must be possessed in order to become a personal good.

3. CONTRARIETY AND THE EVENTUATION OF VIRTUE

In the previous section the discussion centred around the relation between the faculty of appetency as the principle of teleological movement and the deliberate organization of human energies for moral development. The complexity of the human soul and the simultaneous manifestation of a plurality of concerns explain why it is possible to have conflicts in ethical pursuits and also highly diversified and contending desires. But the pursuit of the highest good in life, happiness, requires that not every urge be satisfied, not all diverse demands and pleasures be followed, but only those passions and actions that lead to and extend the virtuous type of life. The consciously purposive conduct could be either virtuous or vicious; and it becomes vicious when it reaches the extreme deviations from assiduously won states of virtue. In this relation between virtue and the extreme deviations from it lies the place of contrariety in moral conduct. As it will be shown, Aristotle built his definition of virtue by re-introducing on the moral level the notion of *mesotis* which he used so amply in his physiological psychology.[25] *Mesotis* there was a natural fact, a natural condition in the form of a neutral *logos* or ratio lying at the centre of the total range of sensibility. One is lead to believe on the basis of this connection, that just as his scientific psychology became the point of departure for his own approach to the question of universality in ethics, and moral judgment in particular, so it appears to be the case with the concept of *mesotis* which now is not the natural neutrality of sensibility but the grounds for an empirical approach to virtue.[26]

[25] H. H. Joachim in his book *The Nicomachean Ethics*, A Commentary (Oxford, 1951), correctly points out that the rational factor in virtue as moral *mesotis* could be most instructively approached when compared with the *mesotis* of sensation in the *De Anima* (423b 27–424b 3), but nowhere in this work did he go beyond this suggestion to explore the connection between the two.
[26] The folklore of Greek popular wisdom abounds in expressions like

Contrariety and the Range of Conduct

The exploration of this theme is the primary aim of the present section. For this reason, no discussion of the many intricate aspects of the concept of virtue or the meaning of happiness is given here, for it would have carried this study to unnecessary length and to repeat what has already been the object of much literature on Aristotle's ethics. The main problem here is the connection between psychological *mesotis* and ethical *mesotis*, between virtue and contrariety. By answering this problem the transition from psychology to ethics will be more clearly understood. It is important at this point to remember that intelligence, prior to its fulfilment as the final cause in man, is but a mere power and that the content of the soul requisite for the mind to become an actuality in the full sense of the term can come only through the gradual inception of intelligible matter. In sensation, *mesotis* is a condition and a beginning inherent in the psychological processes of elementary cognition. Without this condition, which in itself is a physiological standard of normalcy in sensibility, awareness of differences and contrasts in the world of process and change would lack any systematic organization; its absence would entail the total deprivation of a stable frame of reference for discriminatory judgment in matters of sensation and recognition.

Since moral conduct presupposes a satisfactory degree of mental development in the agent, it appears that moral behaviour in contrast to psychological behaviour has no ideal pattern of reference and discrimination from its outset because it does not and cannot have a natural *mesotis* comparable to that of sensation. In sensation, the organism is basically passive with regard to the inception of forms, because it is the influx of sensations that causes the responses and the qualitative modifications in the organs and faculties whereby the latter, from the state of powers, become operative processes. The particular organs of sensation abandon the natural *mesotis* in order to effect ratios, mental events corresponding to the structural configurations of subjects-in-process that make the knowable environment. But in ethical

---

'nothing in excess' which apparently shows that Aristotle did not invent the moderation aspect of virtue. However, there is a vast difference between the popular conception of virtue in Greek folklore and poetry and the originality and depth of meaning Aristotle gave this term in his philosophy of morality. In doing so he followed Plato and also went beyond his teacher's interests and approach.

Contrariety and the Range of Conduct

life, which is emphatically active,[27] the human being performs both voluntarily and deliberately. The range of moral conduct becomes increasingly ordered, delimited and systematically organized in proportion to the agent's maturity. This maturity is evidenced by such intellectual activity that shows unmistakably that the ultimate end of life has been adequately envisaged and that stability of character is consciously strengthened through deliberate choice of the appropriate means.[28]

The morally desirable and pleasant organization of conduct is a task most difficult, cumbersome, and prolonged because, as it was mentioned in the previous section, man is endowed with a multiplicity of natural desires and a plurality of appetitive operations all of which do not by nature contribute to the pursuit of the final good. The relative absence of intelligence and the predominance of the nutritive and sensitive factors during the early stage of the agent's life make it plain why the moral *mesotis* is not biologically given. The new *mesotis* is achieved through virtue and as such it is only a possible emergent, not a physiological fact. Man is only potentially moral, a characteristic which he owes exclusively to the nature of his soul. In the eventual attainment of virtue as the indispensable means for happiness lies the teleology of the moral process whereby man comes to possess a state of character comparable to the psychological *mesotis*. Moral *mesotis* becomes then the ideal frame of reference for moral judgment and discriminations; in its final and complete form, it is the highest state of ethical stability in determining the right course of action away from contrary extremities; it is justice:

'Justice is a kind of mean, but not in the same way as the other virtues, but because it relates to the intermediate amount (*mesotis*), while injustice relates to the extremes. Injustice on the other hand is similarly related to the unjust, which is excess and defect, contrary to proportion, of the useful or hurtful. For which reason

[27] Happiness as the final and best end of the ethical life demands activity performed excellently and nobly. The emphasis on activity is clear from the definition of happiness: 'The human good turns out to be an activity of soul in accordance with virtue, and if there are more than one virtue, in accordance with the best and most complete.' *Nic. Eth.* 1098a 16–18; see also 1098b 33, sqq.

[28] Virtue belongs to the means for moral life; virtues are goods as means for the pursuit of happiness which is the end. *Nic. Eth.*, Book I, ch. 8.

Contrariety and the Range of Conduct

injustice is excess and defect, viz. because it is productive of excess and defect—in one's own case excess of what is in its own nature useful and defect of what is hurtful, while in the case of others it is as a whole like what it is in one's own case, but proportion may be violated in either direction. In the unjust act to have too little is to be unjustly treated; to have too much is to act unjustly.'[29]

The origin of moral conduct and its range of operations lies in the psychological make-up of men and their power to commit in action performances that collectively form a series contained between the contrary extremities of excess and defect. Men are motivated to act by the principle of pleasure and pain;[30] and finally when they attain moral excellence it is again with pleasures and pains that they are concerned.[31]

'If the virtues are concerned with actions and passions, and every passion and action is accompanied by pleasure and pain, for this reason also virtue will be concerned with pleasures and pains. This is indicated by the fact that punishment is inflicted by these means and it is the nature of cures to be affected by contraries.'[32]

We may now proceed to examine more closely the material of the moral *mesotis*. Here the material is not the operations of the special senses but actions and passions.[33] The total range of every passion or emotion, as the collection of its discreet manifestations, could be said to fall within extremes that mark the boundaries of the moral capacity of human nature. The intensity of emotion could be either maximum or minimum. For example, consider fear as an emotion in the concrete situation of war. To feel no fear at all would be inhuman, to feel an extremely intense fear would destroy sensitivity and perhaps cause insanity; both are

---

[29] *Nic. Eth.* 1133b 33–1134a 13.

[30] Ordinary conduct shows that men often do bad acts for the pleasures these ensue and frequently avoid good acts for the pains they involve. *Nic. Eth.* 1104b 9–11.

[31] The moral agent while concerned with the pleasures resulting from his actions must (i) act with knowledge, (ii) choose the act for its own sake, and (iii) be virtuous so that the act is the outcome of his decidedly firm and stable character. *Nic. Eth.* 1105a 27–32.

[32] *Nic. Eth.* 1104b 13–18. Happiness, it must be remembered, 'is the best, noblest, and most *pleasant* thing in the world'. Also, 1099a 14.

[33] *Nic. Eth.* 1106a 14–1107a 27.

Contrariety and the Range of Conduct

cases that go beyond the limits of awareness and the boundaries of experience.

Since the right *meson* or mean for each passion and emotion is not given, as in sensation, apparently man must establish it for himself. That is, man must answer the question of how much of this or that emotion he ought to experience under given conditions. Since conditions vary and individuals display differences in capacity, there cannot be an objective mean with respect to each emotion absolutely. Therefore, the *mesotis* has to be relative to the individual agent. It must, therefore, be neither the excess of an emotion nor its defect; and the correct place it should occupy in the range of the total possible extension of the passion or emotion will necessarily vary with the uniqueness of the situation. Hence, in each particular case, the right mean is one and the number of its deviations indefinite.[34] One finds the right mean either through logical reflection or by depending on the wisdom of men of prudence. The possession of a permanent ability to respond stably to all variations of specific passions and actions makes one virtuous in that respect.

'Virtue then is a state of character concerned with choice, lying in a mean (*mesotis*), i.e. the mean relative to us, this being determined by a rational principle, and by that principle by which the man of practical wisdom would determine it.'[35]

In its essential nature and scientific definition, virtue is a *mesotis*.[36] Yet, in a certain sense virtue is also an *extreme*, i.e. it is so with regard to what is *best and right*.[37] What Aristotle suggests here is that in the stable continuity of human virtuous conduct as a process, virtue is the highest point in man's development and the best organization of his passions and actions. Therefore, virtue must not be interpreted as a compromise between vices, but rather as the ideal intelligent response to the possibilities of action. Vices on the other hand result not from instability but from a deliberate and steady pursuit of extremities of given passions as intentional deviations from a virtuous *mesotis*.[38] Wrong

[34] *Nic. Eth.* 1106a 24–b 7; also 1106b 28–35.
[35] *Nic. Eth.* 1106b 36–1107a 2; also 1139a 22.
[36] *Nic. Eth.* 1107a 6–7.   [37] *Nic. Eth.* 1107a 7–8, 23.
[38] Vices and virtues, collectively, might be considered as contrary genera. The difficulty in this use of contraries has been discussed in ch. 4, section 2, pp. 55–6, text and footnotes.

Contrariety and the Range of Conduct

action implies thinking and acting out of knowledge of some kind.[39]

Since the passions are many, a plurality of virtues, *mesotētes*, is required but the rational element in all of them is the same; *logos* as prudence is the determining factor of all means,[40] and the standard for judging the integrity of the virtues. But before inquiring into the place of *logos* in virtue, we must first turn to the relation between virtue and the range of conduct. Deliberation functions within the framework of man's ultimate conception of the meaning of life and it implies a wider conception of the good, apparent, or final.[41] Deliberation in this sense implies responsibility for whatever acts are done because such acts are neither external nor committed under compulsion. This points to the fact that man is capable of self-determination; i.e. freedom to give a chosen direction to the powers of the soul. Unlike the natural forces which are irrational, the powers of the soul are characterized by a capacity to operate in opposite directions which makes them from the beginning powers of contrary movements. But the irrational forces, we are told, are determinate powers that operate by necessity, for example fire, which as an activity burns by necessity.[42]

In the case of human beings, it is not proper to speak of their capacities as irrational in the sense that natural forces are irrational, because men are endowed with cognitive powers and rational dispositions modifying on the whole the nutritive and appetitive aspects of the soul which are irrational only when contrasted with reason. Due to these interpenetrations of powers in human beings, the emotions and desires can become manifest in contrary and conflicting directions. The presence of both rational and non-rational powers in the soul accounts for not only moral contrariety but also for the twofold division of the concept of virtue.

'Virtue, then, being of two kinds, intellectual and moral, intellectual virtue in the main owes both its birth and its growth to teaching (for which reason it requires experience and time), while moral virtue comes about as a result of habit, whence also its name *ethike* is one that is formed by a slight variation from the

---

[39] *Nic. Eth.* 1147a 24–b 19.
[40] ὁ ὅρος τῶν μεσοτήτων.
[41] *Nic. Eth.* 1113a 45–b 2.
[42] *Met.* 1045b 27–1048a 24.

Contrariety and the Range of Conduct

word *ethos* (habit). From this it is also plain that none of the moral virtues arises in us by nature; for nothing that exists by nature can form a habit contrary to its nature. For instance the stone by nature moves downward and cannot be habituated to move upwards, not even if one tries to train it by throwing it up ten thousand times; nor can fire be habituated to move downwards, nor can anything else that by nature behaves in one way be trained to behave in another. Neither by nature, then, nor contrary to nature do the virtues arise in us; rather we are adapted by nature to receive them, and are made perfect by habit.'[43]

Now the decisive factor which determines the outcome of contrary possibilities of a power is either *orexis* or purposive choice. What makes an outcome moral in its effects is not nutritive or sensitive *orexis* but appetive intelligence which in fact is identical with deliberate choice.[44] Consequently there is a certain type of action which when it determines the mean between contrary possible directions man becomes positively moral; this type of action stems from the distinctively human faculty of intelligence and for this reason it is the element of *proairesis* in conduct that changes the psychological powers into moral qualities. A moral *mesotis*, therefore, prior to the development of intelligence would amount to a contradiction, that is, man would appear to have intelligence as a power and as complete actuality at the same time and prior to his maturity. The development of intelligence then is exactly what gives to the life of man its significance and makes it *worth* living. And virtue as a *mesotis* then must be arrived at only after considerable labour and the continuous practice of appropriate acts. The real means for the good life actually exist within man himself, though other external things are contributive to that effect in no small measure.[45] Moral life, for this reason, is in the final analysis a most personal affair because no one can force anybody else to become intelligent.

For the best life man needs two types of virtue, practical virtue or *phronesis* and theoretical virtue or *sophia*; both moral virtue and intellectual virtue. Happiness for Aristotle is clearly activity in accordance with excellence of that which possesses *logos*, which is either intelligence as such or the appetitively modified intelligence. Further the good life does not mean forming any habits

[43] *Nic. Eth.* 1103a 14–26. [44] *Nic. Eth.* 1139b 4.
[45] *Nic. Eth.* 1099a 31–b 6; 1178a 24–1178b 7.

in random but only those which are permanent states of character and in agreement with the highest expression of human entelechy.

'States of character arise out of like activities. This is why the activities we exhibit must be of a certain kind; it is because the states of character correspond to the differences between these. It makes no small difference then whether we form habits of one kind or of another from our very youth; it makes a very great difference, or rather *all* the difference.'[46]

The approach to virtue as *mesotis* of the indeterminate contrarieties of powers helps understand how the special virtues similarly arise through proper organization of the diverse orectic processes of the soul.[47] Both excess and deficiency in these powers is avoided through the right mean, and action is intelligently directed whenever the occasion arises. Evil thus appears to be any point within the contrariety delineated by excess and deficiency in the total range of possibilities of a certain power, except for that right mean which alone is instrumental to the good life. For this reason each specific virtue is more than a sheer state of soul; its maintenance demands continuity of activity. The virtuous life needs constant vigilance and alertness to steer a clear course away from both sides of the mean, on either direction of which there lies the indefinite range of contrary possibilities. And without steadfastness of habit the dangers of error increase immensely. The virtuous character then is not the man who has a set of inflexible *mesotētes*; he would be a most stubborn monstrosity of moralistic dogmatism. The good man's qualities are not fixed points, but virtuous responses to specific conditions; in his decisions he pays attention to all particular factors in action; the agent, the action itself, the occasion, the instrument, the object and the manner.[48] In addition the virtuous character is one

---

[46] *Nic. Eth.* 1103b 21–6.

[47] The analysis of the application of *mesotis* in the special moral virtues, which occupies a substantial portion of the *Nicomachean Ethics*, is beyond the purpose of the present study. Suffice it to note that the powers which are the material for moral virtue are the pleasures and pains as conditioned in specific types of actions and passions, either bodily or psychical. The psychical ones are such emotions as desire, anger, fear, confidence, envy, joy, love, hatred, regret, emulation, and pity. *Nic. Eth.*, Book III, ch. 4.

[48] *Nic. Eth.*, Book III, ch. 1.

Contrariety and the Range of Conduct

who has been able to *order* his virtues in an all-rounded fashion. He does justice to his whole personality by inter-relating the virtues into a rational order, by regarding the completeness of virtuous personality. Aristotle follows the path of his teacher whose main moral preoccupation was philosophical virtue, virtuous unity in its ideality. In this sense, Aristotle's investigations into the various distinctive forms of virtue is not opposite to the Platonic theory but complementary to it.[49]

The wholly virtuous person is an ideal which Plato expressly emphasized as the unity of virtues.[50] But it is seldom if ever that human life, in its flux and constant change, approximates it. Intelligent conduct, in Aristotelian terms, is life gradually extending excellence over the powers of the soul under the guidance of the ideal of the unity of virtues; it is not therefore practical to condemn a man because he is not wholly virtuous, though it is proper to criticize him when he consciously refuses to increase his virtuousness. Men are neither wholly bad nor wholly good, because some could be virtuous in one respect and not virtuous in another.[51] To Aristotle, ethics is practical and instrumental. It is not the absolute[52] that concerns the theorist of morality, but the study of the conditions and principles of prudent action that lead to happiness by helping man develop virtue. The powers of the soul at the end should come under the intelligent control and guidance of prudence so that the indeterminacy of their vast contrarieties may become determinate and channelled behaviour, with clarity in order and succinctness in expression. In this sense, man's whole life resembles the making of a work of art.

4. MORALITY AND INTELLIGIBILITY

By associating morality with the ideal of human intelligibility, Aristotle completed within the framework of Greek science,

---

[49] Joachim, *The Nicomachean Ethics*, pp. 113–14.
[50] *Protagoras*, 331 sqq.   [51] *Nic. Eth.* 1129b 33.
[52] The 'good' has as many meanings as the term 'is'. In *Nic. Eth.*, Book I, ch. 6, Aristotle proceeds to apply the theory of predication to the term 'good' and discusses it with reference to the following six categories: substance, quality, quantity, relation, time, place. This analysis is presented as an argument against the Platonic position which treated the good absolutely.

physics, psychology, and political inquiry, the humanistic and naturalistic approach to morality prevalent in the philosophical thinking of his times. That ethics is universal is a conclusion scientifically drawn from the study of human psychology; it is confirmed by the conduct of the intelligent citizens of a state guided by the principle that man is a logical animal seeking the completion of his rationality in both thinking and practice. Ethics is universal at least in the sense that morality is distributive as a way of intelligent living open to all human beings. Yet ethics as an ideal, even if only approximated, is an achievement which requires the concentrated and conscious effort for human development. As such it is the result neither of a supernatural gift-granting power nor of a hidden force in nature pushing human beings toward the moral goal by necessity. The moral life is consequently a natural process *desired* and *willed*, but when developmentally viewed, its fruition is contingent upon the co-ordinate development of intelligence.

In so far as the intelligent and moral life is a process, one of many, its understanding brings into the discussion the principle of contrariety. The metaphysical contrariety of form-privation, as a generic trait of subjects-in-process, relates the developmental aspect of morality to a general theory of process. But the analysis of the psychological contrarieties, as cases of the special contrarieties, has thrown additional light on the theme of moral fulfilment by rendering clear the nature of human faculties and powers that make man a distinctive type of being which alone is capable of the good life. With the principle of *mesotis* in virtue, moral contrariety has come to delineate the range of moral conduct which is that of free and responsible determination of choice. Man alone, by being moral, is the *locus* of all contrarieties; the metaphysical, the categorical, the elemental, the biophysical, and finally the moral. And when intelligence is fulfilled, *nous* comprehends all processes and all principles including that of contrariety. Psychologically, *nous* or intelligence could be viewed as process, as entelechy striving toward its completion, as form desiring its total consciousness in operation; therefore, intelligence is not an exception to the rule which demands the metaphysical contrariety of form-privation as a necessary condition for the understanding of any process whatever. But it seems that only intelligence, as fulfilment and virtuous activity, by becoming *complete* tends to

Contrariety and the Range of Conduct

escape the rule and, by knowing all principles of intelligibility, it encompasses contrariety.[53]

The psychological grounds of Aristotle's theory of knowledge preclude the possibility of having a *mesotis* and therefore contrariety in the intellectual virtues. Virtuous intelligence is no more an actualization but an actuality, the eventuation of which occurs not through the inception of forms but basically by the active manipulation and organization of forms as mental actualities. Rational content, unlike emotions, is not open to a number of possibilities for action one of which would be the ethically correct one. Doubtless reason is a process in the sense already discussed but its content is not the nutritive or exclusively orectic passions and actions but formal and cognitive actualities. Since intelligence is both content and the principles of the intelligibility of content, it both contains and apprehends contrariety. It contains contrariety because intelligence alone of all the faculties develops exclusively in accordance with the most universal contrariety, the metaphysical one. It apprehends it because *nous* as intuitive reason grasps all principles of understanding. Contrariety as grasped by *nous* is a formal principle of rendering intelligible all determinate processes and delimited developments: elemental, biological, psychological, and moral. Intelligence itself, as the actuality of human soul, is the consciousness of all principles of science and of the metaphysical contrariety, through which all processes are understood.

It is not a paradox, therefore, that there is no *mesotis* for the intellectual virtues and it would be no surprise to the reader of the *Nicomachean Ethics* if there is no mention of *mesotis* in Book IV, where Aristotle presents his analysis of these virtues. The connection between moral and intellectual virtues must be sought not in the extension of the notion of *mesotis* to reason but in the fact that reason is the formal *locus* of the principle of contrariety and the ultimate judge for the right *mesotis* in the moral virtues. The plurality of powers and activities and their inherent

---

[53] Human *nous* does not transcend contrariety because human beings, as subjects-in-process, belong to the class of sublunary events. *Nous* divine makes no choices. For this reason, it is constant perfection and eternally ideal rational activity. But human *nous* besides sustaining its rationality in the form of logic must use logic as an instrument to extend knowledge and turn action into ethical conduct in society.

indeterminateness necessitate in each case a *mesotis* for effective moral conduct. Every *mesotis* then points to a common rational principle which is the ultimate formal standard for every moral virtue. Aristotle's appeal to right reason is then easily understood. In the last analysis, both amount to the same things. The definition of right reason (*logos*) in virtue is designed to cover two cases of individuals, either those who are moral and maintain their stability, i.e. the *phronimoi*, or those who are becoming morally educated and not fully possessing intelligence as a complete actuality.

To possess intelligence fully is to have intellectual virtues, in which case the thinking soul functions without blemish in its two inter-related activities. In the first, when its object is the first principles, i.e. the unchanging and necessary *archai*, it is scientific intelligence. But when its object is the contingent and changeable reality, the thinking soul functions as calculative and deliberative intelligence. To function excellently in either of these concerns is to have virtue in that respect. Since man is distinctively logical he must be so in everything he does either contemplatively or practically.[54] He must think knowledge truly in the sphere of necessity and demonstrable science,[55] and in the sphere of changeability where truth holds 'for the most part'. In this latter realm of probable truth, intelligence must try its best to know what generally happens and what is likely to happen because these truths which are acquired through reflection and deliberation are most instrumental to doing, producing, and especially to good conduct.[56] The ideal co-ordination of the two spheres of thinking would be that in which one is able to bring into the realm of conduct or probable truth the exactness and demonstrability of the pure sciences. By doing so moral choice becomes increasingly accurate and ethics as certain as possible.

The purpose of moral activity, then, is not to turn ethics into an exact science but to enlighten conduct and enrich it with the rational constancy of intelligence. If it were possible for practical intelligence to become absolutely demonstrable, choice would lose its moral significance and virtuous action would be reduced

[54] *Nic. Eth.* 1139a 3–17.
[55] *Nic. Eth.* 1139a 12; 1139b 23, 25; 1140b 34.
[56] *Nic. Eth.* 1140b 26; 1144b 14. For the object of *doxa*, see *Post. An.* 88b 30; *De Int.* 21a 32; *Pr. An.* 49b 6–9.

to a chapter in deductive reasoning. But the conditions for moral life are such that they exclude this possibility. Science and morality share necessarily in intelligence but differ fundamentally in one respect. In science the ends and means are inseparable; *nous* contains logic as its tools but also grasps the principles of its operations, which are unchangeable contents *qua* forms and permanent possessions of the soul. But in moral action intelligence moves outwardly; it chooses among possible courses of action, one of which alone is in conformity with the principle of right reason.[57] In science the universal is possessed, in ethics the universal is continuously being sought and envisaged after the ideal of *nous* itself. Hence intelligence is excellent when it is *sophia* or intellectual wisdom, and *phronesis* or practical wisdom.[58] And the fully intelligent person is one who knows how to know (*a*) through his established ability to demonstrate[59] his power to grasp immediately the first principles of all knowing,[60] his power to rise to *theoria* or speculative vision, and (*b*) through his stability to bring intelligence into the problematic situation of conduct.

It appears then that moral and intellectual virtues form a continuity. There is no gap between them especially when intelligence is seen developmentally. The moral aspects of intelligence do not stop with the rise of virtue in practical behaviour.[61] For Aristotle, intelligence in conduct as regulated by *phronesis* is both essential and preparatory for the type of life which finds its final expression in philosophy. Here intelligence understands itself fully as both practical excellence and utter rationality. In the philosophical life activity is in accordance with the ultimate demands of the human soul for its fulfilment and yields happiness. The movement of *nous* is no longer one of actualization but of actively sustaining a rational vision complete and perfect. Ideally speaking, the good life is the integrated life of reason in which intelligent action as statesmanship and theoretical activity as philosophy are inextricably fused in every citizen. At this point the Platonic ideal of the philosopher-king is re-stated not with the zeal of the social reformer for a certain political utopia, but with the confidence of a scientist who saw in human nature

[57] *Nic. Eth.* 1139a 35-6.   [58] *Nic. Eth.* 1139b 14-1143b 17.
[59] *Nic. Eth.* 1139b 31-2.   [60] This is intuitive reason, 1140b 31-1141a 8.
[61] *Nic. Ethics.* 1144a 1-1145a 11.

Contrariety and the Range of Conduct

distributively the *arche* for the good life, the possibility for collective intelligence and happiness.

Aristotle was convinced that to live morally one needed all the knowledge one could get about both nature and human nature, the cosmos and the soul. To be a scientist of nature or any subject matter at all, does not entail loss of sight of the moral issues or civil obligations as the Platonic Socrates insinuated in his reserved attitude toward the great Ionian tradition of natural philosophy. To be a well-rounded scientist is in the long run as good as being a responsible citizen. Science liberates and moralizes by turning the light of knowledge on man's struggle to be what he is capable of realizing as a citizen of any city of man and a logical animal in nature. What Plato as a philosophical myth-maker expressed in the *Timaeus* Aristotle accomplished through a life replete of research and investigation into the nature of man and the universe. The much sought for unity for the two previous directions of thought, the Ionian quest for nature and the Sophistic curosity about human nature, Plato was the first to attain in his dramatic exposition of ideas which run through all his great works. Aristotle reached the same goal but through the strict procedures of scientific activity. His findings enabled him to demonstrate the indispensability of natural knowledge for philosophy and human culture in general. The dry and intricate style, if often boring and repetitious, of the *De Anima*, *The Physics*, the two *Analytics*, the *Metaphysics* and the other works in no way diminishes the immense value of his thought and his contribution toward a human conception of the good life.

Plato, it is said, was devoted to the message of his divine Socrates. And so was Aristotle to his great teacher. The master's steady vision of the living universe of ideas received in the hands of the Macedonian disciple the status of a convincingly human reality which starts with the logic of the rationality of the universe and conquers the certainties of the world of process in between. But the steady vision of the universe is a course of action befitting the perfect nature of pure *nous* alone. Man is in process and moves from potentiality to actuality. Since he cannot be totally divine he can be supremely human and becomingly divine. His intelligence is passionately concerned with the possibilities of human nature and the grand order of heavenly perfection. Hence the noble thinker never forgets to bring his wisdom to his fellow

Contrariety and the Range of Conduct

human beings; and never does he deny to translate his personal *theoria* into social action and intellectual friendship. And so the social *locus* of virtue is always the city of man; the purpose of the city is to bring about such desirable and appropriate changes in the citizens as to make society a community of active thinkers. The enlightened citizen then becomes a statesman who invariably departs from the principle according to which 'The good for man is an organized life in which the essential powers of man find harmonious development.'[62]

The test of practice is that of rendering this universal potentiality of mankind into a real and shared ideal. When this is done effectively and traditionally, social intelligence acquires the stability of the ideal activity of *nous*, which is life in its fullest sense. In a well-ordered society the aim of education is that of preserving the painfully won wisdom and extending thoughtfully the boundaries of knowledge. Education warrants a perpetual invitation to new visions by training the youth in the pursuit of the good life in *praxis* and *theoria*. But the ideal is always one: to reach *ousia* through intelligence.

[62] *Pol.* 1269a 29–34; 1314a 25–9; 1317a 40–b 2.

EPILOGUE

Καὶ δὴ καὶ τὸ πάλαι τε καὶ νῦν καὶ ἀεὶ ζητούμενον καὶ ἀεὶ ἀπορούμενον. τί τὸ ὄν, τοῦτό ἐστι τίς ἡ οὐσία . . .
Met. 1028b 2–4.

THE role which Aristotle played in Greek philosophy and culture is undeniably great; its greatness applies equally to the subsequent philosophical developments. It would not be inappropriate to borrow from his terminology and apply his own useful concepts to his own works. The entire Aristotelian corpus could be compared to an organism of an intellectual nature and it exhibits a living unity of form and matter; it has an essence which is philosophical. The philosophy of Aristotle could be compared to a 'substance' (οὐσία) which has a 'telos' (τέλος), an end of its own to fulfil. And it did accomplish its entelechy (ἐντελέχεια) in all the plurality of the demands of this end. However, its 'eidos' (εἶδος) was of a unique kind. It seemed to partake of the eternal perfect circular movement that the Intelligences of Book Λ of the *Metaphysics* exemplify. His philosophy survived the intellectual era in which it was born and developed. Its exceptional nature keeps fulfilling itself like the everlasting unmoved movers. It outlived the Ancient Greek Era and became an active intellectual force and a functioning philosophical current in our long cultural tradition.

The philosophy of Aristotle has become an integral part of another greater intellectual organism of a more inclusive 'substance'; that of the vast and ever-growing body of western philosophy. Its wisdom has been assimilated within the accumu-

Epilogue

lating and expanding human mind. This type of re-fulfilment is not a mere helpful instrument for a better understanding of Greek philosophy; it is also an admirable means for the appreciation of a philosopher who in his own terms stands for the creative individual who with care and devotion erects the amazing world of a great vision. This latter character of his work has an enhancing effect on the student's vision: it resembles those unique monuments of art which capture our imagination and deepen our sense of life by disclosing to the inner eye certain hitherto unthinkable possibilities of the universe.

The chief *aporia* of what substance is, after all its generic traits have been examined, remains to be answered by each generation through its genuine metaphysicians. Its generic traits have by no means been exhausted in Aristotelian metaphysics or in any of the other subsequent attempts down to the present. The reason is simple: substance is cumulative, and its generic traits are by no means fixed once and for all. And as it accumulates, it always requires a fresh consideration and reconstruction. This being the nature of being, it follows that metaphysics must keep in line accumulatively. And there will always be a need for metaphysics. The fundamental Aristotelian *aporia* will always be answered by mankind; but no generation is destined ever to master it fully. Aristotle, the great knower, probably knew this secret deep in his heart. His analysis of wisdom made him superbly wise.

Substance is in process and it is dynamic, functional, always individual. Its intelligibility, as the unit of distributive being, is contingent upon the principle of contrariety as the criterion of process. Contrariety in turn is sustained because substance is determinate. But what, again, is substance in the totality of its determinations and in the integration of its generic traits and plurality of principles? Only divine *nous*, the complete and most cherished vision, could reveal. But could there be such knowledge?

Both the *aporetic* substance and the divine *nous* will remain unknown. The first simply does not exist as a whole unit, because it is not a locus or a delimited process; the second is cognitively incomprehensible, because it defies the conditions of human intelligibility. But man can dream. And from his dreams he can form an attitude and a view towards *nous*. If he is idle and tired, he will resort to simple prayer and humility. If he is strong and determined, he will set out on the unending quest. This quest,

Epilogue

as a work of *envisaging and seeking nous*, inspires man with awe, and compels him to strive for a completion in ideality, so that he will rest only in the highest possible degree of comprehensiveness. Aristotle knew that mankind cannot attain *nous* in actuality and, to compensate for this impossibility, he stated his end in an insight which was at once the product of a strong creative nature and the result of an indefatigable scientist. He made *nous* the guiding principle and the ideal which always lies ahead of all inquiry. Thus, he asserted once again in his personal achievement the value of the Greek *theoria*. And in so far as man continues to be a culture-making and metaphysical animal, *theoria* will remain the consummation of his intellectual labour and the blessed reward of the highest, severest, and the most creative of all disciplines:

ΦΙΛΟΣΟΦΙΑ

APPENDIX

CHAPTER I, *pages* 1-18

Note 1. As an illustration one might refer to the position which John Dewey has taken towards Aristotle in his *Reconstruction in Philosophy*. In spite of the startling similarities between them, his position exhibits the dimensions of a severe hypercriticism. Vigorously attacking the limitations of the ancient scientific mind whose fixed terms and narrow method he considers responsible for the retardation of social progress over a number of centuries, Dewey writes on page 65:

'Terms which sound modern, words like potentiality and development abound in Aristotelian thought, and have misled some into reading into his thought modern meanings. But the significance of these words in classic and medieval thought is rigidly determined by their context. Development holds merely of the course of changes which take place within a particular member of the species. It is only a name for the predetermined movement from the acorn to the oak tree.'

And further down he continues:

'So potentiality never means, as in modern life, the possibility of novelty, of invention, of radical deviation, but only that principle in virtue of which the acorn becomes the oak. Technically, it is the capacity for movement between opposites. Only the cold can become hot; only the dry can become wet; only the babe can become a man; the seed the full-grown wheat and so on. Potentiality instead of implying the emergence of anything novel means merely the facility with which a particular thing repeats the recurrent processes of its kind, and thus becomes a specific case of the eternal forms in and through which all things are constituted.'

For more on this see Dewey's *Quest for Certainty*, pages 3-20.

Appendix

He continues his charges, in a similar fashion, against the four causes. But it is worth inquiring here what it is that Dewey is arguing against. His preoccupation with reconstructing the total scientific and philosophical tradition for the sake both of present successful adjustments and of the facilitation of future progress through active manipulation of the cultural heritage and under the direction of the experimental method of science, gives us the real cue to understanding his biased attitude. He is attacking the Aristotelian philosophy from the standpoint of a pragmatist who is accustomed to criticize ideas in terms of their consequence.

The case Dewey makes out is like that of a historical critic who would complain that a given period did not anticipate the consequences which its view of life would have on subsequent generations. Undoubtedly, Aristotle was committed to certain philosophical convictions and he shared within his own tradition a certain scientific myth. It is precisely the consequences that the Aristotelian commitments and convictions had on the subsequent development of science and philosophy that Dewey is arguing against; namely, the firm belief in a fixed and unmoved Reality, the acceptance of a world of which science was invited to understand the permanent character, and philosophy to reveal the ultimate determinations, the trust in a logic with no alternatives (John Dewey, *Logic, The Theory of Inquiry*, pp. 81–9). The fundamental contrast he draws between the ancient and the contemporary thinker is that the latter 'does not try to define and delimit something remaining constant *in* change, he tries to describe a constant order of change' (*Reconstruction in Philosophy*, p. 67). In another passage he charges Aristotle with being largely responsible for the 'spectator conception of knowledge'. He thinks that this provided the ancients with the basis on which they 'transformed knowing into a morally irresponsible estheticism' (*ibid.*, p. 103).

The above contrasts and remarks may be significant in the context in which Dewey uses them and may be quite suggestive for an interpretive survey of the history of western philosophy and science from the point of view of Dewey's instrumentalism. They may also be valuable to the social critic. However, there is only partial truth in this type of criticism of Aristotle's philosophy, for it omits in its hasty judgments certain considerations without which there is a danger of ignoring the essential merits and the powerful concepts of a philosophy which is still in use and

Appendix

operation in a number of capacities. The consequences of Aristotelianism on scientific and social development may be evaluated from more than one point of view, and Dewey is right only in so far as his observations are justified by his selected context. One is equally right to ask the question whether Aristotle is to be held responsible for the inefficiency of the following generation in extending, amplifying, criticizing, and reconstructing his contributions in the field of philosophy and scientific method. Nor should the man of the remote future accuse Dewey of retarding the development of philosophy on account of the 'limited and fixed' character of the experimental method his instrumentalism stands and falls with.

Philosophers cannot be blamed for the reconstructions and re-evaluations their successors fail to make. Again, in the light of our present demands—just as future generations will regard our own standing in the light of their intellectual demands—much that Dewey has to say about ancient science seems plausible and valid. His sound criticism of the scientific myth of the ancients deserves recognition. But one may equally suspect a possible dogmatic tendency in his own bias which is similarly dictated from a certain point of view, from a selected context which in turn involves a scientific myth more plausible, up-to-date, 'reconstructed', but nevertheless a myth.

Dewey, carried away by his too sweeping, although interesting, criticisms of Aristotle, has forgotten to make his acknowledgments to his forerunners, as Aristotle did when he reconstructed the entire scheme and formulation of problems of his predecessors. It took the sharp and 'reconstructive' attitude of his immediate successors to depict his debts. Professor J. H. Randall, Junr. (*The Philosophy of John Dewey*, The Library of Living Philosophers, edited by A. Schilpp, pages 101–2), concludes his article on Dewey's interpretation of the history of philosophy with the following paragraphs, which I quote fully for their direct bearing on the point emphasized here.

'Dewey himself seems to be working primarily with the conceptions of Aristotle. In his naturalism, his pluralism, his logical and social empiricism, his realism, his natural teleology, his ideas of potentiality and actuality, contingency and regularity, qualitatively diverse individuality—above all, in his thoroughgoing functionalism, his Aristotelian translation of all the problems of

Appendix

matter and form into a functional context—to say nothing of his basic social and ethical concepts—in countless vital matters he is nearer to the Stagirite than to any other philosopher. Where he has used the instruments of a century of critical effort—the empiricist's analysis, the post-Kantian appeal to a more human experience, the biological and social conceptions of human nature, the lessons of a rapidly changing culture—it has been to carry the Aristotelian attitude still further in the direction in which Aristotle criticized Platonism. It were not difficult to exhibit Dewey as an Aristotelian more Aristotelian than Aristotle himself.

'Yet one would hardly realize this from his words. His use of Aristotelian ideas has been remarkably fruitful. But, however effective in developing his own position, most of what he has explicitly said about Aristotle has conveyed little real historical illumination; it has been far more relevant to Saint Thomas than to the Greek. Much of what he points to is there; much is not, and is to be found only in the scholastic tradition. It would scarcely be proper and pertinent, even if true, to maintain here that the total impression he gives of Aristotelian thought is nevertheless false. It would be more to the point to ask, why should Dewey view Aristotle through the eyes of the Neothomists? Why should he not see Aristotle for what he is, the greatest functionalist in the philosophical tradition?—he who of all thinkers today can best claim to be the representative of Aristotelian thought, the truest follower of him who likewise in his time most effectively and suggestively brought the criticism of the best scientific thought to bear on the classic tradition.'

Note 2. A. The narrow view of κίνησις.

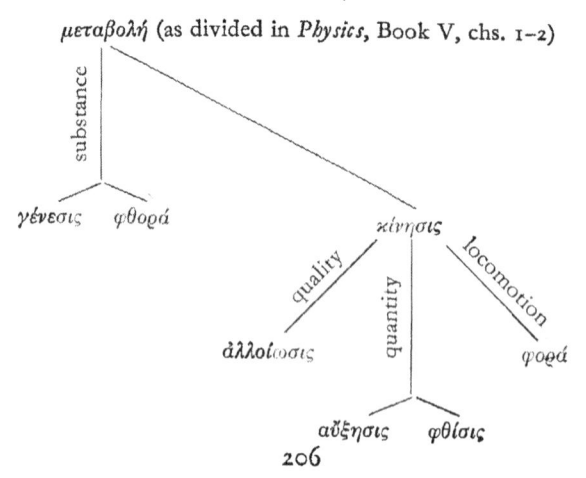

μεταβολή (as divided in *Physics*, Book V, chs. 1–2)

- substance
  - γένεσις   φθορά
- κίνησις
  - quality → ἀλλοίωσις
  - quantity
    - αὔξησις   φθίσις
  - locomotion → φορά

Appendix

B. *The wide view of* κίνησις (in Book III, ch. 1).

κίνησις is used as the generic term equivalent to μεταβολή, and is divided into the following types.

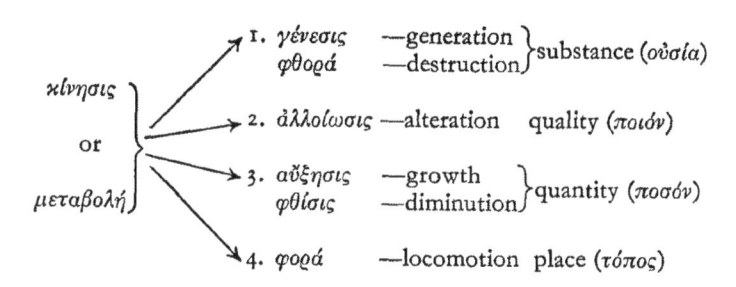

κίνησις or μεταβολή
- 1. γένεσις —generation
     φθορά —destruction } substance (οὐσία)
- 2. ἀλλοίωσις —alteration   quality (ποιόν)
- 3. αὔξησις —growth
     φθίσις —diminution } quantity (ποσόν)
- 4. φορά —locomotion   place (τόπος)

The question is: Did Aristotle pass from a narrow view of κίνησις (as in A) toward a wide one (B), where κίνησις is equal to μεταβολή, or did he proceed from a wide view to a narrow one? P. Tannery believes that Aristotle passed from A to B. W. D. Ross (*Phys.*, Intr., pp. 7–8) brings evidence to establish the view that Aristotle's development was from B to A, that is from the wide to the narrow, because the narrow view of κίνησις (subsumed under μεταβολή) is found in passages of later works. (*Phys.* 260a 27; *De Caelo* 310a 23; *De An.* 406a 12; *Phys.* VIII, 265a 11; *De Gen. et Corr.* 319b 31; 336a 19; *Met.* H 1042b 4.) In the passages given he says that 'μεταβολή, not κίνησις, is the general term under which generation is brought' (*Phys.*, Intr., p. 8). For an elaborate discussion on this see W. D. Ross, *Aristotle's Physics*, Introduction, pp. 45–7.

Note 3. Hamelin, who wrote a whole chapter on the 'opposition of concepts', missed the distinction referred to and was unable to see how certain problems connected with contrariety are not 'real' problems at all. An example is his treatment of the possession-privation contrariety. He writes in *Le Système d'Aristote* (Paris, Librairie Felix Alcan, 1920, p. 139):

'Il est vrai que dans certains cas la privation et l'habitude admettent un term moyen. Mais ce ne sont plus l'habitude et la privation proprement dites et telles que nous les avons considérées. C'est cette espèce particulière d'habitude et de privation que se confond avec les contraires (*Met.* 1055b, 8–11); c'est cette espèce d'habitude et de privation dont le sujet et la notion ne sont pas bien precises. Par exemple l'homme peut n'être ni bon

Appendix

ni méchant; le bien et le mal appartiennent a des genres differents, et Aristote pense sans doute que sous l'idée d'homme sont compris les enfants encore sans raison, aussi bien que les adultes (voir *ibid.*, 1055b, 20—fin du chap.).'

Note 4. For the reader's information, remarks illustrating certain modern interpretations of the relation between the two types of Aristotle's metaphysical theory are presented here.

W. D. Ross in *Aristotle's Metaphysics*, I, pp. 252–3, writes as follows:

'Aristotle has in the main two ways of stating the subject-matter of metaphysics. In one set of passages it is stated as τὸ ὄν ᾗ ὄν, the whole of being, as such. This view is expressed throughout Book Γ, and occasionally elsewhere (E 1025b 3, K 1060b 31, 1061b 4, 26, 31); it is implied also in the description of σοφία as being occupied with the first causes and principles, *sc.* of reality as a whole (A 981b 28, 982b 9). But more frequently metaphysics is described as a study of a certain part of reality, viz. that which is χωριστόν (exists independently) and ἀκίνητον, while physics studies things that are χωριστά but not ἀκίνητα, and mathematics things that are ἀκίνητα but not χωριστά. This view of the subject of metaphysics is expressed most clearly in E 1026a 15, but is implied in such passages as K 1064b 4, Λ 1069b 1, *Phys.* 192a 34, 194b 14, *De An.* 403b 15. On this view metaphysics studies not being as a whole but the highest kind of being, and when viewed in this way it may be called θεολογική (E 1026a 15, K 1064b 3). These two views of the business of metaphysics have been made (by Natorp) a ground for splitting up the *Metaphysics* into two. In E an attempt is made to reconcile the two views. The question is raised (1026a 23) whether first philosophy is universal or deals with a particular class of things, and the answer is given that in studying one kind of being, οὐσία ἀκίνητος, it is φιλοσοφία πρώτη καὶ καθόλου οὕτως ὅτι πρώτη. In studying the nature of pure being, form without matter, philosophy is in effect coming to know the nature of being as a whole.

'Both views are genuinely Aristotelian, but the narrower view of the scope of metaphysics is that which is more commonly present in his works, and more in keeping with the distrust of a universal science expressed in the *Posterior Analytics*.'

P. Natorp, in the nineteenth century, stated that there is an insufferable contradiction in Aristotle's metaphysical theory (see *Philosophische Monatshefte*, xxiv, 1888, pp. 49–53). Natorp explained

Appendix

the origin of the 'contradiction' through a philological interpretation of the text of the *Metaphysics* propounding the view that one could arrive at two types of text which in turn could support two mutually exclusive types of metaphysical theories; one type is a Platonizing and the second is an Aristotelian one. To this second text certain Platonizing members of the Peripatetic school added at a later date certain Platonizing corrections. (See P. Natorp, *Platon's Ideenlehre*, Eine Einführung in den Idealismus, Leipzig: Dürr, 1903.)

E. Zeller regarded the contradiction a genuine one which, however, could not be explained away by Natorp's philological interpretation. Zeller was of the view that Aristotle had actually attempted an unsuccessful synthesis of two mutually exclusive functions of metaphysics; therefore, under the apparent unity there still remains in Aristotle's theory a thoroughgoing contradiction of two antithetical meanings of Being. (See Edward Zeller, *Archiv für Geschichte der Philosophie*, vol. II, 1889, pp. 270–1.)

G. E. Grote (*Aristotle*, 1883, p. 423), differing from both Zeller and Natorp, remarks that there is nothing insolubly incompatible between the two functions and pursuits of first philosophy.

W. Jaeger's view is far more sound and suggestive than those of Zeller and Natorp. He advances the sound argument that the 'insufferable' contradiction could really be discarded through a developmental approach to Aristotle's thought. Jaeger tried to demonstrate that Aristotle came upon his own distinct views through developing from one type of first philosophy built on Platonic conceptions to another type, in which Being was examined in what is termed here as Being in the 'distributive' sense. While the 'early' Aristotle was interested primarily in the supersensible Being, in his later stage of metaphysical development he attempted to include in the scope of his interest all types of being and basically preoccupied himself with the understanding of principles and pervasive traits of distributive being, i.e. the ontological analysis. (See W. Jaeger, *Aristotle*, translated by Robinson, pp. 7, 210, 214–19.)

For detailed references on historical material concerning the various controversies and interpretations given to the notion of Being in Aristotle's *Metaphysics*, see J. Owens, *The Doctrine of Being in the Aristotelian Metaphysics*, pp. 1–23, 303–14.

Appendix

CHAPTER II, *pages* 19–30

Note 1. Of the modern critics, P. Natorp (*Philosophische Monatshefte*, XXIV, 1888, pp. 52–3) argues that strictly speaking, the Aristotelian metaphysics cannot on theoretical grounds be identified with theology. This he sees as a consequence of the insufferable contradiction in the *Metaphysics* in connection with the notion of being, i.e. being as pure empty concept and being as concrete existent. See also W. Jaeger, *The Theology of the Early Greek Thinkers*, pp. 4–10, 194–5, notes 14–29; W. Jaeger, *Aristotle*, pp. 98 ff. (for Aristotle's early attitude toward life and religion); 138 ff. (for Aristotle's theological tendency in his early period); 156 ff., 161 ff., 222 ff.

Note 2. The principle of the internal source of change in beings is called by Aristotle the 'nature' of a thing (*Phys.* 192b 28–33), and it can never be conceived apart from a subject (*Phys.* 192b 34) which is always necessarily involved in process. Nature is a highly complex concept and has a *meaning* which ranges from the notion of *form* that can be stated in the definition of a subject-in-process to all the dynamic developments of that idea. When nature is seen from the point of view of 'ends', then the 'nature' of a thing is what a thing can be after its potentialities have been realized and it has completed its goal. Again nature, seen in terms of a developing career, is the *continuous* unfolding of a subject's form, the struggle for the completion of its total process, which involves all the determining factors and causes—material, efficient, formal, final—that are distinguishable in the analysis of a process.

Here are the principal meanings of nature given in *Metaphysics*, Book Δ, ch. 4. 'Nature' means:

1. The genesis of growing things.
2. That immanent part of a growing existent from which its growth first proceeds.
3. The source of the fundamental process in natural existents which is present in them in virtue of what they are as such (i.e. their essential nature).
4. The primary material of which any natural being consists or out of which it is made, which is relatively unshaped and cannot be changed by its own potency.
5. The *essence* of natural beings, as with those who say nature is the primary mode of composition.

6. By an *extension* of five, every essence in general has come to be called a *nature*, because the nature of a thing is one kind of essence.

And Aristotle summarizes thus in *Met.* 1015a 13-19.

'... nature in the primary and strict sense is the essence of things which have in themselves, as such, a source of movement; for the matter is called the nature because it is qualified to receive this, and processes of becoming and growing are called nature because they are movements proceeding from this. And nature in this sense is the source of the movement of natural objects, being present in them somehow, either potentially or in complete reality.'

Note 3. The direction which their speculations took was dictated by an attitude, a predilection for seeing nature from the point of view of the end result of their inductive search for a source of origination. The value of a speculative view consists in its ability to see nature in its totality and then to proceed to account for plurality, i.e. the value of a vision. The cosmological 'totalism' of the pre-Socratics and the appealing stories it gave rise to, such as the fascinating obscurities of the Platonic *Timaeus*, became for Aristotle the target for an ingenious attack. Aristotle came out with a clearer view of distributive being. This does not mean that natural processes were of no concern to the pre-Socratics or even that Plato ever taught a doctrine of 'nature as a whole'. The point emphasized here is that neither Plato nor the pre-Socratics stated a clear-cut position in respect to a metaphysics of distributive being without resorting either to stories or to assigning prominence to mathematics. Aristotle's criticism yields neither a cosmological story of inclusive material principles nor a theory of nature deducible from mathematical structures.

Note 4. It has been said that in Aristotle's view of metaphysics, contrariety is the principle of organizing intelligibly the cognizable functions of being in the sense of a subject-in-process. Contrariety is a principle of being, in so far as being is a substance known through its manifold manifestations, which are functions in operation and co-operation, developing in determinate ways so that certain fulfilments are attained and certain ends are achieved. Being is thus pluralistically conceived.

Loci are not 'opposed' to one another. Nor are particular

Appendix

functions and processes within a locus 'opposed' to one another. However, the intelligibility of a function involves the concept of contrariety, just as does the intelligibility of the subject-in-process. The particular functions and processes are irreducible because the ultimate types of signification, or categories, are irreducible genera. Each category gives rise to a contrariety. Since the category of substance is the fundamental category, it was stated that its corresponding contrariety is the fundamental and most comprehensive one. The first contrariety, though, does not demand the reduction of the other categorical contrarieties to it—just as the 'nature' of a subject does not dictate the vanishing of the subject's plural functions. Since things are what they can be known to be, the criterion of contrariety is ontologically supported by the fact that the natures of things are such that they can be known and are known in so far as they are determinable.

Contrariety is ontologically grounded, but it is not reducible to a material principle. Nor is the material principle reducible to the conceptual nature of contrariety. Aristotle contributed largely toward a plural approach to the question of first principles. He raised contrariety to the status of a first principle through an original approach to the whole question, i.e. by accepting as first principles all those ultimate presuppositions and assumptions which are necessary and undemonstrable points of departure that mankind uses as beginnings of understanding. And since understanding has something to understand (the hypothesis, as Aristotle calls it), the subject matter to be understood along with all the principles requisite to render it cognizable constitute the domain of first principles. Thus, there is an interdependence and irreducibility that, among other features, characterize first principles. Distributive being is the subject matter that is to be cognized. Wherever there is substance there is always contrariety which makes its cognition possible. Against this ontological background Aristotle was able to present a metaphysical analysis of contrariety and was also able to reconstruct and correct the misconceptions about it that rendered this principle either superfluous or made it a mere instrument in a world story.

Contrariety is a kind of difference. (*Met. Δ*, chs. 1, 2; especially the second part of ch. 2. Also *Met.* 1055a ff.) Plato had also formulated a definite view that the contraries constitute a kind of difference. He says in the *Philebus* (12E 2–13A ff.): 'Colour as such

Appendix

does not differ at all from colour in its entirety; but we all know that black in respect to white is not only different but it happens also to be the most contrary.' The study of contrariety cannot be successful apart from the inquiry into substance as the subject-in-process. For it is substances that differ, and it is their functions that are the processes which comprise change; and difference is in the field of change.

Note 5. Substance understood in terms of unity and oneness is stated aporetically in the following passage (*Met.* B 1001a 4–9):

'The inquiry that is both the hardest of all and the most necessary for knowledge of the truth is whether being and unity are the substances of things, and whether each of them, without being anything else, is being or unity respectively, *or* we must inquire what being and unity are, with the implication that they have some other underlying nature.'

The proper answer to this question requires the use of the notion of subject-in-process (*hypokeimenon*) as well as the concept of metaphysical contrariety. Aristotle in the same passage proceeds to demonstrate the inadequacies of other views offered as answers to the question raised and advocates the primacy of being and of unity. The uncritical handling of principal philosophical concepts such as 'being' and 'unity' led many of his predecessors to arbitrary monisms, reductionistic cosmologies, and various unattainable pluralisms. The answer to the above *aporia* is suggested in *Met.* Z 1040b 16–24, and Iota, ch. 2, where he states that being and unity *as such* are not substances in themselves but attributes. In M 1083a 20–1085a 2, he argues that unity and number *as such* cannot have separate existence. See also W. D. Ross, *Arist. Metaph.*, vol. I, p. 224. If all unity is referable to substance, then all contrarieties are connected with the various senses and basic distinctions of substance. Further, contrariety is applicable to the ways of talking about unity and, its counterpart, plurality.

CHAPTER III, *pages* 31–48

Note 1. Other scholars also agree with this interpretation of Aristotle's treatment of his predecessors. See H. Cherniss, *The Riddle of the Early Academy*, pp. 30–59; F. M. Cornford, *Plato's*

Appendix

Theory of Knowledge, p. 31; O. Schwegler, *Metaph. Arist.* III, p. 30; J. Owens, *The Doctrine of Being in Aristotle's Metaphysics*, pp. 107 ff., 358, note 98.

Note 2. The following discussion on the difference between Logic and Dialectic is largely based upon F. M. Cornford's *Plato's Theory of Knowledge*, pp. 262–73.

Aristotle not Plato first used formal logic. Formal logic may be described as the study of

1. propositional forms, not their content, i.e. it studies the patterns or types under which statements can be classified;
2. the constituents of these propositional forms (subjects, predicates, relations between terms, etc.);
3. formal relations of inference between propositional forms.

Plato does not use symbols or construct propositional forms. The factors he recognizes are these:

1. The immutable structures or forms or kinds, eternally combined or disjoined in the system of truth or reality; these are the meanings to which common names are conventionally attached.
2. Our thoughts (διάνοια) about these objects, our acquaintance with them, reasonings (λογισμός) about them, judgments (δόξαι) in which such reasonings terminate; all these are mental existents.
3. Statements (λόγοι), the vocal expression of thoughts and judgments, consisting of spoken names and verbs. The meanings of common names and verbs are the forms. Statements are not propositional forms, but actual significant statements, existing only while we utter them.

The science of dialectic does not study formal symbolic patterns, it is not logic (the science of *logoi* or *logismoi*).

(*a*) It studies the structure of the real world of forms. Its technique of collection and division operates in that structure.

(*b*) Its rules are those of correct procedure in making division (they are not laws of inference or laws of thought).

(*c*) All its statements are actual significant statements and are either true or false; viz. 'Motion is Rest' or 'Existence is Motion'. All this is in fact 'Ontology'.

(*d*) The structure of forms is conceived as a hierarchy of

Appendix

genera and species, amendable to the methods of collection and division. (The preliminary process of collection is described in the *Phaedrus* 265D.) Then the dialectician surveys the collection and 'clearly discerns' by intuition the common (generic) character 'extended throughout' of them, which he will select for division; it is a unity which is complex, divisible into specific forms characterized by their differences, which species are mutually exclusive and incompatible. With these many specific forms is contrasted the 'one form connected in a unity through many wholes' (δι' ὅλων πολλῶν). Wholes means many specific completely defined forms. However, the single generic form blends with each specific form, is dispersed through them, and yet in virtue of its own nature, it is connected in a unity traversing them all (viz. animal: man, ox, horse, etc.) (*Sophist* 253 C, D).

The Structure of the World of Forms

1. The highest, generic form must be a whole of which the specific forms are parts;
2. The highest form in a table of division must be the richest, not the poorest, in content;
3. Every specific form must be likewise a whole of parts, complex and definable.

'Real' is confined to the forms.

Existence covers both the realm of forms (real) and of change.

Note 3. Reasoning and its species (*Top.* I, ch. 1). Reasoning is an argument in which certain things being laid down, something other than these necessarily comes about through them. (*Top.* 100a 25.)

(*a*) *Demonstration:* its premises are true and primary.

(*b*) *Dialectical reasoning:* it reasons from opinions generally accepted. A dialectical *proposition:* (1) consists in asking something that is held by all men or by most men or by the philosophers; (2) includes views which are like those generally accepted; also (3) includes propositions which contradict the contraries of opinions that are taken to be generally accepted; and (4) includes all opinions that are in accordance with the recognized arts (*Top.* I, ch. 10).

(*c*) *Contentious reasoning:* it starts from opinions that seem to be generally accepted, but are not really such.

Appendix

Species of dialectical argument (*Top.* I, ch. 12).

1. Induction. 2. Reasoning.

Induction is a passage from individuals to universals.

Note 4. Aristotle distinguishes three senses of sameness (*Top.* I, ch. 7). It applies:

1. *numerically*, when there is more than one name, but only one thing;
2. *specifically*, where there is more than one thing, but they present no differences in respect of their species, as one man and another;
3. *generically*. Those things are generically the same which fall under the same genus, such as a horse and a man.

On sameness see also *Top.* VII, chs. 1, 2.

'... as sameness is a term used in many senses, see whether things that are the same in one way are the same also in a different way. For there is either no necessity or even no possibility that things that are the same specifically or generically should be numerically the same, and it is with the question whether they are or are not the same in that sense that we are concerned (*Top.* VII, 2, 152b 30–4).

Note 5. F. M. Cornford in his *Principium Sapientiae* (Cambridge University Press, 1952, pp. 188–9) gives the following list of assumptions in the cosmological accounts of the early thinkers:

(1) In the beginning there is a primal unity, a state of indistinction or fusion in which factors that will later become distinct are merged together.
(2) Out of this unity emerge, by separation, pairs of opposite things or 'powers'; the first being the hot and the cold, then the moist and the dry. This separating out finally leads to the disposition of the great elemental masses constituting the world-order, and the formation of the heavenly bodies.
(3) The opposites interact or reunite, in meteoric phenomena and in the production of individual living things, plants and animals.

Note 6. In order to prove this point he proceeded as follows: He divided the views on this issue into two kinds: (1) theories which admit elemental transformation into each other like the Pythagorean (*De Gen. et Corr.* 334b 4 and 330b 13–19) theory and

Appendix

his own, and (2) views which deny transformation, like that of Empedocles (*De Gen. et Corr.* 315a 4–8; also Joachim's commentary p. 68, 1; 15a 4–8). This second view cannot explain the genesis of homogeneous organic substances except through a mechanical synthesis, which, according to Aristotle is totally unsatisfactory (*De Gen. et Corr.* 334a 20–30). A non-mechanical explanation would have to show that the organic substances are neither the original elemental constituents, nor a conglomeration of the elements, nor of the common underlying substratum of which they are ramifications. At this point he introduces potentiality and actuality and has his explanation resting on the following notions: (*a*) genesis (*De Gen. et Corr.*, Book A, ch. 10) of organic homogeneous substances is a different synthesis than that of the elemental transformation and (*b*) elemental mixture must be distinguished from generation and destruction, growth and decay, change or process, and mere mechanical mixture.

Mixture proper means that two distinct elemental bodies, i.e. fire, water, came together and through their mixture there results a single outcome where its properties differ from those of the constituents. The new properties are fused throughout the whole product, which finally must be capable of resolving itself into its original components by means of a process of separation (*De Gen. et Corr.* 327a 1; 328a 17). The elements are combinable, because there is a distinction between a complete and a relative status of the hot-cold, dry-moist contrarieties, and also there is a reciprocal interdependence of these contraries (*De Gen. et Corr.* 334b 8–24). Hence, the completely hot is potentially cold because its substratum is also that of the cold, and the substratum has within it the tendency to pass from one contrary to the other. The relatively hot is an intermediate which partakes both hot and cold; it is neither one completely, but it is both potentially. Now, this is how the homogeneous substances emerge from the elements (*De Gen. et Corr.* 334b 17–31):

'Thus all the other bodies will result from the contraries, or rather from the "elements," in so far as these have been "combined": while the elements will result from the contraries, in so far as these "exist potentially" in a special sense—not as matter "exists potentially" but in the sense explained above. . . . It is thus, then, that *in the first place* the "elements" are transformed and that (in the second place) out of the "elements" there come-to-be flesh and bones and the like—the hot becoming cold and the cold becoming hot when they have been brought to the "mean." For at the "mean" is neither hot nor cold. The "mean," however, is of considerable extent and not indivisible (i.e. not a point). Similarly, it is *qua* reduced to a "mean" condition that the dry and the moist, as well as the contraries we have used as examples, produce flesh, bone, and the remaining compounds.'

The Aristotelian view of the relation between simple bodies and organic homogeneous substances owes its merits as an explanatory hypothesis to the assumption that the simple elements are speculative abstractions, products of a careful analysis. Once these elements are granted *hypostasis* in connection with a given temporal point of reference, then the entire position collapses. However, the artificiality of the propounded theory is obvious; it was erected as the result of a rationalistic attempt to establish a theory capable of explaining the relation between elemental transformations and the origins of organic substances, and thus to provide the links between the first and the second synthesis. Still the entire theory of the elements is a mere abstraction and the contrarieties arbitrarily chosen.

The fact is that the early cosmology has now become stoichiology. There is no temporality attached to this stoichiology, and in this respect his position marks a serious advantage over the cosmic stoichiologies of his predecessors. It might appear to the modern student as a childish and artificial elaboration; nevertheless, in its origin it remains a qualitative chemistry grounded on observation. W. D. Ross (*Aristotle*, p. 127) observes that 'Aristotle has no theory of definite chemical affinities, still less any notion that elements can combine only in fixed proportions'.

It is essential to see that the bringing into the picture of the contrariety potentiality-actuality was done after and only after some elemental mixture was theoretically presented. Only a mixture of some kind is capable of admitting a qualitative contrariety. Once the qualitative contraries are assumed, then actuality-potentiality and action-passion can operate, because all the sufficient conditions are present, namely, the substratum capable of process. However, we must note, contrariety is inconsistently applied to the analysis of elements, because in fact no single element is a distinct substratum containing a contrariety such as hot-cold or moist-dry. If one of these contrary pairs was present

Appendix

in a single element, it would be impossible for the latter to be. Yet the contrary pairs hot-cold, dry-moist as such do not occur isolable from the elements. Therefore, it is impossible for the elements to be processes in the way other 'natures' are; again they are hardly analysable in terms of a substratum and a pair of contraries. These two points have sufficiently disclosed the artificiality of Aristotle's theory of elements as well as the inconsistent application of contraries as compared with that in his ontological analysis.

CHAPTER IV, *pages* 49–67

Note 1. Process of process, or change of change, or change of motion has meaning for Aristotle only in the sense of change in the subject's change. As he says:

'But naturally the *subject* of change may incidentally carry with him his change of one kind into a change of another kind that he enters into while the first change is going on; for instance, he may shift from the process of recollecting something and so arriving at knowledge to the process of forgetting it and so arriving at ignorance (*Phys.* 225b 30–3, Loeb translation).

The notion of change of change, or change of motion, is also found in modern science. Calculus as a branch of mathematics, which deals with variable quantities and their rates of change, was worked out to solve problems of change of motion. The phenomenon of acceleration, for example, is change of motion or change of a given velocity.

However, there is a fundamental difference between the Aristotelian conception of process of process and that of modern science. The difference is due to the fact that while both views accept an ultimate subject to which change refers this ultimate reality is not the same. The Aristotelian subject of change is always an individual substance which retains its identity (due to its essence) throughout the course of change. The Aristotelian substances were replaced in Newtonian science by properties and relations of substances conceived in terms of *time*, *space*, and *mass*, which, in the Aristotelian view, were accidental to substance. This is evident in Newton's second law:

'Change of motion (i.e. rate of change of momentum=ma)

Appendix

is proportional to the moving force impressed, and takes place in the direction of the straight line in which such force is impressed.'

Infinitesimal calculus, unknown to Aristotle, was developed in different forms by Newton and Leibniz to meet the problems raised by modern science's mathematical and mechanical conception of the 'subject' of change of change.

Note 2. There is no distinct type of process in respect of relation. If change is observed in relation it is always due to change in one of the *relata*. A given substance may remain unchanged and yet change in respect of relation because one of its correlatives happened to change. From the point of view of process, the category of relation is a negligible one. This seems to be the reason that Aristotle, when referring to change and process, gives only a partial list of categories; namely, only those in which process is possible. The secondary character of relation is not brought out in the *Categories*, perhaps because its author realized that he was not writing a work on the philosophy of nature, but on logic.

In *Met.* 1088a 27–35 Aristotle writes:

'A sign that the relative is least of all a substance and a real thing is the fact that it alone has no proper generation or destruction or movement, as in respect of quantity there is increase and diminution, in respect of quality alteration, in respect of place locomotion, in respect of substance simple generation and destruction. In respect of relation there is no proper change; for, without changing, a thing will now be greater and now less or equal, if that with which it is compared has changed in quantity.'

In *Cat.* 6b 15–20, however, Aristotle states:

'Relatives sometimes have contraries. Virtue is contrary to vice, either term itself being a relative; knowledge to ignorance also. By no means all relative terms can, however, be said to have contraries. "Double" and "triple" have none, nor, indeed, any terms of that sort' (Loeb translation).

The passage calls for interpretation. The relative contraries of vice and virtue are not *termini* of process or change. There are the contrary genera mentioned in *Cat.* 14a 20–5. The contrary genera of this type appear to be obtained through division by genera. *Pr. Anal.* I, ch. 31. Compare *Sophist*, 219A ff.; *Politicus*, 258B ff. See also notes 14, 15, page 55.

Appendix

E. Cassirer in connection with Aristotle's category of relation writes in *Substance and Function, and Einstein's Theory of Relativity* (Dover Publications, unabridged edition, 1953, pp. 8-9):

'Only in a fixed thing-like substratum, which must first be given, can the logical and grammatical varieties of being in general find their ground and real application. Quantity and quality, space and time determinations, do not exist in and for themselves, but merely as properties of absolute realities which exist by themselves. The category of relation especially is forced into a dependent and subordinate position by this fundamental metaphysical doctrine of Aristotle. Relation is not independent of the concept of real being; it can only add supplementary and external modifications to the latter, such as do not affect the real "nature". In this way the Aristotelian doctrine of the formation of the concept came to have a characteristic feature, which has remained in spite of all the manifold transformations it has undergone. The fundamental categorical relation of the thing to its properties remains henceforth the guiding point of view; while relational determinations are only considered in so far as they can be transformed, by some sort of mediation, into properties of a subject or of a plurality of subjects. This view is in evidence in the textbooks of formal logic in that relations or connections, as a rule, are considered among the "non-essential" properties of a concept, and thus as capable of being left out of its definition without fallacy. Here a methodological distinction of great significance appears. The two chief forms of logic, which are especially opposed to each other in the modern scientific development, are distinguished ... by the different value which is placed upon *thing-concepts* and *relation-concepts*.'

CHAPTER V, *pages* 68-83

Note 1. Anaxagoras, who systematically worked with cosmic qualitative contrarieties as the material cause of things, did not have an adequate number of premises, because it was impossible to produce everything from the contrarieties, and thus he had to make the efficient cause a separate and unique principle. One could give credit to Anaxagoras for his ingenious introduction of *nous*, but so far as consistency with regard to the contraries is concerned, he violated the rule by insisting on the aloofness of *nous*. Aristotle makes another remark. His predecessors used contrariety in such a way that none of them could satisfactorily

Appendix

account for the perpetuation of coming-to-be or genesis according to the demands of distributive being. Nor again, could they explain the nature of the cause of generation in a precise analysis that could account for the plurality of functions in a subject-in-process. Generation and its perpetuation as a recurring phenomenon could not be explained by the pre-Aristotelians without resorting to a third element or eliminating one of the contrary terms.

Note 2. Hamelin thinks that Aristotle formulated the theory of opposition in order to provide the foundations for a logic of attribution. He says (*Le Système D'Aristote*, p. 131):

'Pour fair voir que l'attribution n'est pas impossible, Aristote était donc forcé de determiner le sens de l'opposition contradictoire, et par suite il était même conduit a réflechir sur l'opposition en general. Voilà pour quelles raisons nous trouvons chez lui toute une theorie de l'opposition.'

This explanation is only partly true, for what might be called the main drive in Aristotle is the fundamental interest in demonstrating in theory and practice that the science of change and process is possible and valid. He answers the Eleatics and Heraclitus not as a dialectician or a visionary, but as a philosopher of process. The logical formulations, finally, are but parts of the *Organon*, and are instrumental to the cognizance of nature and being, i.e. process.

CHAPTER VI, *pages* 84–102

Note 1. The distinction between ἀριθμῷ ἕτεραι and ἀριθμῷ ἕν appears in *Met.* 999b 25 ff. It is found in connection with *aporia* 9, i.e. whether the principles are one in kind (εἴδει ἕν) or in number (ἀριθμῷ ἕν). Again, ἀριθμῷ ἕτεραι, meaning numerically different individuals within species, might be usefully contrasted with ἕτερα τῷ εἴδει which means (1) things whose proximate substratum is different, (2) things which belong to different categories of being. However, the two classes of things meant by 'different in species' are not analysable into one another or into some one thing (*Met.* 1024b 10–16). For a fuller discussion of the 'other' (ἕτερον), see *Top.* E 4. 133b 15; *Met.* 1018a 37 ff.; 1054b 14; 1058a 35, b. 15. For the numerically one individual see *Met.* 1052a

Appendix

31 and 999b 33, where it is said that 'There is no difference of meaning between numerically one and individual.' Also *Phys.* 228b 12-15, 'Sometimes we mean to imply by calling a thing "one" that it is complete in itself, whether we have the genus or the species or the individual in view.' The individual existent could be any *one* material thing, one plant, one man, one geometrical figure, one number. 'To be one is just to be a particular thing' (*Met.* 1054a 20). In order to avoid unnecessary perplexities in the development of the argument, we concentrated on the things that differ and are within contraries. Such things are (1) the substances in process, and (2) the particular processes within each substance as their locus.

Note 2. A perfectly static world with motionless constituents could not possibly give rise to difference. Anaximander's Boundless apart from the efficacy of the rarefaction and condensation forces remains undifferentiated. Even in a pluralistic stoichiology like that of Empedocles and of Anaxagoras, the elements taken in themselves would remain homogeneous and would give rise to no difference at all if it were not for the differentiating capacity of efficient principles. Empedocles introduced the *archai* of love and strife, while Anaxagoras restricted his principle to *nous*. The world, apart from the efficient principle which causes differentiation of the presupposed homogeneous 'stuff', whether monistically or pluralistically conceived, would literally remain a universe, but never be a cosmos. The efficient principle is the basis for explaining the rise of differences. One of the differences between Aristotle's position and that which most of the pre-Socratics take is that Aristotle did not want to explain away the notion of difference, but accepted it with the calmness of the pluralist whose purpose is not to reduce phenomena, but to understand them.

Note 3. In Plato's view, the singular cannot be known. One of Aristotle's main points in his philosophy was to establish the knowability of the unit of distributive being. This he did by making the universal (the one, i.e. the common form) present in the singular (the unit of distributive being).

In the *Philebus* (15B; 16C E) Plato restricted scientific knowledge to the ideas-forms. The forms are placed between the 'one' and the numerically many or infinite individuals. For Plato only ideas are definite things while the singulars (the many, the units of distributive being) are infinite or indefinite and hence are not objects of scientific knowledge (On *Ideas*, Fr. 182; 1509a 12–15).

Aristotle probably had in mind the views expressed in the *Philebus* when he attempted a reconstruction of the Platonic approach to the knowability of the singular. He did so by first reformulating the problem in the eighth *aporia* of *Met.* B in the light of the theory about equivocals. He states: 'For in so far as they (singulars) are something *one and the same* and in so far as something universal is present, do we come to know all things' (*Met.* B 999a 28–9).

The singulars, now the units of distributive being, are known by virtue of possessing universal traits and characteristics. Plato begins from the idea (the one and being) and embarks on the project of making it known as the *one and the same* and as manifested in the plurality of temporal things. Aristotle ascribes an altogether different content to the notion of *one and the same*, which he considers to be an equivocal term. In the back of his mind is the unit of distributive being which he is out to render knowable by means of the knowledge of the universals. His question is how the many singular units of distributive being can be known in the sense of *one and the same*. (See also *An. Pr.* II, 21, 67a 19–67b 12; *An. Post.* II, 19, 100a 6–8; *Top.* I, 17, 108a 14–17.)

This is the logical justification of the universal as the grounds for scientific knowledge, or the ground for knowledge of the singular. In any syllogistic process, the middle term is always a universal, otherwise demonstration is impossible. He states (*An. Post.* I, 77a 6–8): 'But it is true to say that there must be a "one of many"; and if there were no universal, there would be no middle term, and so no demonstration.' By 'one' now he means the universal concept present in the 'many' units of a given class of beings. (See also *Met.* A2, 994b 20–31.) This also tells us why there is more need for the 'major' premise to contain a universal (*An. Pr.* I, 31, 46a 39–46b 2). Knowledge is of the universal (*An. Post.* I, 18, 81b 6–7). Universals are perceived only *per accidens* (*Met.* M. 1087a 19–20). However, the universal is in the sensation (*De An.* III, 1, 425a 24–7; and *An. Post.* II, 19, 100a 17–100b 5). The theory of the inception of forms (universals) solves the enigma and explains how in terms of psychology scientific knowledge is possible.

Appendix

Note 4. Aristotle has stated careful distinctions of the various kinds of premises or *archai* necessary to the demonstration of truth.

A. *The axioms*, or *common principles*. These general axioms fall into two kinds.

(1) Those pervasive principles extended over all types of being, and here belong the principles of non-contradiction and of the excluded middle. (See *An. Post.* 71a 14; 77a 10–12, 30; 88b 1.)
(2) Here also belong certain generalities which are valid for whatever comes under a given genus of the categories. (See *An. Post.* 76a 41; 76b 20; *Met.* K 1061b 20; *Cat.* 6a 26.)

B. There are the *theses* or proper principles to particular sciences. The theses are subdivided into two types:

(1) Terminological principles or nominal definitions concerning the particular terms of a given science that correspond to the subject matter. (See *An. Post.* 76a 31–6.)
(2) The *hypotheses* of assumptions of the subject matter which correspond to the nominal definitions. (See *An. Post.* 76b 35–77a 4.)

While hypothesis is a necessary preliminary for knowledge in connection with a particular science, it is not a necessary preliminary to all knowledge, for we *know* the other principles. Any attempt to reduce all hypotheses to mathematics is a grave mistake. (See *Met.* M 1083b 6 ff. where he criticizes Plato, the Pythagoreans and Speusippus; also *Met.* N 1090a 16–65.) Metaphysics is a distinct science for it has a hypothesis or subject matter of its own: being *qua* being and its generic traits.

CHAPTER VII, *pages* 103–134

Note 1. The notion of the unity of the soul forms the basis for Aristotle's refutation of the theories that attribute motion to the soul. In the concluding paragraph of chapter 2 of Book I of the *De Anima* he states that 'thus practically all define the soul by three characteristics, motion, perception and incorporeality'. In the next chapter he proceeds to examine the soul and its relation to motion.

Appendix

'We have to consider in the first place the subject of motion. For, unless I am mistaken, the definition of soul as the self-moving, or as that which is capable of self-motion, misrepresents its essential nature: it is quite impossible for soul to have the attribute of motion at all. To begin with, it has been already stated that a thing may cause motion without necessarily being moved itself. A thing always moved in one of two ways; that is, either indirectly, through something else, or directly, of and through itself. We say things are moved through something else when they are in something else that is moved; as for instance, sailors on board a ship: for they do not move in the same sense as the ship, for the ship moves of itself, they because they are in something else which is moved. This is evident if we consider the members of the body: for the motion proper to the feet and so to men also is walking, but it is not attributable to our sailors in the case supposed. There being thus two senses in which the term 'to be moved' is used, we are now inquiring whether it is of and through itself that the soul is moved and partakes of motion' (*De Anima*, 405b 31–406a 12).

Aristotle discusses in the subsequent chapters, which are admirable examples of his analytical and critical ingenuity, the various theories of his predecessors arguing for the motion of the soul and brings out with remarkable thoroughness the difficulties these theories entail for a psychological approach to the phenomena of life. They are the difficulties inherent in ancient psychological dualism, which he rejects, because of the many contradictions to which the theories lead, in favour of his new psychophysical philosophy of organic life. Since the older theories attribute motion to the soul, Aristotle introduces boldly his own theory of motion and without any hesitation uses it as the criterion to judge the adequacy of these theories. And motion is of four kinds corresponding to the four categories of place, quality, quantity and substance. It follows then that the motion of the soul must be either of the four types. If so, then such motion must involve a contrariety, and by further implication the soul must be a process either in the sense of a subject-in-process or a process in a locus. In the first case the soul becomes both the body and the soul, an obvious absurdity, and in the second, it becomes identical with a faculty, which is equally false, because the outcome is less than what we started with at the beginning.

Aristotle was aware of such absurdities to which psychological dualism leads when seen through his system. But the problem here is not what theoretical problems emerge from holding a psychological dualism with the kind of philosophy of process he held. The discussion is directed only toward the relation between motion and soul in the views of his predecessors. With indirect motion he does not bother at all. The argument revolves around direct motion. Take, for example, the analysis of the motion of the soul with respect to motion in place. Such motion leads to crucial difficulties because they introduce problems regarding place and rest. For example, in what kind of space does the soul move? And if it rests, where does it rest? Then he points out correctly that such theories inevitably link the soul with a downward or upward movement. Once the new view of natural place is added to the movement of the soul, the soul's corporeality follows by necessity. No wonder then certain pre-Aristotelians identified the soul with some or all the elements. Democritus made the soul a kind of atom. Empedocles, partly because of his theory of perception, defined it as being composed of all the elements.

With consistency Aristotle brings out one by one the absurdities and theoretical shortcomings in the systems of his predecessors. And it must be noted that his analysis is concentrated with equal vigour on both the explanatory inadequacies and the discrepancies in the logic of the theories discussed in the *De Anima*. There is no need to reproduce here in detail the refutation of the theories. Suffice it to note only the key assumptions on which the refutation rests:

(a) The psycho-physical unity of the organism.
(b) The theory of the unity of the soul as the principle of the structural configuration of the organism.
(c) The theory of process and the four categorical contrarieties.

Note 2. Aristotle did not fix the number of faculties. His approach to the question of faculties differs essentially from Plato's. The latter based his view on the division of the soul into parts. There is the rational part which is immortal, and the irrational part made up of passion and appetite, which is mortal. The Pythagorean influences are obvious in this case. This Platonic division of the soul has become the foundation of the early Aristotelian work on ethics known as *Eudemian Ethics*. Even in the *Nicomachean Ethics* he still speaks of practical or moral virtues

Appendix

and 'intellectual' virtues (1102a 5–1103b2). For the definition of moral virtue, see 1105b 19–1107a 8; and for the distinction between practical wisdom and philosophic wisdom, see 1140a 24–1141a 20. Aristotle, the psychologist, oriented by his empirical and biological interests, was more interested in stating what he found rather than dividing the whole into expedient parts. The faculties are numerically indefinite, functionally united and distinguishable only in analysis.

'A question at once arises in what sense it is proper to speak of parts of the soul and how many they are. For in one sense they appear to be an infinite number of parts and not merely those which some distinguish, the reasoning, passionate and concupiscent parts, for which others substitute the rational and the irrational. For, if we examine the differences on which they base their divisions, we shall find that there are other parts separated by a greater distance than these; namely, the parts which we have just discussed, the nutritive, which belongs to plants as well as to animals, and the sensitive, which cannot easily be classed either as rational or irrational. Imagination, again, is logically distinct from them all, while it is difficult to say with which of the parts it is in fact identical or not identical, if we are to assume separate parts in the soul. Then besides these there is appetency, which would seem to be distinct both in concept and in capacity from all the foregoing. And surely it is absurd to split this up. For wish in the rational part corresponds to concupiscence and passion in the irrational. And, if we make a triple division of soul there will be appetency in all three parts' (*De Anima* 432a 22–432b 6; see also 433b 1–5).

The passage quoted is important not only for the bearing it has on Aristotle's empirical approach to the problem of the number of faculties but also because it points to two other notions which evidently prevent us from turning Aristotle into a faculty psychologist of the modern rationalist type. These notions are: (i) negatively, there are no pure faculties working independently of each other, like the separate parts of a machine all of which contribute to the accomplishment of the work; (ii) the faculties while distinguishable in discourse for the purposes of analysis and of guiding our conduct are unified by virtue of the 'oneness' of the soul and hence it is perhaps better to say that they function co-operatively and interpenetrate one another. This interpenetra-

Appendix

tion and interdependence makes possible the harmonious development of the organism, and in the case of man, the total fulfilment of his nature in the virtuous personality. It is true, however, that Aristotle has admitted the possibility of pure *nous*, which in a sense could be regarded as a faculty. The difficulty of *nous* is further complicated by the immortality attributed to this faculty. But this is a separate problem and need not be discussed here.

Aristotle did not seem to favour a fixed number of faculties. Depending upon the type of analysis and the particular point he wishes to emphasize in the discussion, we see that there are three possible ways of enumerating the faculties.

(a) In *De Anima* 414a 29-32, where the faculties are five in number: nutrition, appetency, sensation, locomotion, reasoning.
(b) In *De Anima* 413b 11-13, only four faculties are mentioned: nutrition, sensation, reasoning, and locomotion.
(c) In *De Anima* 415a 14-415b 7, the faculties are three: the nutritive, the sensitive, and the rational.

To put the matter briefly, (a) plants live and reproduce; (b) animals live, reproduce and have sensation. It must be observed that not all animals possess all of the senses, but all animals have the faculties of touch and taste. Only animals capable of locomotion possess in addition to touch and taste, the senses of smell, hearing, and sight. The additional faculties indicate that these animals are stimulated by a medium external to the body. *Distance*, therefore, seems to be the differentia that Aristotle is using here. Perhaps G. R. T. Ross has stretched his interpretation too far by insisting that ultimately there is no differentia at all. (See G. R. T. Ross, *De Sensu and de Memoria*, commentary, pp. 129-30, 1. 436b 20.) W. D. Ross, answers correctly the question of the number of faculties and why Aristotle actually reduces them to three:

'Desire is thus the cause of movement. But desire presupposes imagination of good or pleasure to be attained-imagination which may be calculative (i.e. deliberative) or merely sensitive. In the latter case the animal acts of the vague "imagination" as soon as it arises (and even the lowest animals have in this sense imagination and desire); in the former the imagined goods are measured against each other. There are three possibilities: (1) unreasoning

Appendix

action from appetite, (2) alternate victory over wish and of wish over appetite (i.e. incontinence), (3) action from the naturally higher desire, viz. wish. Desire, then, and bodily movement may be regarded as secondary effects of sensation. The four main faculties are thus reduced to three—nutrition, sensation, thought' (*Aristotle*, 146).

Note 3. When Aristotle is discussing psychology and biology he is interested primarily in the subject matter, not its evaluation in terms of a hierarchy of faculties. All types of soul are significant for the investigator. The question about the value of faculties and their place in a hierarchical stratification is misleading when raised in the context of psychology. Souls are 'principles' and do not compare with each other. When the problem of hierarchy of faculties makes its appearance it must be understood that we are abandoning psychology and are entering ethics. The human soul is more complex than that of a plant. One faculty cannot be judged against another when the faculties are taken from two different organisms. The value of individual faculties has its place only in the economy of a whole organism. To speak about 'higher' faculties is to make a value judgment. A value judgment in turn can be made only by a certain type of organic being possessing the power of rational reflection and capable of moral conduct. But now this is no more psychology than discussing the phenomena of life is a theory of elements. The term 'higher faculties' is misleading when used in the context of psychology. No doubt, such expressions appear in the *De Anima*, but they should be interpreted as ancillary to an ethical theory rather than as indispensable, ingredients of a philosophy of organism.

The opening sentences of the *De Anima* betray an attitude of preference and they point to an evaluation of faculties:

'Cognition is in our eyes a thing of beauty and worth, and this is true of one cognition more than another, either because it is exact or because it relates to more important and remarkable objects. On both these grounds we may with good reason claim a high place for the inquiry concerning the soul. It would seem, too, that an acquaintance with the subject contributes greatly to the whole domain of truth and, more particularly, to the study of nature, the soul being virtually the principle of all animal life.'

What is evaluated in this passage is not types of organisms, plants against animals or animals against rational animals, but

Appendix

kinds of knowledge, i.e. actualized outcomes and achievements of rational processes, and then these kinds of knowledge are classified in terms of their worth. Usually Aristotle moves 'upward' starting from sense perception, through memory and art to culminate finally with the supreme insights of the theoretical philosophies. (See also *Met.* A, ch. 1; *Anal. Post.* 99b 34–100a 9; also *Top.* VIII, 1, 157a 8; *Anal. Post.* 78b 34–79a 6.) The highest of all sciences is that of *first principles*, referred to as first philosophy and traditionally known as metaphysics; mathematics and physics follow. (See *Met.* 1025a 32; 1064b 1–6.) The criterion of 'highest' is not simply inclusiveness and universality but also 'firstness' in abstraction and ultimateness in presuppositions in the sense of comprising the widest set of generic traits of being. This science yields the 'highest' and best kind of wisdom. In *Met.* 983a 6, he says: 'The most divine science is also the most honourable.'

Not infrequently do we encounter examples of interpretations of Aristotle's thought which depart from the notion of higher faculties which then advance from this point a causal and teleological relation between different types of existents. This philosophical and often theological prejudice is evident in the following passage from W. A. Hammond's *Aristotle's Psychology*. He writes there:

'The lower functions exist teleologically for the higher. Man, consequently, is the apex of creation, because all forms of life terminate in him as the complete development of what is contained implicitly and imperfectly in the lower organisms' (p. xxi).

Upon reading this passage one wonders whether the author is writing about Aristotle or some other philosopher. To omit some serious objections one could easily advance against the use of certain terms such as 'creation', 'contained implicitly and imperfectly', there are two basic notions that must be mentioned here and which refute Hammond's interpretation based as it is on a misunderstanding of the meaning of 'faculties' in Aristotle's psychology. (*a*) Each organism exists for the sake of the fulfilment of its own form; throughout its span of life the unity of its soul remains intact, and hence it does not exist for a 'higher form' outside of it. (*b*) In man there is but one soul with many activities. This soul does not contain implicitly any lower souls which

Appendix

serve a higher one. Therefore, it is not correct to infer from the presence of the nutritive and sensitive faculties in man that all organic and inorganic existents exist for the sake of man's fulfilment of his rational soul. Here is another example of such 'bad' Aristotelianism.

'With it (i.e. the soul) ends the process upwards from lifeless ὕλη to ὕλη which now lives; and with it again begins another process upwards from *mere* life, as in vegetables, to the life which has ·intelligence (νοῦς) in its sublimest energy. That the body should live, organs are necessary. That further determination or development of soul should take place—that, for example, it should rise from its lowest grade such as plants exhibit to the next above it—that of sentiency which all animals exhibit—further organs are necessary' (Beare, J. I., *Greek Theories of Elementary Cognition*, Oxford, 1906, p. 222).

But to return to our problem concerning the notion of 'higher' faculties, the fact remains that these become higher for a given individual human being not because the psychologist has termed them so, but only after these faculties, as powers in operation, are actualized by virtue of the process which enables the first entelechy to reach its fulfilment. Broadly speaking, we witness here an education and fulfilment of certain special faculties, characteristic of man, which have been termed 'higher'. This education is a moral achievement and as such it is not so much a fact of psychology as it is a matter of ethics. In ethics it is called virtue and it is a precondition for the state of ethical conduct called happiness. It is not difficult, therefore, to see how teleological psychology has been so instrumental for the construction of an ethical theory of self-realization. Psychology lends to ethics, but this does not necessarily imply that ethics is derived from psychology. To imply such connection between the two disciplines is to misunderstand Aristotle both as a biologist and a moral philosopher. Ethics is an exclusively human enterprise, and though it presupposes knowledge of man's biological nature, it concerns him not *qua* organism but *qua* rational.

Note 4. Cherniss expresses this subject-environment interaction clearly in the following passage:

'Aristotle's own explanation of change represents it as the actualization in the substrate of the quality potentially present; this quality is the contrary of a quality actually present, these two

Appendix

qualities, as contraries, implying each other. Consequently, interaction from the point of view of actuality is the assimilation of dissimilars but from the point of view of potency the assimilation of similars; and Aristotle introduces these two sides of the theory as separate possibilities before combining them by means of his doctrine of potency-actuality into a single explanation' (*Aristotle's Criticism of Pre-Socratic Philosophy*, p. 358).

CHAPTER VIII, pages 135–169

Note 1. The notion of *mesotis* seems to be related to the Empedoclean theory of symmetry in sensation. According to Empedocles sensation is based on the principle that like acts upon like. Sensible objects 'radiate' particles which enter the sensing organ through the pores in the organism. This entering is possible only on the condition that a certain symmetry or commensurability exists between the particles received and the dimensions of the pore. In the case of vision, however, the eye also pours forth elemental stuff, i.e. water and fire. Due to this simultaneous pouring of particles there occurs a meeting of radiations which causes the phenomenon of vision. The objects are composed of four elements and so are the organs of sight. This explains why necessarily like senses like in Empedocles. The speculative aspects of this materialistic explanation of a psychological process were obvious to Aristotle, a fact that did not make Empedocles' theory better than the one propounded by the Atomists. See Diels, *Die Frag. Der Vors.* (Empedocles), A 84; also *De Gen. et Corr.* I, 8, 324b 25 sqq.

Note 2. It is doubtful whether a hierarchical stratification or an evolutionary approach to the senses could be adequately defended. Beare, for example, speaks of Aristotle's theory of 'evolution of the soul' and remarks that 'we seem to be led up by him to the parallel thought of an ascending scale within the sentient soul—a scale which reaches from touch at its lowest to sight at its highest extremity' (*Greek Theories of Elementary Cognition*, p. 230).

Obviously, Beare reads into Aristotle more than the text allows. The passage on which he bases his inference is found in *De An.* 435a 18. A close and careful reading of this passage hardly supports Beare's position, which he seems to rest on a conclusion drawn from the order in which Aristotle arranged the particular senses for purposes of presentation. Beare, in spite of his remarkable acquaintance with the primary sources of ancient philosophy, had confused Aristotle's analysis of the soul in its distributive setting with an anthropocentric interest which we find in the *De Anima* and other treatises, especially the ethical ones. Yet Beare's approach to the inter-relations of the senses is misleading and definitely not in agreement with Aristotle's scientific approach to questions of psychology.

It is possible to speak of an 'order' of the senses because of the way in which the inception of the form without matter occurs increasingly. This order would start from touch, proceed to taste, smell, hearing, and end with sight (*De An.* 429a 2). This order, however, is not followed in the exposition presented in the *De Sensu* where he begins with hearing, passes on to vision, taste, touch, and ends with smell. Touch precedes the other senses in the sense that it is universally present in all animal life, whereas the same cannot be said of the other senses (*De An.* 414a 2–4; 415a 3–6). Biologically, touch is more important than sight, and in this meaning, it is more fundamental, for without it the animal world would perish (*De An.* 434b 11–24; 435a 12–b19). Taste is not completely distinguishable from touch; because of what the other senses entail in terms of the cognitive development of man they are both biologically indispensable and ethically significant (*Part. An.* II, 656a 6 sqq. and *Top.* III, 118a, 7 sqq.). But in the last analysis so are the senses of touch and taste. In the *De Anima* he says that:

'Our sense of taste is more exact because it is a modification of touch and the sense of touch is the most exact of man's senses. In the other senses man is inferior to many of the animals, but in delicacy of touch he is far superior to the rest. And to this he owes his superior intelligence. This may be seen from the fact that it is this organ of sense and nothing else which makes all the difference in the human race between the natural endowments of man and man. For hard-skinned men are dull of intellect, while those who are soft-skinned are gifted' (421a 21–6, Hicks's translation. Compare *Part. An.* 660a 12 sqq.).

This contention is related to his belief that the heart is the seat of intelligence and thinking in general. Touch, then, and thinking are both seated in the heart. To what extent this coincidence affects the exactness of touch is not clear at all, but it may well

Appendix

serve as an explanation for his insistence on the superiority of touch in man; man alone has intelligence. While the animals have hearts, they do not possess higher intelligence. In other passages he admits that hearing is the most important sense for the development of intelligence, yet it is with sight that sensibility culminates. He remarks in the *De Sensu*:

'In animals with the power of locomotion, are found the senses which are mediated by something external, to wit, smell, hearing, and sight. These exist uniformly for the purpose of self-preservation of the animals possessing them, in order that they may become aware of food at a distance and go in pursuit of it and that they may avoid what is bad and injurious. Where intelligence is found they are designed to subserve the ends of well-being; they communicate to our minds many distinctions out of which develops in us the intelligent apprehension alike of the objects of thought and of the things of the practical life. Of these three sight is *per se* more valuable so far as the needs of life are concerned, but from the point of view of thought and accidentally, hearing is the most important. The characteristics are many and various which the faculty of sight reports, because all bodies are endowed with colour; thus by this sense especially are perceived the common sensibles (by these I mean figure, magnitude, motion, and number).

'But hearing gives merely differences in sound and, in a few cases, in articulate utterance too. Hearing, however, has the greatest share in the development of intelligence, though this is an accidental function. Speech being audible is instrumental in causing us to learn; but this function it possesses not *per se* but accidentally, for speech is a complex of words, every one of which is a conventional symbol. A consequence is that of those who from birth have been without one or other of those two senses, the blind are more intelligent than deaf-mutes' (436b 19–437a 19. G. T. R. Ross's translation).

The ethical considerations that loom in the background of this passage are easily suspected. Elsewhere he says that 'the moral value of visual pleasures exceeds the pleasures of touch' (*Nic. Ethics* 1076a 1). Sight is fundamental as a medium for the accumulation of knowledge and, as he informs us in *Met.* A 980a 21–b26, it is even desired for its own sake. To conclude, the hierarchical stratification of the senses is definitely not the result of his psychology; in so far as a hierarchy can be extracted, even an inconsistent

Appendix

one, it is primarily restricted to human psychology, and as such, it should be interpreted in the light of Aristotle's ethical concerns and not his comparative psychology and biology.

Note 3. The following quotation from Boring's recent historical work illustrates how the author has not been able to overcome the difficulties of an historian who failed to see the relation between Aristotle's treatises on special subjects and his philosophy of scientific method and metaphysics. It is apparent that he reads into Aristotle's discursive distinctions, meanings that are not genuinely Aristotelian but perhaps of some later Aristotelianism, medieval or other. Boring's vocabulary is surprisingly un-Aristotelian when he speaks of Aristotle.

'It was Aristotle who declared that the soul is unitary, thus influencing Descartes, making it difficult for Helmholtz to prove that the nervous impulse takes time for its transmission, supporting the holistic argument in the contest between elements and wholes which continued from William James to Gestalt psychology. It was Aristotle who declared that the soul is free, thus taking sides against philosophers and against the scientists who wished to tie the soul to the uniformities of nature. It was Aristotle who reinforced the basic dichotomy between form and matter which characterizes all materialistic thinking. Aristotle said that the mind is a tabula rasa, a blank tablet as yet unwritten on by experience, thus supporting the school of empiricism, which began with Hobbes and Locke. Aristotle laid down the basic principles of memory—similarity, contrast, and contiguity—which have not yet ceased to dominate theoretical thinking about learning. Aristotle said that there are five senses, one of them (touch) being more complex than the others, and that basic distinction is still with us, no matter how much the five may have to be subdivided. There have in the history of psychology been many nominations of a sixth sense, but none of a seventh, for no one ever accepted a sixth as good gospel. And then Aristotle said that the seat of the soul is in the heart, but in that he said something that seems nonsense to the modern. Galen's view that the brain is the organ of mind long prevailed against Aristotle, and nowadays of course we have enough evidence to know what we mean when we assert the mind is in the brain or that it is not.

'The shift within philosophy from Aristotelian dogma came along in the seventeenth century with the emergence of science, in the century of Kepler, Galileo and Newton. It began with Descartes' revolt against "the ancients" and his revision of the

Appendix

conception of the human mind as partly free and rational and partly mechanically automatic' (E. G. Boring, *A History of Experimental Psychology*, N.Y. Appleton-Century-Crofts, Inc., Second Edition, 1950, p. 159).

Note 4. With a factual sensation no error occurs. A sensation is, as it were, the given, the datum, the 'beginning' of experience. The first appearance of error happens with concurrent stimuli originating in the same object and causing the mind to be called upon to make inferences. To put the matter more concretely, error does not occur with the facts of experience but with the correlating, conjoining, discriminating, interpreting and deducing in experience. Error does not occur on two levels: (*a*) that of mere sensation (mere sensation is an abstraction from the total activity of sensation); (*b*) that of the most refined and fulfilled operations of our mentality, the practice of demonstrable science (*De An.* 428a 17). Error occurs in the activities and operations that lie between the facts of sensation and the perfect deductions of science. Error then is either imperfect judgment or hasty inference (*De An.* 425b 1–3). The faculty of common sense is held responsible for a great variety of errors especially when it operates in its combinatory and discriminative capacity. Memory and recollection are powers which can cause error because neither of the two has the immediacy and factuality of sensation (*De Mem.* 451a 10; 452b 27; 452b 5). Another source of error is the impact of emotions on judging and discriminating, regardless as to whether these operations involve sensations or images. Fears and desires misinterpret facts, i.e. make more than sensation warrants. That is why a man approaching me from the distance is taken to be the enemy I feared would attack me (*De Somniis* 450b 8), or to be my father whose arrival I have wished and expected. The same illusions also occur in cases of illness when organic disturbances or emotional disruptions interfere with the normal pattern of sensation; here illusory stimuli arise to cause sensations which would not occur if the cause of inner disturbance were absent. What would ideally eliminate error is of course the perfect functioning of our psychological powers; the proper combination and discrimination of sensations; the careful inferring of only what these sensations entail; the proper retention of images; the impeccable memory and accurate recollecting; the control of fears and strong emotions which when present in the subject

Appendix

should not be allowed to become part of sensibility and thus modify the act of judging; and finally, the smooth and unimpeded operations of the cognitive functions as they build inductively the universals and then reach inferences deductively through a masterful awareness of the syllogistic and according to a strict observance of the law of contradiction and excluded middle. Error for Aristotle is psychological. The accomplishment of its systematic elimination is an essential objective of, and a condition for, the good life.

Note 5. Roughness and smoothness, sharpness and bluntness, are not literally common sensibles, though they appear to be sensed by more than one sense. They are not *common* like unity, magnitude, movement, and rest. Perhaps they are in the final analysis qualities accidentally inceived by two different organs in a manner appropriate to the particular senses involved. Aristotle's solution to this problem is not clear.

Note 6. Mathematics studies quantity in two ways: (*a*) As *number*; numbers are discrete quantities viewed as units and they constitute the subject matter of arithmetic (*Cat.* 4b 20–3; *Met.* 1085b 15–22). (*b*) As magnitude; magnitudes are continuous because their parts have common boundaries, viz. solids, surfaces, and lines, and they constitute the subject matter of geometry (*Phys.* 227a 10–17).

It is important to remember that quantities considered in themselves do not admit of contraries, i.e. they do not admit of terms like 'more' or 'less' (*Cat.* 5b 11–6a 11). Furthermore, the use of terms like 'much', 'little', 'great', 'small', are not quantitative but relational. To be aware of the relational aspects of quantities implies that the faculty of common sense has functioned in two capacities: (*a*) of sensing common sensibles, and (*b*) of discriminating and comparing. The terms mentioned, therefore, are not contraries but 'terms of relation'.

'*As such*, things are not great or small. They are so by comparison only. Thus a hill is called small, a grain large; but we really mean greater or smaller than similar things of the kind, for we look to some external standard. If such terms were used absolutely, we never should call a hill small, as we never should call a grain large. So, again, we may very well say that a village has many inhabitants, a city like Athens but few, though the latter are many times more; or we say that a house contains many,

Appendix

while those in the theatre are few, though they greatly outnumber the others. While "two cubits", "three cubits long" and the like, therefore, signify quantity, "great", "small" and the like signify not a quantity but rather a relation, implying some external standard or something above and beyond them. The latter, then, plainly, are relative' (*Cat.* 5b 16–30, Loeb translation).

We may now turn to the ways in which quantities have 'being'.

Any mode of quantity depends upon the existence of subjects-in-process (*Cat.* 2a 34–b6). It is sensible bodies that possess both qualities and the other aspects given in common sense. For example, motion exists only as property of a subject-in-process and never by itself, which is also true of colour, weight, heat, etc. Similarly, lines, surfaces, and numbers are dependent upon and presuppose existing things; existing substances alone are separate (*Met.* 1069a 18–24; 1077b 4–9). Even if we call quantity, relation, quality, and the other categories 'being' in some sense, we must do so only in a secondary sense (*Met.* 1071a 7–27; 1027a 10–34).

What we call mathematical objects are actually the outcomes of abstraction. The axioms of mathematics treat quantities not *qua* separate entities or first substances but *qua* quantities which ultimately go back to the sensible objects. As H. G. Apostle writes:

'In this way the objects of mathematics are arrived at by abstraction. We take a substance, let us say a man, and in thought we disregard all that belongs to him *qua* living and rational; what remains is a physical body, still capable of being moved from one place to another, and in this it has much in common with other bodies, such as stones, chairs, and metals. Further, we remove in thought its principles of motion and along with them the sensible qualities, such as whiteness, heat, hardness, weight, and their contraries. What remains now is an immovable solid, continuous in three dimensions. This solid has length, width, depth, and also surfaces, lines, and points. We may remove in thought continuity itself, thus arriving at something which is indivisible, the unit' (*Aristotle's Philosophy of Mathematics*, p. 14). See also *Met.* 1026a 23–7; 1077b 15–1078a 9.

Note 7. There is nothing super-natural about Aristotle's god. His pure *nous* is free from the magic and mythology of religion. *Nous* is, from man's viewpoint, an ideal vision of perfect intelligibility. Yet, *nous*, from the scope of all nature, is the form of

Appendix

forms, the comprehensiveness of all structures and principles; it is nature at its best, formally perfected, and hence causing movement without needing to move; it is like the educator who moves the student towards him as the centre of attraction because of his serenity and wisdom. Aristotle's god is doubtless an ideal scientist. See also J. H. Dunham, *The Religion of Philosophers* (Univ. of Pennsylvania Press, Philadelphia, 1947), pp. 40–71.

CHAPTER IX, *pages* 170–199

Note 1. Aristotle, as it is evidenced through his later works, including his writings on biology, came to treat the notion of teleology in a way which shows again his gradual abandonment of the Platonic conception and use of the term. In spite of the fact that Book Lambda of the *Metaphysics* contains much of Platonic teleology, his scientific use of the concept points to the fact that teleology must be *distributively* and *pluralistically* understood. The initial universal purposiveness, the comprehensive design gave way to an ontology of specific purposes inherent in the subjects-in-process *qua* members of the species. Entelechy, then, distributively seen is another generic trait of being, a permeative ontological feature, and a universally useful explanatory principle of understanding. The critical analysis of this notion again as both a principle of understanding and a trait of being belongs to the science of metaphysics. G. Sarton in his *History of Science*, pp. 533–5, has an interesting discussion of Aristotle's teleology, but he makes a number of errors because of his failure to see that Aristotle as a scientific metaphysician saw teleology in its distributive sense.

If there is an inclusive meaning of teleology, it is so only with regard to human psychology, not to a cosmological theory. It is the new complexity of the human soul that gives teleology a new encompassing meaning. Human entelechy fulfilled as philosophic vision is the broadest encompassing view of the inter-relations of all natural processes. But it does not follow from this that there exists in nature an end of all ends and an entelechy of all specific entelechies, i.e. a principle of all principles! If man in his successful scientific moments accomplishes a theoretical system of purposiveness, it does not mean that individual entelechies are no longer concrete and independent as the formal ends of beings. The fact that an intellectual vision of order, of a totality of inter-related

Appendix

structures, is possible as a psychological event in man does not necessarily imply that there is a destiny of the universe as a whole. The universe is not proved to be an 'animal', an organic individual thing, and hence it has not a destiny as such. Providential plans and universal destinies might have a place in prophetic lyricisms and cosmological religions, but are no legitimate parts of scientific metaphysics.

To the extent that Thomas Aquinas was trying to establish an end of ends or purpose of purposes he was being not an Aristotelian but was working with a form of Platonism. Not only he failed to see the limits that distributive teleology placed before philosophical theory, but tried instead to prove his point by taking literally the analogy between organ and organism and projected it into the universe. Thomas made an illicit generalization based on analogical thinking: the organs are to the organism as the genera are to the mind of God; the specific teleologies are purposively related to the inclusive design or *telos* of the universe. The Thomistic emphasis on end of ends is one of value rather than of fact; and the ontology which it presupposed is a Neoplatonic conception of the hierarchy of being, which, in spite of its appeal to certain ways of thinking, produces no scientifically acceptable evidence in its favour. See also S. Lamprecht, *Our Philosophical Traditions* (p. 182), especially the chapter entitled 'The Thomistic Synthesis'.

BIBLIOGRAPHY

I. TEXTS, TRANSLATIONS, AND COMMENTARIES

BEKKER, IMMANUEL (ed.). *Aristotelis Opera.* Vols. I–V. Berlin: Reimer, 1831–70.

BONITZ, HERMANN. *Index Aristotelicus.* Berlin: Reimer, 1870. (In Prussian Academy *Aristotelis Opera,* v. V.)

BURNET, I. (ed.). *Platonis Opera.* 5 vols. Oxford: Clarendon Press, 1941.

Commentaria in Aristotelem Graeca. 23 vols. Berlin: Reimer, 1882–1909. With Supplementum Aristotelicum (3 vols.) 1882–1903.

CORNFORD, FRANCIS MACDONALD. *Plato's Theory of Knowledge.* The *Theaetetus* and the *Sophist* of Plato translated with a running commentary. London (Kegan Paul, Trench, Trubner & Co.) and New York: Harcourt, Brace & Co., 1935.

Γεωργούλης, Κ. Δ. *'Αριστοτέλους Πρώτη Φιλοσοφία.* Introduction and Translation. Thessalonika: Alexios K. Pikopoulos, 1935.

DIELS, HERMANN (ed.). *Die Fragmente der Vorsokratiker, Griechisch und Deutsch.* 5th ed., Walther Kranz. 3 vols. Berlin: Weidmann, 1934–7.

—— *Elementum,* eine vorarbeit zum griechischen und lateinischen thesaurus. Leipzig, druch von Teubner, 1889.

DIOGENES LAERTIUS. *Lives of Eminent Philosophers.* With an English Translation by R. D. Hicks (in the Loeb Classical Library). London (Heinemann) and New York: Putnam, 1925.

HAMMOND, W. A. (ed.). *Aristotle's Psychology.* London and New York: 1902.

HETT, W. S. *Aristotle, on the Soul, Parva Naturalia, on Breath.* (In the Loeb Classical Library.) Cambridge: Harvard University Press, 1935.

HICKS, R. D. *De Anima.* Introduction, Text and Commentary. Cambridge: University Press, 1907.

JOACHIM, H. H. *Aristotle: The Nicomachean Ethics.* A Commentary. Oxford: Clarendon Press, 1951.

—— *De Generatione et Corruptione,* a revised Text with Introduction and Commentary. Oxford: Clarendon Press, 1922.

JOWETT, B. *The Dialogues of Plato.* Translated into English with an Introduction by Raphael Demos. 2 vols. New York: Random House, 1937.

MCKEON, RICHARD (ed.). *The Basic Works of Aristotle.* New York: Random House, 1941.

—— *Introduction to Aristotle.* Modern Library. New York: Random House, 1947.

ROSE, VALENTINUS (ed.). *Aristotelis Fragmenta.* Leipzig, 1886.

Bibliography

Ross, G. R. T. (ed.). *Aristotle, de Sensu and de Memoria.* Text, Translation, and Commentary. Cambridge: 1906.

Ross, William David. *Aristotle.* Introduction and Selections. New York: Charles Scribner's Sons, 1938.

—— *Aristotle's Metaphysics.* A revised Text with Introduction and Commentary. 2 vols. Oxford: Clarendon Press, 1924.

—— *Aristotle's Physics.* A revised Text with Introduction and Commentary. Oxford: Clarendon Press, 1936.

—— *Aristotle's Prior and Posterior Analytics.* A revised Text with Introduction and Commentary. Oxford: Clarendon Press, 1949.

Ross, W. D., and Smith, J. A. (ed.). *The Works of Aristotle.* 11 vols. Oxford: Clarendon Press, 1908-31.

Schwegler, Albert. *Die Metaphysik des Aristoteles.* Grundtext, Ubersetzung und Commentar, nebst erlaüternden Abhandlungen. 4 vols. Tübingen: L. F. Fues, 1847-8.

Stewart, J. A. *Notes on the Nicomachean Ethics of Aristotle.* 2 vols. Oxford: Clarendon Press, 1892.

Theophrastus. *Metaphysics.* With Translation, Commentary and Introduction by W. D. Ross and F. H. Fobes. Oxford: Clarendon Press, 1929.

Tredennick, Hugh. *The Organon.* (In the Loeb Classical Library.) Cambridge: Harvard University Press, 1949.

Welldon, J. E. C. *The Nicomachean Ethics of Aristotle.* Translated with an analysis and critical notes. London: Macmillan, 1930.

Wheelwright, Phillip. *Aristotle.* (Introduction and Selections.) New York: Odyssey Press, 1951.

Wicksteed, P. H., and Cornford, F. M. *Aristotle, The Physics.* (In the Loeb Classical Library.) 2 vols. Cambridge: Harvard University Press, vol. I, 1929, vol. II, 1935.

II. GENERAL

Adamson, R. *The Development of Greek Philosophy.* Edited by W. R. Sorley and R. P. Hardie. Edinburgh, 1908.

Alexander, H. G. 'Language and Hypostatization.' *Proceedings of the XIth International Congress of Philosophy.* Vol. V. August 1953. Pp. 185-90.

Allan, D. J. *The Philosophy of Aristotle.* London: Oxford University Press, 1952.

Apostle, H. G. *Aristotle's Philosophy of Mathematics.* Chicago: The University of Chicago Press, 1952.

Armstrong, A. H. *An Introduction to Ancient Philosophy.* London: Methuen, 1947.

Beare, J. I. *Greek Theories of Elementary Cognition.* Oxford: Clarendon Press, 1906.

Boring, E. G. *A History of Experimental Psychology.* (2nd edition.) New York: Appleton-Century-Crofts, 1950.

Burnet, John. *Greek Philosophy, Thales to Plato.* London: Macmillan, 1932.

Carteron, H. *La Notion de Force dans le Système d'Aristote.* Paris: Librairie Philosophique, J. Vrin, 1923.

Bibliography

CASSIRER, E. *Substance and Function, and Einstein's Theory of Relativity*. Unabridged Edition. New York: Dover Publications, Inc., 1953.

CHERNISS, H. *Aristotle's Criticism of Plato and the Academy*. Baltimore: Johns Hopkins Press, 1944.

—— *Aristotle's Criticism of Pre-Socratic Philosophy*. Baltimore. Johns Hopkins Press, 1935.

—— *The Riddle of the Early Academy*. Berkeley and Los Angeles: University of California Press, 1945.

CHRIST, WILHELM VON. *Studia in Aristotelis Libros Metaphysicos*. Berlin: G. Bethge, 1853.

COLLINGWOOD, ROBIN GEORGE. *The Idea of Nature*. Oxford: Clarendon Press, 1944.

CORNFORD, FRANCIS MACDONALD. *From Religion to Philosophy*. London: E. Arnold, 1912.

—— *Principium Sapientiae*. The Origins of Greek Philosophical Thought. Cambridge: University Press, 1952.

—— *The Unwritten Philosophy and other Essays*. Edited with an introductory memoir by W. K. C. Guthrie. Cambridge: University Press, 1950.

DEMOS, RAPHAEL. 'The Structure of Substance according to Aristotle', *Philosophy and Phenomenological Research*, V (1944–5), 255–68.

DEWEY, JOHN. *Logic, The Theory of Inquiry*. New York: Henry Holt & Co., 1949.

—— *The Quest for Certainty*. London: Allen and Unwin, 1929.

—— *Reconstruction in Philosophy*. Mentor Books, 1950.

DUNHAM, J. H. *The Religion of Philosophers*. Philadelphia: University of Pennsylvania Press, 1947.

DURANT, WILL. *The Story of Philosophy*. Chapter 2, 'Aristotle and Greek Science', pp. 41–75. Garden City: Garden City Publishing Co., 1943.

EDEL, ABRAHAM. *Aristotle's Theory of the Infinite*. New York: n.p., 1934.

FREEMAN, KATHLEEN. *The Pre-Socratic Philosophers. A Companion to Diels' Fragmente*. Oxford: Blackwell, 1946.

FULLER, B. A. G. *A History of Philosophy*. Revised edition. New York: Henry Holt & Co., 1945.

GOMPERZ, THEODOR. *Greek Thinkers*. Authorized Edition. 4 vols. Translated by G. G. Berry. New York: Charles Scribner's Sons, 1912.

GROTE, GEORGE. *Aristotle*. Edited by A. Bain and G. Robertson. Third Edition. London: John Murray, 1883.

HAMELIN, OCTAVE. *Le Système d'Aristote*. Paris: Librairie Felix Alcan, 1920.

HANTZ, HAROLD D. *The Biological Motivation in Aristotle*. New York: privately printed, 1939.

'Ισηγόνη, A. M. 'Η Τελολογικὴ κατ' 'Αριστοτέλη 'Εκδοχὴ τοῦ Ψυχικοῦ Βίου. (Doctoral Thesis: University of Athens.) Rhodos: n.p., 1951.

JAEGER, WERNER W. *Aristotle:* Fundamentals of the History of his Development. Translated by Richard Robinson. Second Edition. Oxford: Clarendon Press, 1948.

—— 'The Pre-Socratic Philosophers as Founders of Philosophical Theology', *Library of the Xth International Congress of Philosophy* (Amsterdam: North-Holland Publishing Co., 1949), I, pp. 1069–71.

Bibliography

JAEGER, WERNER W. *Studien zur Entstehungageschichte der Metaphysik des Aristoteles.* Berlin: Weidmann, 1912.

—— *The Theology of the Early Greek Philosophers.* Oxford: Clarendon Press, 1948.

JOHNSON, EDITH HENRY. *The Argument of Aristotle's Metaphysics.* New York: Lemcke and Buechner, 1906.

KAPP, ERNST. *Greek Foundations of Traditional Logic.* New York: Columbia University Press, 1942.

LAMPRECHT, STERLING P. 'Metaphysics: its Function, Consequences and Criterion', *The Journal of Philosophy.* Vol. XLIII, No. 15, July 18, 1946.

—— *Our Philosophical Traditions.* New York: Appleton-Century-Crofts, 1955.

MILL, J. S. *A System of Logic.* (New Impression, 1949.) New York: Longmans, Green and Co., 1949.

MOODY, ERNEST A. *The Logic of William of Ockham.* London: Sheed & Ward, 1935.

MURE, GEOFFREY R. G. *Aristotle.* London: E. Benn, 1932.

NATORP, PAUL. *Platons Ideenlehre.* Eine Einführung in den Idealismus. Leipzig: Durr, 1903.

—— 'Thema und Disposition der Aristotelischen Metaphysik', *Philosophische Monatshefte*, XXIV (1888). Pp. 37–65.

NUYENS, F. *L'Evolution de la psychologie d'Aristote.* (French translation.) Paris: Louvain, 1948.

OWENS, JOSEPH C. Sc. R. *The Doctrine of Being in the Aristotelian Metaphysics.* With a preface by Etienne Gilson. Toronto, Canada: Pontifical Institute of Medieval Studies, 1951.

Παπανούτσος, 'Ε. Π. Γνωσιολογία. Athens, Greece: Ikaros, 1954.

RANDALL, JOHN HERMAN, Junr. 'Dewey's Interpretation of the History of Philosophy', *The Philosophy of John Dewey.* The Library of Living Philosophers. Edited by A. Schilpp. New York: Tudor Publishing Co., 1951. Pp. 75–102.

—— 'Metaphysics: Its Function, Consequences, and Criterion', *The Journal of Philosophy.* Vol. XLIII, No. 15, July 18, 1946.

ROBIN, LEON. *Greek Thought and the Origins of the Scientific Spirit.* London, New York: A. Knopf, 1928.

ROSS, WILLIAM DAVID. *Aristotle.* Fifth edition, revised. London: Methuen, 1949.

SANTAYANA, GEORGE. *Dialogues in Limbo.* Chapter 10, 'The Secret of Aristotle'. New York: Charles Scribner's Sons, 1925.

SARTON, GEORGE. *A History of Science.* Cambridge: Harvard University Press, 1952.

—— *Introduction to the History of Science* (3 vols. in 5). Baltimore: Williams and Wilkins, 1927–48.

SHUTE, C. W. *The Psychology of Aristotle.* New York: Columbia University Press, 1941.

SHUTE, RICHARD. *On the History of the Process by which the Aristotelian Writings arrived at their Present Form.* Oxford: Clarendon Press, 1888.

SOLMSEN, FRIEDRICH. *Die Entwicklung der Aristotelischen Logik und Rhetorik.* Berlin: Weidmann, 1929.

Bibliography

SPICER, E. E. *Aristotle's Conception of the Soul*. London: University of London Press, 1934.

STOCKS, JOHN LEOFRIC. *Aristotelianism*. Boston: Marshall Jones Company, 1925.

TAYLOR, ALFRED EDWARD. *Aristotle*. London (T. C. & E. C. Jack) and New York: Dodge Publishing Co., 1912; 2nd ed., 1919. Pp. 1-91.

—— *Aristotle on his Predecessors*. Chicago: Open Court Publishing Co., 1910.

TRENDELENBURG, A. *Geschichte der Kategorienlehre*. (Historische Beiträge zur Philosophie) Erster Band. Berlin, 1846.

Veatch, Henry. 'Aristotelianism', *A History of Philosophical Systems*. Edited by V. Ferm. New York: Philosophical Library, 1950. Pp. 106-17.

WALLACE, EDWIN. *Outlines of the Philosophy of Aristotle*. London: Clay, 1883.

WINDELBAND, W. *A History of Philosophy*. (Translated by J. H. Tufts.) New York: The Macmillan Co., 1901.

ZELLER, EDUARD. *Aristotle and the Earlier Peripatetics*. 2 vols. Translated by B. F. C. Costelloe and J. H. Muirhead. London: Longmans, Green & Co., 1897.

—— ' "Bericht", on Natorp's Thema und Disposition der Aristotelischen Metaphysik', *Archiv für Geschichte der Philosophie*, II, 1889. Pp. 264-71.

INDEX I

Actualization, 20, 21, 25, 29, 46, 57, 58, 66, 70, 74, 80-1, 83, 115, 116, 117, 120, 125-6, 131, 138, 147, 159, 163, 169, 178, 182, 184, 197, 232-3
Affirmation-negation, 59, 88, 91, 95-7, 99
Appetence, 170, 180-5, 187, 190-1, 227-30

Becoming, 51-2, 63, 73-4, 80. See also Actualization, Change, Elements, Process
Being:
    distributive, 10, 11, 14, 15, 19, 21, 22, 25, 26, 27, 41, 46, 60, 61, 71, 73, 101, 105, 118, 134, 156, 209, 211, 221, 224
    as a whole, 10, 40-1, 46, 241
    generic traits of, 17, 64, 99, 101, 104, 151, 167, 201, 231
    eternal, absolute, 17, 18, 20-2, 36, 41, 78, 83
    levels of, 19, 22-3, 114n.
    See also Metaphysics, Substance, Process, Subject-in-process

Categories, 49, 51, 60, 61-7, 71, 73, 76, 86, 90, 135, 156-63, 212, 220-1, 222, 224, 226, 239
    do not constitute contraries, 86, 97
    See also Substance, Quality, Quantity, Place, Categorical contrarieties
Cause, 20, 21, 22, 26, 37, 45, 60, 75, 77, 116, 118

Change, 10n, 27, 38, 40, 42, 49-50, 51, 52-4, 56, 58, 61, 86, 94, 116, 122-3
    interelemental, 16, 42-8, 110, 122, 216-19
    substantial, 12, 13, 16, 18, 46, 51, 53, 94n., 162, 206-7
    qualitative, 12, 14, 23, 26, 51, 53, 66-7, 111, 113, 119, 122, 125, 127, 138, 152, 162, 207
    quantitative, 12, 14, 51, 53, 64-5, 122, 162, 207
    locomotive, 12, 14, 23, 51, 53, 65, 112, 119, 146, 207, 227
    and relatives, 56, 220-1. See also Process
Choice, 20, 22, 191, 194, 196-7
Contradiction, 40, 51, 53, 80, 87-90, 96, 99-102, 110, 165, 224, 238
Contrariety:
    in pre-Aristotelian thinkers, 5-7, 34, 35-48, 64n.
    Aristotle's reconstruction of, 8, 15-16, 25, 32-35, 42, 45, 47-8, 69-70
    meanings of, 12-13, 32-4, 37, 46, 47, 86, 100, 129n.
    and difference, 85 ff., 151
    in discourse, 13, 25, 45, 59, 76, 96, 100 ff., 111
    in cosmology, 14, 27-8, 30, 34, 37-42, 69, 216-19, 221
    and elements, 15-16, 27, 37-48, 133
    error in Aristotle's theory of, 45-8, 218
    studied by metaphysics, 13n., 17, 19-22, 28-30, 45, 69, 71, 99

247

Index I

Contrariety (*contd.*):
  a principle in process, 6, 13, 16, 25, 46, 58, 75, 77, 86, 89, 109, 211–13
  and being, 13, 36, 46, 47, 48–9, 69–72, 76, 82, 99–100, 118, 211–13
  a principle of intelligibility, 9, 13, 18, 29, 35, 36, 42, 45–6, 47, 58, 62, 69, 70, 96, 99–101, 112, 136, 140, 195
  metaphysical or primary, 7, 11, 12–13, 14, 29–30, 33–4, 55–6, 63, 69–83, 88–9, 100, 118, 120, 133, 163, 194–5, 212, 213. See also possession-privation, potentiality-actuality
  categorical, 8, 14, 46, 49, 61–7, 71, 90, 97, 118, 212, 227
  excluded from eternal motion, 17, 65, 83
  in psychological processes. See Soul
  in conduct. See Ethics, Mean, Mesotis
Contraries:
  defined, 32–3, 55–8, 70, 80, 87, 91–3
  theory of, 49–55, 63, 87, 90–1, 156
  as principles, 8, 13, 15, 33, 34, 38–9, 42, 45, 47, 55, 58, 62n., 64, 69, 72, 75–7, 118, 125, 128
  termini of process, 8, 13, 14, 25, 45, 51, 57, 61, 87, 92, 116, 122, 129
  not co-existing, 8, 70, 72, 76, 80, 92, 93–4, 96, 111n.
  in discourse, 8, 13, 25, 57, 76, 80, 95–6
  neither true, nor false, 95
  in elements and being, 46–8, 55n., 56, 64, 65, 122. See also Elements, Substance, Process
  in genus, 55–6, 86, 89, 94, 220. See also Ethics and Mesotis
  specific, 12, 13, 28, 86, 92, 101, 110, 112, 194
  derivative, 57–8
  and intermediates, 89, 90, 92–3, 94, 96, 97n., 145. See also Contrariety
Cosmology, 15–16, 25–7, 33–5, 37–42, 64, 112, 132n., 171–4, 210, 213, 216, 223

Dialectic, 35–7, 214–16
Difference, 28, 30, 42, 57, 83–7, 90, 93, 128n., 140, 151–2, 186, 212–13, 222–3
Dry-moist, 43, 110, 122, 142, 216–17

Education, 184, 232
Elements:
  theory of, 14–16, 22–3, 24, 26, 34–5, 37–48, 79, 105, 131, 142, 216–19
  and qualitative chemistry, 109, 110, 218
  and psychology, 110, 122 ff., 131, 141, 155, 223, 227
Error, 237–8
Ethics, 93, 170–99, 232
Excellence, 116, 163, 168, 170, 179–180, 188, 191. See also Virtue
Excess-defect, 187–9, 192

Form, 11–12, 13, 22, 24, 59, 63, 65, 74–6, 78, 80, 83, 89, 98–9, 163, 197, 214, 223–4, 240
  and soul, 104, 115, 116–17, 119, 125, 127, 231
  inception of, 126–34, 136–7, 138, 156 ff., 184, 186, 224, 234
  as ratio, 129–30, 136n., 138–40, 141–9, 151, 162, 163, 165, 186
  form-matter, 26, 75, 107, 120, 200
Form-privation. See Metaphysical contrariety

Generation-destruction, 10, 12, 14, 16, 38–9, 42, 44, 50–1, 54, 63, 66n., 81, 103, 113, 115, 118, 162, 206–7, 216, 220
  absolute, 51, 54
  See also Substance, Process, Change
Genus, 55–6, 57, 58, 61n., 82, 85–7, 89, 90, 94, 101, 121, 215, 220

248

Index I

God, 6, 20, 24, 83, 167–8, 239–41
Good, 177, 178–80, 183, 184–5, 187, 189–90, 191–3, 196, 197–9
Growth-decay, 23, 38, 51, 65, 113–14, 115, 119, 120–1, 216. See also Generation-destruction, Quantity, Change.

Happiness, 171, 177, 170–80, 185, 186, 187n., 188n., 197–9, 235, 238
Hot-cold, 34, 43–4, 61, 110, 122, 142, 216–17

Identity, 118, 124, 151–3
Immortality, 6, 7, 167
Intelligence, 110, 116, 119, 120–1, 135, 137, 138, 140, 163–9, 170, 172, 177, 178, 180–5, 190–3, 195–6, 235
   practical, 181, 182, 189, 191, 194, 196–7
   See also Nous
Intelligibility, 25, 29, 32, 36, 42, 59, 70, 110, 112, 127, 128, 132n., 140, 167, 193–9, 201, 212, 239

Judgment:
   in cognition, 127, 129, 137n., 140, 150–1, 153 ff., 159–61, 186, 237–8
   in conduct, 185, 187, 190, 192
Justice, 187–8
Justice-injustice, 55n., 74, 179

Knowledge, 60, 71, 81, 83, 85, 98–102, 105, 110, 125–6, 130–4, 155, 161n., 164 ff., 175, 183–4, 196, 220, 223–4, 225, 231, 237
   range of, 129, 130n., 133, 135, 142n., 150, 165–6

Language, 85, 96, 97–100, 109n., 110, 157, 235
Life, 114, 115, 118, 121 ff.
Life-death, 7, 109
Logos, 42, 70, 80, 82, 99, 109n., 128, 130n., 140, 153, 158, 167, 170, 175–6, 185, 190, 191, 196

Mathematics, 20–2, 27, 30, 82, 98, 137n., 160, 176, 211, 219, 225, 231, 238–9
Matter, 11, 20, 22, 26, 27, 41, 63, 65, 75, 79–81, 114, 137, 232
   types of, 20, 81–3, 111n., 115, 184
   and elements, 15–16, 23–4, 37–42
   primary, 79, 127
Mean, 47, 129, 187, 189, 192, 218
Mesotis:
   in sensation, 130, 135, 139, 141 ff., 153, 156, 160, 182, 185–6, 233
   in conduct, 170, 185–93, 194 ff.
Metaphysics or First Philosophy, 16–18, 19, 22, 25, 26, 28–30, 42, 68, 69–70, 73n., 99, 101–2, 104–5, 208–9, 210, 225, 231, 240–1
Mixture, 23, 39, 43, 48, 216–19
Movement, 10, 55, 206–7
   linear, 11, 17, 22, 47, 52–3, 58, 62, 83, 95
   eternal, 10, 17–18, 20, 37, 45, 46, 53, 65, 240
   and contrariety, 23, 58, 65–6
   and soul, 111, 112–13, 117–19, 164, 180–3, 226–7
Movement-rest, 22, 33, 38, 53, 112, 154, 159, 214, 238

Nature, 22, 46, 58, 113, 121, 210–11, 222
   as internal principle, 25, 28, 59, 63, 65, 74, 78, 113, 210–11
   and levels of being, 22 ff., 105, 114n., 167–8
   and human nature, 110, 128n., 171–2, 176–7
   See also Process, Substance, Change
Nous, 17, 20–1, 39, 66n., 106, 128n., 132n., 136, 142n., 163, 165–9, 175, 194–5, 197–9, 201–2, 221, 223, 229, 231, 239

One, 28, 29, 33, 39–41, 42, 43, 63, 70, 153, 160n., 213, 222–4

249

Index I

One-many, 28, 33, 38–9, 128n., 151–2, 153, 213
Opposites, 7, 28, 50, 53, 56, 73–4, 95, 111
Opposition:
　theory of, 84–102, 207–8, 222
　types of, 91, 93–5, 99, 119
Organism, 22–5, 26, 77, 104, 106, 111–14, 118, 121, 125, 136, 138, 158, 168, 177, 227, 230
Otherness, 57, 90, 128, 131, 222–3

Perception. See Soul
Permanence, 54
Physics, 20–2, 29–30, 111, 231
Physiology of senses, 110, 128 ff., 131n., 141, 149, 158
Place, 10, 14, 23, 45, 49, 51, 61, 65–6, 118, 157–9, 221
Pleasure-pain, 6, 143, 180, 184, 188, 235. See also Appetence
Possession, 59, 88–90, 91, 93. See also Metaphysical contrariety, Privation.
Potentiality-actuality, 14, 48, 58, 65, 76, 77–8, 83, 119, 125, 133, 139, 148, 163, 166, 198, 205, 218, 232–3
Principle, 13, 22, 26, 32, 42, 64, 70–1, 75, 83, 100–2, 105, 126, 164, 168, 184, 195, 196–7, 212, 225, 230–1, 240
Prior-posterior, 49, 58–61
Privation, 13, 45, 55n., 57, 67, 74–6, 79–81, 87–90, 93–5, 111n. See also Metaphysical contrariety
Process, 10–1, 25, 28–9, 33, 42, 51, 52–5, 56, 59, 62, 65, 69, 83, 94, 99, 110, 112, 114, 116, 118, 120, 125, 127, 137, 158–9, 166, 178, 180, 183, 186, 194, 199, 206–7, 210, 219–20, 222, 225
　types of, 10, 12, 22, 25, 37, 45–6, 49, 51, 53–5, 99, 110–11, 113, 127, 165
　and contraries, 8, 13, 25, 36, 45, 51, 53, 58, 66, 89, 92, 100, 112, 139

Process, psychological, 110, 112, 135, 138–9, 180
　See also Substance, Change, Movement, Nature, Telos
Psychology, 103–10, 124, 129, 136, 171, 177–8, 194, 232

Quality, 10, 14, 26, 49, 51, 61, 66–7, 157, 159, 221, 239
　and sensation, 126n., 127, 128n., 129, 133, 140, 141 ff.
Quantity, 10, 14, 49, 61, 64–5, 127, 157, 160, 221, 238

Relation, 36, 51, 61, 127, 158, 160–2, 220–1, 238–9
　and correlatives, 91, 99, 126n., 137, 161

Sameness, 36–7, 216, 224
Self-realization, 171, 178 ff., 197 ff., 232
Similarity, 85, 93
Soul, 23, 74, 104–34, 136 ff., 178 ff., 225–7, 231–2
　Aristotle's reconstruction of, 107–112, 115, 131–2, 226–7, 233
　as actuality, 115, 116, 119, 132n., 135–6, 139, 164, 177–8, 180, 186, 191, 194, 240–1
　types of, 115, 118, 120
　not contrary to body, 111, 118
　and contrariety, 110, 112, 115, 118, 120, 125, 127, 133, 139, 140–50, 164, 177, 181n., 184, 226
　powers of, 110, 112n., 115–6, 117n., 120, 124, 126, 136, 137n., 138, 151, 165, 167, 181, 190, 193, 228–9, 237
　processes of, 112, 118, 133, 137, 163, 183, 186, 232
　nutritive, 110, 113, 120–4, 140n., 143
　sensitive, 124–34, 136–69, 180–1, 183–4, 186
　particular senses, 136–40, 234 ff.
　touch, 141–3
　taste, 143–4

250

Index I

Soul, smell, 144–5
  hearing, 136, 145 ff.
  sight, 92–3, 94, 127, 147–50
  common sense, 150–6, 160, 163, 235, 237
  hierarchy of souls, 121n., 140n.
  hierarchy of faculties, 230–2
  hierarchy of senses, 233–6
  and sensible object, 110, 124, 125, 130, 132, 154
Subject-in-process, 11–12, 22, 42, 45–6, 51, 55n., 56, 58, 60, 62–3, 69, 71, 73, 74–7, 85, 87, 89, 92, 98–9, 101, 112, 114, 116, 120, 125, 138, 157, 167, 186, 210, 213, 226, 239, 240
  and grammatical subject, 11, 60–1, 85, 96, 98 ff.
  See also Substance, Being, Process
Substance:
  individual and distributive, 8, 9–10, 12, 14, 21, 26, 28, 32, 35, 41, 54–5, 58, 60, 71, 73, 77, 79, 118, 125, 127, 152, 156, 160, 201, 219, 223
  as locus of process, 12, 13, 25–6, 29, 33, 42, 46, 51, 59, 60, 66, 73, 80, 85, 87, 100, 112, 120, 129, 201, 211–12, 223, 226, 240
  no contrary to it, 51, 53–5, 56, 62, 70, 131

Substance (*contd.*):
  delimited by contraries, 12, 13, 33, 36, 55, 57, 61–4, 72, 75, 80, 89
  and soul, 111, 114–15, 125–7
  See also Metaphysical contrariety
Synthesis, levels of, 23–5

Telos, 12, 21, 24–5, 29, 59, 67, 77–9, 87, 99, 116, 118–19, 125–6, 130n., 133, 136, 142n., 170, 178, 180–5, 187, 200, 205, 231, 240–1
Theology, 20–2, 208
Time, 24, 221
Truth, 59–60, 63, 93, 95, 96, 97, 225, 230

Unity, 26, 28, 30, 151, 154, 159–60, 213, 238
  and soul, 112, 114–20, 125, 128
Universals, 97–9, 109n., 137, 138, 152, 163, 165–6, 176, 197, 216, 223–4, 238

Virtue, 178, 179, 185, 187, 189, 190–3, 196 ff., 199, 227–8, 232
Virtue-vice, 55n., 56, 89, 161n., 185, 189, 220. See also Genus

Wisdom, 139n., 166–9, 174, 184, 189, 191, 197, 201, 228, 231, 240

INDEX II

Alexander, H. G., 109
Anaxagoras, 34, 38, 39, 40, 41, 44, 61, 66, 123, 132, 142, 221, 223
Anaximander, 38, 39, 41, 43, 223
Anaximenes, 38, 39, 40, 41, 43, 153
Apostle, H. G., 20, 239
Aquinas, Thomas, 206, 241
Aristotle, quoted:
   Categories, 12, 60, 62, 63, 64, 73–4, 92–3, 94, 95, 220, 238–9
   De Anima, 114–15, 117, 119, 120–1, 122, 124, 129, 132, 146, 155–6, 164, 180, 181–2, 225–6, 228, 230, 234
   De Generatione et Corruptione, 46–7, 217–18
   De Interpretatione, 36, 98
   De Sensu, 143, 145, 147
   De Generatione Animalium, 24
   De Partibus Animalium, 23–4, 78, 136
   Historia Animalium, 113–4
   Metaphysics, 21, 27, 28, 29–30, 32, 33, 36, 56, 57, 58–9, 62, 69–70, 72, 82, 86, 87, 90, 94, 96, 100–1, 152, 161–2, 200, 211, 213, 220, 223, 224
   Nicomachean Ethics, 180, 183, 187–8, 190–1, 192
   Physics, 11, 22, 49–50, 51, 52–4, 61, 62, 65, 66, 70–1, 73, 77, 80, 123, 219
   Politics, 179, 199
   Posterior Analytics, 56, 101, 224
   Topics, 216

Beare, J. I., 107, 232, 233, 234
Bekker, I., 21

Bonitz, H., 21
Boring, E. G., 141, 236, 237

Cassirer, E., 221
Cherniss, H., 117, 213, 232
Christ, W., 21
Cleisthenes, 173
Cornford, F. M., 10, 37, 152, 213, 214, 216

Democritus, 44, 123, 139, 145, 227
Dewey, J., 203–6
Descartes, 236
Diels, H., 15
Diogenes of Apollonia, 38, 43
Diogenes Laertius, 9
Dunham, J. H., 240

Eleatics, 34, 222
Empedocles, 15, 27, 34, 38, 39, 41, 42, 44, 122, 123, 132, 142, 217, 223, 227, 233
Eudemus, 15, 106

Galen, 236
Galileo, 236
Geulincx, 157
Gorgias, 174
Grote, G., 157, 209

Hammond, W. A., 231
Hamelin, O., 207, 222
Heraclitus, 6, 39, 40, 41, 42, 43, 132, 222
Hesychius, 9
Hicks, R. D., 182
Hippo, 43
Hobbes, Th., 236

Index II

Ion of Chios, 44

Jaeger, W., 17, 21, 34, 106, 112, 209, 210
James, W., 236
Joachim, H. H., 44, 185, 193, 217
Jowett, B., 6

Kant, 128, 157, 158, 160, 206
Kapp, E., 158
Kepler, 236

Lamprecht, S., 241
Leibniz, 220
Locke, 236

Melissus, 43
Mill, J. S., 157

Natorp, P, 208, 209, 210
Neoplatonism, 114, 241
Neothomism, 114, 241
Newton, 219, 236
Nuyens, F., 130

Owens, J., 209, 214

Papanoutsos, E. P., 157-8
Parmenides, 34, 39, 40, 41, 42, 44, 71, 153
Plato, 2, 6, 7, 8, 15, 21, 27, 31, 32, 34, 36, 42, 44, 106, 142, 145, 175, 176, 178, 186, 193, 198, 206, 209, 211, 212, 214, 223, 224, 225, 227
  quoted, 5, 36, 213

Platonists, 17, 34, 70, 103
Plotinus, 153
Pre-Aristotelians, 34, 69, 70, 107, 108, 115, 222, 227
Pre-Socratics, 5, 16, 25, 32, 33, 70, 103, 132, 171, 172, 173, 176, 211, 223
Protagoras, 174, 193
Pythagoreans, 34, 44, 70, 216, 225, 227

Randall, J. H., Jr., 10, 205
Ross, G. R. T., 229, 235
Ross, W. D., 10, 21, 51, 56, 58, 86, 87, 88, 127, 130, 131, 143, 207, 208, 213, 218, 229

Sarton, G., 114, 240
Schwegler, O., 21, 214
Simplicius, 9, 15, 43
Socrates, 5, 6, 26, 31, 137, 142, 174, 175, 176, 198, 211
Sophists, 15, 136, 198
Speusippus, 225
Spicer, E. E., 107, 154
Stuart, J. A., 117

Tannery, P., 10
Thales, 43, 153
Trendelenburg, A., 157

Welldon, J. E. C., 183
Windelband, W., 157

Xenophon, 175

Zeller, E., 87, 88, 107, 209

The
International Library
OF
PSYCHOLOGY, PHILOSOPHY
AND SCIENTIFIC METHOD

Edited by
C. K. OGDEN, M.A.
Late Fellow of Magdalene College, Cambridge

The International Library, of which over one hundred and fifty volumes have been published, is both in quality and quantity a unique achievement in this department of publishing. Its purpose is to give expression, in a convenient form, to the remarkable developments which have recently occurred in Psychology and its allied sciences. The older philosophers were preoccupied by metaphysical interests which for the most part have ceased to attract the younger investigators, and their forbidding terminology too often acted as a deterrent for the general reader. The attempt to deal in clear language with current tendencies whether in England and America or on the Continent has met with a very encouraging reception, and not only have accepted authorities been invited to explain the newer theories, but it has been found possible to include a number of original contributions of high merit.

Published by
ROUTLEDGE & KEGAN PAUL LTD
BROADWAY HOUSE: 68-74 CARTER LANE, LONDON, E.C.4.
1963

INTERNATIONAL LIBRARY OF PSYCHOLOGY, PHILOSOPHY AND SCIENTIFIC METHOD

All prices are net

A. PSYCHOLOGY

GENERAL AND DESCRIPTIVE

The Mind and its Place in Nature. By C. D. Broad. £2 15s.

Thought and the Brain. By Henri Piéron. Trans. by C. K. Ogden. £1.

The Nature of Laughter. By J. C. Gregory. 18s.

The Gestalt Theory and the Problem of Configuration. By Bruno Petermann. Illustrated. £1 5s.

Principles of Gestalt Psychology. By K. Koffka. £3.

Analysis of Perception. By J. R. Smythies. £1 1s.

The Psychology of Character: with a Survey of Personality in General. By A. A. Roback. *Revised Edition.* £2 10s.

ANALYSIS

The Practice and Theory of Individual Psychology. By Alfred Adler £1 5s.

Psychological Types. By C. G. Jung. Translated with a Foreword by H. Godwin Baynes. £2.

Character and the Unconscious: a Critical Exposition of the Psychology of Freud and Jung. By J. H. van der Hoop. £1.

LANGUAGE AND SYMBOLISM

The Symbolic Process, and Its Integration in Children. By J. F. Markey. 14s.

The Meaning of Meaning: a Study of the Influence of Language upon Thought and of the Science of Symbolism. By C. K. Ogden and I. A. Richards. £1 8s.

Principles of Literary Criticism. By I. A. Richards. £1 5s.

The Spirit of Language in Civilization. By K. Vossler. £1.

CHILD PSYCHOLOGY, EDUCATION, ETC.

The Growth of the Mind: an Introduction to Child Psychology. By K. Koffka. Translated by R. M. Ogden. £2.

The Language and Thought of the Child. By Jean Piaget. Preface by E. Claparéde. *Third Edition (revised and enlarged).* £1 5s.

Moral Judgment of the Child. By Jean Piaget. £1 12s.

The Child's Conception of the World. By Jean Piaget. £1 10s.

The Child's Conception of Number. By Jean Piaget. £1 5s.

Judgment and Reasoning in the Child. By Jean Piaget. £1 5s.

The Origin of Intelligence in the Child. By Jean Piaget. £1 12s.

The Child's Conception of Space. By Jean Piaget. £2 2s.

The Child's Conception of Geometry. By Jean Piaget, Bärbel Inhelder and Alina Szeminska. £2 5s.

The Mental Development of the Child. By Karl Bühler. 15s.

The Psychology of Intelligence. By Jean Piaget. 18s.

The Psychology of Children's Drawings: From the First Stroke to the Coloured Drawing. By Helga Eng. *Second Edition.* £1 5s.

ANIMAL PSYCHOLOGY, BIOLOGY, ETC.

The Mentality of Apes, with an Appendix on the Psychology of Chimpanzees. By W. Koehler. With 9 plates and 19 figures. £1 5s.

Theoretical Biology. By J. von Uexkuell. £1 4s.

ANTHROPOLOGY, SOCIOLOGY, RELIGION, ETC.

Crime and Custom in Savage Society. By B. Malinowski. With six plates. 18s.

Sex and Repression in Savage Society. By B. Malinowski. £1 1s.

B. PHILOSOPHY

Philosophical Studies. By G. E. Moore. £1 10s.

The Philosophy of "As If": a System of the Theoretical, Practical, and Religious Fictions of Mankind. By H. Vaihinger. Translated by C. K. Ogden. £1 10s.

Five Types of Ethical Theory. By C. D. Broad. £1 10s.

Speculations: Essays on Humanism and the Philosophy of Art. By T. E. Hulme. Edited by Herbert Read. With a frontispiece and Foreword by Jacob Epstein. £1 1s.

The Metaphysical Foundations of Modern Physical Science, with special reference to Man's Relation to Nature. By E. A. Burtt. £1 8s.

Bentham's Theory of Fictions. Edited with an Introduction and Notes by C. K. Ogden. £1 10s.

Ideology and Utopia: an Introduction to the Sociology of Knowledge. By Karl Mannheim. £1 8s.

The Philosophy of Peirce. Selected Writings. Edited by Justus Büchler. £1 15s.

Ethics and the History of Philosophy: Selected Essays. By C. D. Broad. £1 3s.

Sense-Perception and Matter: A Critical Analysis of C. D. Broad's Theory of Perception. By Martin E. Lean. £1 5s.

The Structure of Metaphysics. By Morris Lazerowitz. £1 5s.

Methods and Criteria of Reasoning. An inquiry into the structure of controversy. By Rupert Crawshay-Williams. £1 12s.

Reasons and Faiths. By Ninian Smart. £1 5s.

LOGIC

Tractatus Logico-Philosophicus. By L. Wittgenstein. German text, with an English Translation en regard, and an Introduction by Bertrand Russell, F.R.S. £1 1s.

The Foundations of Mathematics, and other Logical Essays. By F. P. Ramsey. £1 3s.

The Nature of Mathematics: a Critical Survey. By Max Black. £1 4s.

Logical Syntax of Language. By Rudolf Carnap. £1 10s.

Bertrand Russell's Construction of the External World. By Charles A. Fritz, Junr. £1 3s.

Logical Studies. By G. H. von Wright. £1 8s.

C. SCIENTIFIC METHOD

Scientific Thought: a Philosophical Analysis of some of its Fundamental Concepts in the light of Recent Physical Developments. By C. D. Broad. £2.

The Limits of Science: Outline of Logic and of the Methodology of the Exact Sciences. By Leon Chwistek. Introduction and Appendix by H. C. Brodie. £1 12s.

HISTORY, ETC.

An Historical Introduction to Modern Psychology. By Gardner Murphy. With a Supplement by H. Kluver. £2.

The History of Materialism and Criticism of its Present Importance. By F. A. Lange. Introduction by Bertrand Russell. £3.

Outlines of the History of Greek Philosophy. By E. Zeller. £1 8s.

Psyche: the Cult of Souls and the Belief in Immortality among the Greeks. By Erwin Rohde. £2 5s.

Plato's Theory of Art. By R. C. Lodge. £1 5s.

The Philosophy of Plato. By R. C. Lodge. £1 8s.

Plato's Phaedo. A translation with an Introduction, Notes and Appendices, by R. S. Bluck. £1 1s.

Plato's Theory of Knowledge. The Theaetetus and the Sophist of Plato. Translated, with a Running Commentary, by F. M. Cornford. £1 8s.

Plato's Cosmology: The Timaeus of Plato. Translated, with a Running Commentary, by F. M. Cornford. £1 12s.

Plato and Parmenides. Parmenides' "Way of Truth" and Plato's "Parmenides". Translated with an Introduction and Running Commentary, by F. M. Cornford. £1 4s.

Aristotle's Theory of Contrariety. By John P. Anton. £1 5s.

A LIST OF BOOKS PUBLISHED IN THE LIBRARY BUT AT PRESENT OUT OF PRINT

Analysis of Matter. By B. Russell.
Art of Interrogation. By E. R. Hamilton.
Biological Memory. By Eugenio Rignano.
Biological Principles. By J. H. Woodger.
Chance Love and Logic. By C. S. Peirce.
Charles Peirce's Empiricism. By Justus Büchler.
Child's Conception of Physical Causality. By Jean Piaget.
Child's Discovery of Death. By Sylvia Anthony.
Colour Blindness. By Mary Collins.
Colour and Colour Theories. By Christine Ladd-Franklin.
Communication. By K. Britton.
Comparative Philosophy. By P. Masson-Oursel.
Concentric Method. By M. Laignel-Lavastine.
Conditions of Knowing. By Angus Sinclair.
Conflict and Dream. By W. H. R. Rivers.
Conscious Orientation. By J. H. Van der Hoop.
Constitution-Types in Delinquency. By W. A. Willemse.
Contributions to Analytical Psychology. By C. G. Jung.
Creative Imagination. By June E. Downey.
Crime, Law and Social Science. By J. Michael and M. J. Adler.
Development of the Sexual Impulses. By R. E. Money Kyrle.
Dialectic. By M. J. Adler.
Doctrine of Signatures. By Scott Buchanan.

Dynamics of Education. By Hilda Taba.
Dynamic Social Research. By J. T. Hader and E. C. Lindeman.
Education Psychology. By C. Fox.
Effects of Music. By M. Schoen.
Eidetic Imagery. By E. R. Jaensch.
Emotion and Insanity. By S. Thalbitzer.
Emotions of Normal People. By W. M. Marston.
Ethical Relativity. By E. Westermarck.
Examination of Logical Positivism. By Julius Weinberg.
Foundations of Geometry. By Jean Nicod.
Growth of Reason. By F. Lorimer.
History of Chinese Political Thought. By Liang Chi-Chao.
How Animals Find their Way About. By E. Rabaud.
Human Speech. By Sir Richard Paget.
Individual and the Community. By Wen Kwei Liao.
Infant Speech. By M. M. Lewis.
Integrative Psychology. By W. M. Marston *et al.*
Invention and the Unconscious. By J. M. Montmasson.
Law and the Social Sciences. By H. Cairns.
Laws of Feeling. By F. Paulhan.
Measurement of Emotion. By W. Whately Smith.
Medicine, Magic and Religion. By W. H. Rivers.
Mencius on the Mind. By I. A. Richards.
Mind and its Body. By Charles Fox.
Misuse of Mind. By K. Stephen.
Nature of Intelligence. By L. L. Thurstone.
Nature of Learning. By G. Humphrey.
Nature of Life. By E. Rignano.
Neural Basis of Thought. By G. G. Campion and Sir G. E. Smith.
Neurotic Personality. By R. G. Gordon.
Philosophy of Music. By W. Pole.
Philosophy of the Unconscious. By E. von Hartmann.
Physique and Character. By E. Kretschmer.
Personality. By R. B. Gordon.
Plato's Theory of Education. By R. C. Lodge.
Plato's Theory of Ethics. By R. C. Lodge.
Pleasure and Instinct. By A. H. B. Allen.
Political Pluralism. By Kung Chuan Hsiao.

Possibity. By Scott Buchanan.
Primitive Mind and Modern Civilization. By C. R. Aldrich.
Principles of Experimental Psychology. By H. Pieron.
Problems of Personality. Edited by A. A. Roback.
Problems in Psychopathology. By T. W. Mitchell.
Psychology and Ethnology. By W. H. R. Rivers.
Psychology and Politics. By W. H. R. Rivers.
Psychology of Animals. By F. Alverdes.
Psychology of Emotion. By J. T. MacCurdy.
Psychology of Intelligence and Will. By H. G. Wyatt.
Psychology of Men of Genius. By E. Kretschmer.
Psychology of a Musical Prodigy. By G. Revesz.
Psychology of Philosophers. By Alexander Herzberg.
Psychology of Reasoning. By E. Rignano.
Psychology of Religious Mysticism. By J. H. Leuba.
Psychology of Time. By Mary Sturt.
Religion, Philosophy and Psychical Research. By C. D. Broad.
Religious Conversion. By Sante de Sanctis.
Sciences of Man in the Making. By E. A. Kirkpatrick.
Scientific Method. By A. D. Ritchie.
Social Basis of Consciousness. By T. Burrow.
Social Insects By W. M. Wheeler.
Social Life in the Animal World. By F. Alverdes.
Social Life of Monkeys and Apes. By S. Zuckerman.
Speech Disorders. By S. M. Stinchfield.
Statistical Method in Economics and Political Science. By P. Sargant Florence.
Technique of Controversy. By B. B. Bogoslovsky.
Telepathy and Clairvoyance. By R. Tischner.
Theory of Legislation. By Jeremy Bentham.
Trauma of Birth. By O. Rank.
Treatise on Induction and Probability. By G. H. von Wright.
What is Value? By Everett M. Hall.